SEEK JUSTICE THAT YOU MAY LIVE

SEEK JUSTICE THAT

YOU MAY LIVE

REFLECTIONS AND RESOURCES ON THE BIBLE AND SOCIAL JUSTICE

JOHN R. DONAHUE, SJ

Paulist Press
New York / Mahwah, NJ

Parts of chapter 8, "The Gospel of Matthew and the Letter of James," are a summary of *The Gospel in Parable: Metaphor, Narrative, and Theology in the Synoptic Gospels* (Philadelphia: Fortress Press, 1988), 109–25. Chapter 9, "Luke–Acts: Guideposts for a Pilgrim Church," incorporates *The Gospel in Parable*, 162–80. Used with permission of the publisher.

Front cover photo credits: Details in band, from left to right, courtesy of: halfpoint/ shutterstock.com; Charles Harker / shutterstock.com (this photo also appears enlarged below); cristianl/iStock.com; Zurijeta/shutterstock.com; Richard Cavalleri / shutterstock.com; and AfricaImages/iStock.com
Cover design by Sharyn Banks
Book design by Lynn Else

Library of Congress Cataloging-in-Publication Data:

Donahue, John R.
    Seek justice that you may live : reflections and resources on the Bible and social justice / John R. Donahue, S.J.
        pages cm
    Includes bibliographical references and index.
    ISBN 978-0-8091-4874-5 (alk. paper) — ISBN 978-1-58768-363-3
    1. Social justice—Biblical teaching. 2. Catholic Church—Doctrines. 3. Bible—Criticism, interpretation, etc. I. Title.
    BS680.J8D66 2014
    261.8—dc23

                                                                    2014018729

ISBN 978-0-8091-4874-5
ISBN 978-1-58768-363-3

Published by Paulist Press
997 Macarthur Boulevard
Mahwah, New Jersey 07430

www.paulistpress.com

Printed and bound in the
United States of America

In Memoriam
Very Rev. Pedro Arrupe, SJ (1907–91)
Superior General (1965–83) of the Society of Jesus
and
Walter J. Burghardt, SJ (1914–2008)

He has told you, O mortal, what is good; and what does the Lord
require of you but to do justice, and to love kindness,
and to walk humbly with your God? (Mic 6:8)

CONTENTS

CONTENTS

Contents

CONTENTS

FOREWORD

Today's world is marked by deep distress. The suffering is evident in the hunger of children touched by the poverty that blights not only inner cities of the United States, but increasingly those neighborhoods that were once seen as middle-class suburbs. The hardship shows its face in the depression and despair of unemployed parents, who have finally given up looking for jobs because their search for work has long been fruitless. The struggles lead millions of refugees fleeing from war and oppression to ask if they will ever again have a place to call home. Whether today's sufferings are greater than in other periods of history can be debated. However, it is certain that many of the burdens people are forced to carry have been caused by other human beings. Much of the anguish in our world, as the Penitential Rite at the Eucharist puts it, is due to "what we have done and what we have failed to do."

The title of John Donahue's book tells us in a few succinct words what our response to this human distress must be: *Seek Justice That You May Live.* Much, maybe even most, of the human suffering we see, if our eyes are open, is the result of injustice. Seeking justice will thus be indispensable if we are to overcome at least some of the hardships people must face daily. And as Donahue shows in a powerfully persuasive way, seeking justice is an essential requirement of Christian faith. It is a key dimension of every Christian's vocation as a disciple of Jesus. It should be one of the central foci of the mission of the Church. The Holy Spirit empowers the followers of Christ in their efforts to bring greater justice to the world, so work for justice is not only a duty; it is a gift. As Pope Francis stresses so vividly in both his words and his deeds, faith in the gospel should overflow joyfully in each Christian's work of justice. Working for justice brings new life.

SEEK JUSTICE THAT YOU MAY LIVE

Justice, of course, is a complex reality. *Seek Justice That You May Live* makes an important contribution by helping readers come to a deeper understanding of how the Bible understands what justice requires. Donahue shines the light of his deep biblical scholarship and strong social/pastoral sensitivity on debates about what justice means and how to put it into action. His book will be an invaluable aid to lay Christians seeking a more reflective grasp of the social dimension of their faith. It will help parish Bible study groups and social action committees come to a deeper understanding of the texts they are reading and of the faith-dimension of the challenges they face. It will enable pastors to come to a more profound understanding of how the biblical Word of God raises the challenge of justice, and it will help them communicate this challenge in the homilies they preach.

Seek Justice That You May Live is also a rich resource for students and teachers of biblical studies, Christian ethics, and pastoral ministry. Donahue surveys and synthesizes the very best scholarship on the way the Bible addresses the meaning of social justice. He presents his synthesis in a way that is clear and accessible. The resource bibliographies in each of the chapters of the book will be invaluable to students seeking to take their study of the Bible's vision of justice to deeper levels. These bibliographies will also help teachers and researchers by providing an indispensable overview of the best contemporary scholarship on the biblical vision of justice and social ethics.

The Christian community today is called to fresh engagement with the challenge of justice raised by the human suffering that mars our world today. Several decades ago I had the privilege of working with John Donahue as we served together as consultants to the United States Catholic bishops in the writing of their 1986 pastoral letter, *Economic Justice for All*. In recent years, issues of social justice have not had the high priority in the life of the Catholic community that the pastoral letter encouraged. Pope Francis, however, has clearly set out to make justice for the poor and other marginalized persons once again a central priority for the Christian community today. In light of the pope's powerful witness to the importance of the social dimensions of Christian faith, the timing of the publication of *Seek Justice That You*

May Live could not be more opportune. Donahue's contribution is an indispensable resource for the renewal of the social mission of the Church both today and in the years ahead. Its publication is a true grace. It will lead the Christian community to deeper insight into its mission and help renew the Church's hope that this mission can help heal the wounds of our world.

David Hollenbach, SJ

PREFACE

For almost four decades, I have been engaged in reflection on how the biblical heritage can address issues of social justice, first in an essay published in *The Faith That Does Justice* (New York: Paulist Press, 1976), then in teaching ministerial students at the Jesuit School of Theology in Berkeley, California, and undergraduates recently at Loyola University Maryland, along with working with the late Walter J. Burghardt, SJ, in his project of retreats mainly for priests and pastoral ministers on "Preaching the Just Word." I also worked as a consultant to the United States bishops' committee that drafted the 1986 pastoral letter, *Economic Justice for All.* In 1993, I published a short pamphlet, *What Does the Lord Require? A Bibliographical Essay on the Bible and Social Justice. Studies in the Spirituality of the Jesuits* (St. Louis: Seminar on Jesuit Spirituality, 1993, rev. ed. 2000).

One of the most encouraging things I have noticed over the past four decades is the expansion of studies of the Bible on issues of social justice. The Church today has become a Bible-reading, Bible-praying community that sustains legions of people engaged in the quest for social justice, as well as earnest seekers from priests in the pulpit to religious education teachers and students who we hope are challenged by the biblical witness. My goal is to present reflections on major biblical themes and significant texts that will draw readers into the richness of the Bible. I am also aware that major areas of social justice are not adequately addressed, for example, injustice toward women, concern for the environment, and the pursuit of peace. I have tried to call attention to fundamental biblical themes and perspectives that challenge the roots of injustice and stimulate conversation on the ways of justice. I have also tried to provide the most up-to-date bibliography available. Since the literature is vast, with rare exceptions, I limit the references to books I have used or examined. Each chapter is then followed by a resource bibliography, which I hope will help people to appropriate the biblical message in their own lives and situations. I think of the work as a handbook for both teachers and students in their personal commitment to the quest for justice.

But, most important, if concerns for social justice are to inform the lives of the pilgrim people of God today, they must arise from the proclamation and study of the Word in religious education and worship. While other ecclesial communities have always tried to ground their faith in Scripture, it is mainly since the Second Vatican Council that contemporary Catholics have become a Bible-reading, Bible-praying community. It is my hope that this present work will be of some help to those preaching and teaching Scripture and to those who find in the Scripture, "a lamp for my feet, a light for my path" (Ps 119:105).

In completing this work, I want to remember with gratitude and admiration Rev. Lawrence E. Boadt, CSP (d. July 24, 2010), a distinguished scholar who never forgot that the Bible was to be opened up for the people of God. He first encouraged me to write this work. I am very grateful also to Dr. Enrique Aguilar, Donna Crilly, and Paul McMahon, editors at Paulist Press, for their guidance and patience during the course of this publication.

John R. Donahue, SJ

ABBREVIATIONS

AB	Anchor Bible
ABD	*Anchor Bible Dictionary*
au. trans.	Author's translation of a particular text
BDAG	Bauer, Danker, Arndt and Gingrich, *Greek-English Lexicon of the New Testament and Other Early Christian Literature*
DSE	*Dictionary of Scripture and Ethics*
ICC	International Critical Commentary
JSB	*Jewish Study Bible*
JSOT	*Journal for the Study of the Old Testament*
NABRE	New American Bible, Revised Edition
NISB	*New Interpreter's Study Bible*
NRSV	New Revised Standard Version
NJBC	*The New Jerome Biblical Commentary*
SBLDS	Society of Biblical Literature Dissertation Series
TDOT	*Theological Dictionary of the Old Testament*

CHAPTER 1

THE WAYS OF JUSTICE

A BRIEF REVIEW OF CHURCH TEACHING
ON SOCIAL JUSTICE

Over the last century and into the present century, the Catholic Church
has responded to the changing social and economic challenges of the
modern world with a wide variety of official teaching, beginning with
the encyclical letter of Pope Leo XIII, On the Condition of Labor,
(*Rerum Novarum*, 1891), continuing through the pontificate of Pope
John Paul II (1978–2005), and in the encyclicals of Pope Benedict XVI,
especially in Charity in Truth (*Caritas in Veritate*, 2009), and continuing in the actions and statements of Pope Francis.[1] The same period
that witnessed the rise of Catholic social teaching, was also the century
during which the Magisterium cautiously accepted the methods and
conclusions of modern biblical scholarship.[2] Catholic social teaching
had been based almost exclusively on the Catholic natural law tradition mediated primarily through scholastic philosophy and theology,
though later enhanced by dialogue with contemporary social ethics.
During the evolution of Catholic social teaching and the development
of Catholic biblical studies, these two great streams of renewal flowed
side by side rather than together.

A major change in the use of Scripture was inaugurated in the

---

1. Throughout this work, the following systems of referencing are used: Works quoted in the text
will be listed by name, short title, and page number, for example, (Berman, *Created Equal*, 6);
other works cited will be found in the footnotes. All works referenced in a chapter can be found
in the bibliography at the end of that chapter. A complete listing of authors cited is in the index.

2. Helpful surveys are Raymond F. Collins, *Introduction to the New Testament* (New York:
Doubleday, 1983), 272–386; and Raymond E. Brown, "Church Pronouncements," in the *New
Jerome Biblical Commentary*, ed. R. E. Brown, J. A. Fitzmyer, and R. E. Murphy (Englewood Cliffs,
N.J.: Prentice Hall, 1990), 1166–75.

documents of Vatican II, held twenty years after Pope Pius XII's encyclical, *Divino Afflante Spiritu*, often called the "Magna Carta" of biblical studies. Following in the footsteps of Pope Leo XIII, the Second Vatican Council mandated that Scripture be the soul of sacred theology, and stressed that "special care should be given to the perfecting of moral theology," and "its scientific presentation should draw more fully on the teaching of Holy Scripture"[3] In the post–Vatican II period, the social teaching of the Magisterium, while never abandoning its debt to philosophical analysis, began to be more explicitly theological and scriptural. The documents did not engage in exegetical discussions but drew on the fruits of exegesis, especially by giving a more christological thrust to moral teaching. J. Bryan Hehir has observed, "After the appearance of *Gaudium et Spes* (Pastoral Constitution on the Church in the World Today), however, the pressure for a more biblically and theologically based social ethic came from within the ranks of Catholic theologians and advocates of social justice."[4]

Select writings of Pope John Paul II indicate ways in which Scripture has been used for social justice. In his first letter dealing with social justice, *Laborem Exercens* (On Human Work, September 19, 1981), John Paul II speaks of human dignity and human destiny in the first two chapters of Genesis and comments, "An analysis of these texts makes us aware that they express—sometimes in an archaic way of manifesting thought—the fundamental truths about humanity."[5] John Paul's most sustained use of the Bible occurs in his encyclical, *Sollicitudo Rei Socialis* (On Social Concerns, December 30, 1987), in commemoration of the encyclical of Pope Paul VI, *Populorum Progressio* (On the Development of Peoples, March 20, 1967). Again the Pope turns to Genesis 1 and 2 to stress that men and women are created in the image of God, and he further notes, "The story of the human race described by Sacred Scripture is, even after the fall into sin, a story of constant achievements which, although always called into question and threatened by sin, are nonetheless repeated, increased and

---

3. *Dei Verbum* 24, (Dogmatic Constitution on Divine Revelation), and *Optatum Totius* 16 (Decree on the Training of Priests).

4. "Forum," *Religion and American Culture* 10 (Winter 2000): 25.

5. *Laborem Exercens* 4.

extended in response to the divine vocation given from the beginning to man and woman (Gen 1:26–28) and inscribed in the image they received."[6]

The parable of the rich man and Lazarus (Luke 16:19–31) is one of the texts most often cited in modern social teaching. At Vatican II, in *Gaudium et Spes* 27, the parable is cited to show that "everyone must consider his [or her] neighbor without exception as another self," so as to not imitate the rich man who had no concern for the poor Lazarus. In *Populorum Progressio* 47, Pope Paul VI expressed a hope for "a world where freedom is not an empty word, and where the poor man Lazarus can sit down at the same table with the rich man." In his world travels, Pope John Paul II used this parable frequently, most notably in his address in Yankee Stadium on October 2, 1979, where he noted that the rich man was condemned because "he failed to take notice" of Lazarus who sat at his door. The pope further stated that this parable "must always be in our memory" and "form our conscience," and said that Christ demands openness "from the rich, the affluent, the economically advantaged to the poor, the underdeveloped and the disadvantaged," and saw this as both an individual and national challenge.[7] The key words in the papal statement are "always be in our memory," and "form our conscience." The biblical material does not give direct precepts, but is necessary to inform the Christian imagination and moral dispositions.[8]

Pope John Paul II returns to this parable in *Sollicitudo Rei Socialis* (1987) stating, "It is essential to recognize each person's equal right to be seated at the common banquet instead of lying outside the door like Lazarus."[9] Though this use of the parable verges on the allegorical, I would argue that intertextually (in the larger context of the Gospel of Luke) its use is legitimate and that it touches human imagination today

---

6. *Sollicitudo Rei Socialis* 29.

7. Pope John Paul II, "Special Sensitivity to Those in Distress," in David M. Byers, *Justice*, 1. The pope himself comments that he has used this parable "on various occasions."

8. See esp. James M. Gustafson, "The Changing Use of the Bible in Christian Ethics," and "The Place of Scripture in Christian Ethics: A Methodological Study," in *Readings in Moral Theology No 4: The Use of Scripture in Moral Theology*, ed. C. Curran and R. McCormick (New York/Ramsey, NJ: Paulist, 1984), 133–78.

9. *Sollicitudo Rei Socialis* 33.

in a way that can evoke a response to the parable analogous to that expected of Luke's original readers.

Other texts most frequently used are a number of references to Genesis 1—2, especially to Genesis 1:26, the Creation of man and woman in the image of God, as a basis of human rights and human dignity, and as one might expect, to the allegory of the sheep and the goats in Matthew 25:31–46, but interpreted in the universalistic sense that all the thirsty, the hungry, and people otherwise marginalized are brothers and sisters of Jesus.

In *Centesimus Annus* (On the Hundredth Anniversary of *Rerum Novarum*, May 1, 1991), John Paul makes sparing use of Scripture, again invoking Genesis to undergird human dignity and the destination of the goods of the earth for common use. He also cites Matthew 25:31–46 (the parable of the sheep and the goats) and the parable of the Good Samaritan (Luke 10:25–32) to stress that everyone is responsible for the well-being of his or her brother or sister (no. 51). More important than citation of specific texts is that the pope sees the whole Christian tradition as affirming "the option or love of preference for the poor" (no. 42), and says that it is because of "her *evangelical duty* [emphasis mine] that feels called to take her stand beside the poor, to discern the justice of their requests" (no. 39).

Though too early to assess completely Pope Benedict XVI's social teaching, some clear guidelines emerge. Clearly *caritas* (love in its most comprehensive sense) is at the center of his theology and social teaching. More than John Paul II, he makes clear distinctions between justice and charity, with the former the main task of civil society and laypeople in the Church, and charity as the animating force for justice. Still, in both encyclicals and public statements, his concern for the poor and marginal is undiminished. Love of the poor is an essential and defining activity of the Church. Benedict declares in *Deus Est Caritas* 25 (God Is Love, December 25, 2005): "Love for widows and orphans, prisoners, and the sick and needy of every kind is as essential to her [the Church's] ministry of the sacraments and preaching of the gospel. The Church cannot neglect the service of charity any more than she can neglect the sacraments and the word."

Later in *Caritas in Veritate* (Charity in Truth, June 29, 2009), he stresses again the role of charity: "The earthly city is promoted not merely by relationships of rights and duties, but to an even greater and more fundamental extent by relationships of gratuitousness, mercy and communion. Charity always manifests God's love in human relationships as well, it gives theological and salvific value to all commitment for justice in the world" (no. 6) and criticizes modern Capitalism as based on the conviction "that the economy must be autonomous, that it must be shielded from 'influences' of a moral character, has led man to abuse the economic process in a thoroughly destructive way. In the long term, these convictions have led to economic, social and political systems that trample upon personal and social freedom, and are therefore unable to deliver the justice that they promise" (no. 34).

Pope Benedict's theology is very influenced by Scripture and Patristic thought, but without a great engagement with specific texts. Rather, he offers a biblical theology based on fundamental themes such as the primacy of love, the presence of Christ in a suffering neighbor, and the importance of hope in confronting the crises of our age.

Pope Francis has proclaimed a vision of social justice with special concern for the poor and marginalized—which he introduced less than a year into his papacy—combined with refreshingly direct language about the structures of injustice. Though he does not cite the Bible often, his statements reflect the concern for the marginalized that permeates the Bible. While the major themes of his teaching are in continuity with the strong social encyclicals of the post–Vatican II popes, his direct manner of speaking and his personal actions and witness have captured the imagination of the world and rekindled hope among those directly involved in empowering the poor and marginalized.

His apostolic exhortation, *Evangelii Gaudium* (The Joy of the Gospel) epitomizes strong statements made on earlier occasions. He begins with a ringing condemnation of "consumerism," "born of a complacent and covetous heart" (no. 2). Previous papal writings have presented low-key criticisms of free-market capitalism, but Francis castigates "trickle down" theories and a "naïve trust in the goodness of those wielding economic power" (no. 54). Echoing the biblical claim that greed is idolatry (Col 3:5), he writes of "the idolatry of money and the dictatorship of an impersonal economy lacking a truly human purpose" (no. 55). He goes on to reject the income gap between the majority and "the prosperity enjoyed by the happy few," who reject the concerns of government for the "common good" (no. 56) and notes that violence arises from great economic disparity (no. 60). At the same time, he is not simply strident and critical but calls for reform that "would require a vigorous change of approach on the part of political leaders" where "money must serve, not rule," and exhorts the rich "to generous solidarity and to the return of economics and finance to an ethical approach which favours human beings" (no. 58). In January of 2013, he wrote to the World Economic Forum at Davos, out of concern for "the frail, the weak and the vulnerable." He praises business as a vocation: "The international business community can count on many men and women of great personal honesty and integrity, whose work is inspired and guided by high ideals of fairness, generosity and concern for the authentic development of the human family. I urge you to draw upon these great human and moral resources and to take up this challenge with determination and far-sightedness."[10]

The most sustained use of the Bible in any Church document on social justice was in the 1986 pastoral letter of the United States bishops, *Economic Justice for All*.[11] Here the bishops recognize the difficulty of bringing the Bible to bear on complex economic and social issues, and call attention to "the Bible's deeper vision of God, of the purpose of creation, and of the dignity of human life in society." While offering no sustained biblical argument, the bishops select five themes from the Bible that are judged especially pertinent to social issues today: (1) Creation of all men and women in God's image, which stamps them with an inalienable dignity; (2) God's formation of a covenant community, which is to live in justice and mutual concern; (3) the proclamation of God's reign by Jesus; (4) along with his formation of a community of disciples; (5) which is to be manifest in a special concern for the poor and marginalized; and (6) which bequeaths to history a legacy of hope and courage even amid failure and suffering. Despite the cursory and selective nature of the biblical treatment and the criticism in some circles that the use of the Bible by the bishops softens the prophetic critique of injustice, the themes selected provide a foundation for further theological reflection.

---

10. Message can be found at http://www.vatican.va/holy_father/francesco/messages/pont-messages/2014/documents/papa-francesco_20140117_messaggio-wef-davos_en.html.

11. *Economic Justice for All* 29.

Furthermore, as Archbishop Rembert Weakland, OSB, (the chair of the committee that drafted the latter document) stressed, no matter how difficult the problems of interpretation and application of the biblical material, "if the document was to influence preaching and daily church life," there should be a scriptural section that would put people in touch with the major texts and social themes of the Bible.[12] Whatever the intellectual power and depth of papal teaching, the encyclicals rarely touch the lives of everyday Catholics. If Catholic social teaching is to form people's consciences, inspire their imaginations, and shape their lives, it must weave biblical theology into its presentations.

DESCRIBING SOCIAL JUSTICE

Even a cursory survey of Church teaching on issues of social justice will show that the Old Testament plays little role in its articulation.[13] While this may indicate an understandable desire to give a christological focus to its theology, rich dimensions will be lost, principally the prophetic heritage, which, as we will see, informs the portrayal of Jesus in the Gospel of Luke. Neglect of the Old Testament also hinders dialogue with the long tradition among Jewish scholars and social activists who have concern for the poor and for justice in human relationships.

Like *goodness* or *love*, there is no concise definition of *justice*; it always deals with the regulation of relationships, and the kinds of justice are determined by the kinds of relationships. Traditional philosophy distinguishes between "commutative justice," and "distributive justice." The former concerns the claims that exist in relations between individual and individual or between groups that are essentially private and nonpolitical, such as voluntary associations. The obligation of commutative justice is one of fidelity to freely formed mutual bonds and of fairness in exchange. It is rooted in the fundamental equality of

---

12. Oral communication from Archbishop Rembert Weakland, OSB, to the committee that helped to draft the pastoral letter.

13. I use "Old Testament" rather than "Hebrew Scriptures," or other descriptions of the Jewish writings because many Jewish scholars do not object to this use by Christians and also the Christian canon of Scripture is larger than the traditional Jewish canon, for example, the inclusion of the Wisdom of Solomon and Sirach (Ecclesiasticus), both of which contribute to the reflection on issues of social justice.

persons.[14] Distributive justice offers principles that provide "moral guidance for the political processes and structures that affect the distribution of economic benefits and burdens in societies."[15] In Catholic social teaching, the norm of distributive justice, then, specifies the demands of mutuality and interdependence in those relations that determine the opportunity of every person to share or participate in essentially public goods. It establishes the equal right of all to share in those goods and opportunities that are necessary for genuine participation in the human community. It establishes a strict duty of society as a whole to guarantee these rights. "Social justice," though related to distributive justice, has developed more recently in Catholic thought as a distinct and more comprehensive category. It now involves not only issues of distribution but is concerned with the rights and dignity of all peoples, concern for the poor, attention to social and economic inequality, and the impact of war and violence.

The Catholic understanding of social justice is very close to a recent secular description as stated in a social justice symposium sponsored by the School of Social Welfare of the University of California at Berkeley:

> Social Justice is a process, not an outcome, which (1) seeks fair (re)distribution of resources, opportunities, and responsibilities; (2) challenges the roots of oppression and injustice; (3) empowers all people to exercise self-determination and realize their full potential; (4) and builds social solidarity and community capacity for collaborative action.[16]

The focus of this book will be on social justice, which can be so comprehensive that no single work can be adequate. It will not address *explicitly* all major concerns embraced by social justice today, for example, feminism and social justice; gender rights and discrimination;

---

14. For an excellent discussion of the divisions of justice, see David Hollenbach, "Modern Catholic Teaching Concerning Justice," in *The Faith That Does Justice*, ed. John C. Haughey (New York, Paulist Press, 1976), esp. 219.

15. Julian Lamont and Christi Favor, "Distributive Justice," *The Stanford Encyclopedia of Philosophy* (Spring 2013 ed.), ed. Edward N. Zalta, http://plato.stanford.edu/archives/spr2013/entries/justice-distributive.

16. Http://socialwelfare.berkeley.edu/sjs/.

issues of ecology; issues of war, peace, and violence; relation of health issues to social justice. The hope is, however, that those concerned about these issues will find material in the biblical texts and bibliographies to appropriate and integrate the Scripture into their own vital commitments.

APPROACHING THE BIBLE

In contrast to general religious and secular understandings, the Bible has a rich vocabulary of justice and injustice, which does not yield to a one-to-one correspondence in English. The two principal biblical terms are variations of the term *tsedaqah* (used 523 times) and *mishpat* (used 422 times), which are very often used interchangeably. Space does not allow adequate exploration of the labyrinth of other terms used for justice and their translations into Greek, Latin, and contemporary versions, so the emphasis will be put on the above terms that give rise to a major translation problem.

Biblical terms do not have the precision of concepts based on philosophical analysis, so distinctions between *justice* and *charity*, or *justice* and *holiness* are much murkier in the Bible. A classic instance of the larger semantic fields and translation problems embraced by these terms is the famous marriage covenant renewal text of Hosea 2:19–20 (NRSV) [NABRE, 2:21–23]:

> And I will take you for my wife for ever; I will take you for my wife in righteousness and in justice (*be tsedeq we be mishpat*) ["with justice and with judgment" (NABRE)] in steadfast love, (*be chesed*) and in mercy (*be rahamin*) will take you for my wife in faithfulness (*be 'emunah*); and you shall know the Lord.[17]

Equally important, as underscored by Walter Brueggemann, is Jeremiah's indictment of the Jerusalem establishment:

---

17. When citing the original Hebrew, I will adopt phonetic transliteration rather than academic transliteration.

Thus says the LORD: Do not let the wise boast in their wisdom, do not let the mighty boast in their might, do not let the wealthy boast in their wealth; but let those who boast in this; that they understand and know me, that I am the LORD; I act with steadfast love, justice, and righteousness in the earth, for in these things I delight, says the LORD. (Jer 9:23–24)

In contrast to the "lethal commitments" of the Jerusalem leaders for their wisdom, might, and wealth, is the triad of self-expression of Yahweh (Brueggemann, *Journey*, 5–6):

Steadfast love (*chesed*) is to stand in solidarity, to honor commitments, to be reliable toward all the partners.

Justice (*mishpat*) in the Old Testament concerns distribution in order to make sure that all members of the community have access to resources and goods for the sake of a viable life of dignity. In covenantal tradition the particular subject of YHWH's justice is the triad "widow, orphan, immigrant," those without leverage or muscle to sustain their own legitimate place in society.

Righteousness (*tsedaqah*) concerns active intervention in social affairs, taking an initiative to intervene effectively in order to rehabilitate society, to respond to social grievance, and to correct every humanity-diminishing activity.

As powerful as Brueggemann's descriptions remain, the English translation of the *tsdq* word group as "righteous," and "righteousness" and *mishpat* as "justice" or "judgment" (generally used by the NRSV) raises problems. The *Oxford English Dictionary* defines *righteousness* as "justice, uprightness, rectitude, conformity of life to the requirements of the divine moral law, virtue, and integrity." The term was first introduced into English biblical translations under the influence of Cloverdale (1535). Today, *righteousness* evokes primarily personal rectitude or personal virtue, and the social dimension of the original Hebrew is lost. This has resulted in a virtual "biblical dialect" where righteousness is relegated to the sphere of religion and personal piety, while justice is more associated with the realm of public, secular discourse. Imagine, for instance, what people's reaction would be if we had a "department of righteousness" or we talked about "social righteousness."

The Hebrew term *tsedaqah* most often conveys an attitude or disposition, while *mishpat*, from the verbal root *shpt* ("to judge"), refers to the effect of a decision or an attitude. The older New American Bible (1970) generally translates *tsedaqah* as "justice" and *mishpat* as "judgment," which is both more accurate and better suited to contemporary discussions of justice. A number of authors suggest when "righteousness and justice" appear together, it is in instances of hendiadyses (two terms conveying a single idea) and should be translated as "social justice" (Leclerc, *Yahweh*, 12). Many of our citations of the Bible are from the New Revised Standard Version, which translates *tsedaqah* as "righteousness" and *mishpat* as "justice," but, in critical passages, the Hebrew will be noted so that the deeper biblical nuances and powerful interpretation of the terms indicated by Brueggemann will be apparent.

The Hebrew terms for *justice* are also *applied* to a wide variety of things. Some examples would be Genesis 24:48: "God...who has led me by the right way;" "just" weights (Lev 19:36: "You shall have honest balances, honest weights, an honest ephah...; Deut 25:15: "You shall have only a full and honest measure," [cf. Ezek 45:10]); "just" sacrifices (Deut 33:19; Pss 4:5; 51:19). Scales are "just" when they give fair measure; paths are "just" when they get you where you should be going. *Justice* is also used in the sense of "victory" or "saving act" (Judg 5:11, "they repeat the triumphs [*sidqoth*] of the LORD"; 1 Sam 12:7, "all the saving deeds of the LORD"). Laws are "just," not because they conform to an external norm or constitution, but because they create harmony within the community.

Acting justly consists in avoiding violence and fraud and other actions that destroy communal life and in pursuing that which sustains the life of the community. God is frequently characterized as "just" (2 Chr 12:6; Neh 9:8; Pss 7:9; 103:17; 116:5; Isa 30:18; Jer 9:24) and seeks and loves justice (Isa 61:8; Pss 11:7; 33:5; 37:38; 99:4), and justice is one of the stipulations of the covenant (Hos 2:21; Jer 9:23–24). The Bible speaks of a just individual who is in "right relation" to God and others, with a special concern for those "others" who are powerless or marginal (Job 4:3–4; 29:12–16; 31:16–19; Prov 31:9). The justice of

Yahweh is not in contrast to other covenant qualities such as steadfast love, mercy, *or* faithfulness but, in many texts, is equated with them.

The centrality as well as the richness of the biblical statements on justice is the very reason why it is difficult to give a strict biblical definition of *justice*. In general terms, the biblical idea of *justice* can be described as *fidelity to the demands of a relationship*.[18] Today, I would specify this by the addition to "demands of a relationship" that arises from God's law and covenant for the people of Israel, and for Christians, the relationship to the Christ event, understood as the meaning that the life, teaching, death, resurrection of Jesus and the gift of the Spirit has for believers.

In the Jewish Scriptures, God is just when he acts as a God should—defending or vindicating his people or punishing violations of the covenant. People are just when they are in right relationship to God and to other humans. In contrast to modern individualism, the Israelite is in a world where "to live" is to be united with others in a social context either by bonds of family or by covenant relationships. This web of relationships—king with people; judge with complainants; family with tribe and kinfolk; the community with the resident, alien, and suffering in their midst; and all with the covenant God—constitutes the world in which life is played out. The demands of the differing relationships cannot be specified a priori, but must be seen in the different settings of Israel's history and its responses to God's Word.[19]

This wider semantic field for justice is a caution against distinguishing too closely between "love" and "justice." The biblical usages suggest that in the Judeo-Christian tradition, *love motivates toward justice, and justice creates the conditions under which love can flourish.* The great social leaders of our recent history illustrate this. Martin Luther

---

18. John Donahue, "Biblical Perspectives on Justice," in *The Faith That Does Justice*, ed. John Haughey (New York/Ramsey: Paulist Press, 1977), 69. It is similar to the perspectives now described by Barbara Johnson, "*tsdq*" TDOT 12, esp. 246–47. See also Joseph A. Fitzmyer, "What Do the Scriptures Say about Injustice?" in *Proceedings of the Jesuit Education 21 Conference*, ed. Martin Tripole (Philadelphia: St. Joseph's University Press, 2000), 99–112. The study by James Bruckner, "Justice in Scripture," (*Ex auditu* 22 [2006], 1–9), is especially helpful.

19. See also the important study of J. M. Walsh, *The Mighty From Their Thrones* (Philadelphia: Fortress Press, 1987), esp. 1–10, who describes *tsedeq* as a "consensus which shapes God's people." Walsh also studies the related concept of *naqam*, "vengeance which is not simply punishment but the restoration of justice."

King, Jr., was motivated by the biblical vision of love of God and neighbor but campaigned against racial injustice with a vision of justice for all people. His legacy, though still unfulfilled, led us along that path of true love and respect across racial barriers. Dorothy Day said that the essence of her work was love, "a harsh and dreadful thing," but she protested against the violence that can destroy a loving relationship and offered a vision of community that bridged barriers of class, gender, and race.[20] People may not feel love for a particular group, for example, people of other religions, the disadvantaged, or immigrants, but justice demands that they be given equal rights and opportunities.

Biblical justice is fundamentally "making things right," not simply recognizing or defining *individual rights*. It is concerned with describing and enacting the "right relation" of human beings to God and to each other. Biblical justice always has a critical or prophetic edge in exposing the structures of injustice and giving a voice to the voiceless. It is not "blind," nor totally impartial. It is partial to those most affected by evil and oppression—symbolized in the Old Testament by the four groups: the widow, orphan, poor, and stranger in the land, and embodied in the New Testament by Jesus' mission to those on the social and religious margin of society. Joshua Berman contrasts Greek and Hebrew notions of Justice: "In the Greek context justice required, as Aristotle opined, that equals be treated as equals, and unequals as unequals" and consideration of justice never crossed social class, which today is one of the main sources of injustice (Berman, *Created Equal*, 6). But the covenantal structure of biblical religion was egalitarian and countered various hierarchies (ibid., 49).

READING THE BIBLICAL TEXTS

While the fruit of the biblical renewal has been to draw people to the Bible, the modes of interpretation and appropriation are diverse, ranging from an unacceptable literalism to equally unacceptable allegorical and theological appropriations seasoned with a large dose of individualism. In treating biblical texts and themes, we will present the

---

20. Dorothy Day, *The Long Loneliness: The Autobiography of Dorothy Day* (San Francisco: Harper and Row, 1981, orig. 1952), 285.

power of the biblical texts in their various literary and historical contexts and suggest initial ways that these texts can speak to our world today. The final chapter will address more fully the issue of appropriation. In presenting the power of the biblical texts and themes in their various literary and historical contexts, we will examine ways in which they can speak to our contemporary world. The final chapter will address more fully the issue of appropriation.

Two macro themes span the whole of biblical revelation: self-disclosure of a transcendent God, who at the same time is manifest in human history and the evil that arises when humans usurp divine power. While the Bible offers no system of ethics, its directives on how life should unfold are rooted in the *kind of God* who is disclosed. Any language about God must acknowledge the utter transcendence and mystery of God, as affirmed by the three great monotheistic religions, Judaism, Christianity, and Islam. The Bible is a narrative of God's self-disclosure, but there are, literally, different "Gods" that adorn its pages. Jack Miles, in his Pulitzer Prize-winning book, *God: A Biography*, guides readers through texts that image God as creator, liberator, conqueror, executioner, wife, friend, recluse, and absent—to mention select main headings.[21] Different cultures throughout history appropriate diverse biblical images of God, without being aware of the inadequacy of any single conception.

Though Jewish and Christian traditions stress the transcendence of God, both affirm divine self-disclosure, which provides the first macro theme. The God who calls to Moses at the burning bush is a God of mystery and power but one whose self-description unfolds in a cascade of verbs:

> I have *witnessed* the affliction of my people in Egypt and have *heard* their cry of complaint against their slave drivers, so I *know well* what they are suffering. Therefore I have *come down to rescue* them from the hands of the Egyptians and *lead them out* of that land into a good and spacious land. (Exod 3:7–8, emphasis mine)

---

21. Jack Miles, *God: A Biography* (New York: Alfred A. Knopf, 1995).

The biblical God is active and present to a suffering people. Though God's presence and desires for humanity will take different forms often conditioned by historical events (for example, the "divine warrior," or "the lamenting God," of Jeremiah), there is an underlying identity. Joseph Jensen, in a fine new book, captures this identity: "To do good in such a view is to imitate God, to do the things that God would do if God were a human being. What these things are can be read in some measure from the things God *has* done, especially in the acts of love and faithfulness toward Israel."[22] In the heritage of Israel, Jesus will continue to reveal the kind of God who sustains our lives and points out how we should live. The image of God that informs this present work is the God who is deeply concerned about injustice and the abuse of power while taking the side of suffering humanity. Such a God spans biblical history from the revelation to Moses to the exaltation of the Son of Man in glory who was present in the suffering and marginal of the world (the parable of the sheep and the goats, Matt 25:31–46).

A second macro theme is a mirror image of the first: the evil of humans seeking or claiming absolute power. In the Creation narrative of Genesis, the human person according to Genesis 2:4b—3:24 is created for life and knowledge. The ultimate test or temptation in this narrative is to "be like God" (3:5), knowing good and evil, which is "knowledge in a wide sense, inasmuch as it relates to the mastery of human existence" (Westermann, *Creation*, 92–93). To know good and evil is to determine what is good and what is evil. Sin is overstepping the limits of the human condition by aspiring to divine power. As the primeval history unfolds, this desire reaches its climax in the attempt to raise a tower to the heavens (Gen 11:1–9). It resurfaces through the Bible in both the constant lure of idolatry and its rejection, culminating in the fall of "Babylon the Great" (Rev 13:1). The quest for domination and the arrogance of power in their various incarnations reenact primal evil.

As we approach a mosaic of biblical texts and themes, we do so with the realization that while we read and interpret the Bible, the Bible reads and interprets us. Karl Barth, one of the greatest theolo-

---

22. Joseph Jensen, *Ethical Dimensions of the Prophets* (Collegeville, MN: Liturgical Press, 2006), 13, in dialogue with John Barton, "Approaches to Ethics in the Old Testament," in *Beginning Old Testament Study*, ed. John Rogerson (Philadelphia: Westminster Press, 1983). (Emphasis in original.)

gians of the past century, once wrote that to ask what the Bible teaches is a dangerous question:

> We might do better not to come too near this burning bush. For we are sure to betray what is—behind *us*! The Bible gives to every man [and woman] and to every era such answers to their questions as they deserve. We shall always find in it as much as we seek and no more....The hungry are satisfied by it, and to the satisfied it is surfeiting before they have opened it. The question, "What is within the Bible?" has a mortifying way of converting itself into the opposing question, Well, what are your looking for, and who are you, pray, who make bold to look?[23]

I hope the following pages will help to raise dangerous questions!

RESOURCE BIBLIOGRAPHY

OFFICIAL DOCUMENTS OF CATHOLIC SOCIAL TEACHING

Documents of the Second Vatican Council, papal encyclicals and other Vatican documents can be found at www.vatican.va.

An excellent collection of magisterial documents through the pontificates of Pope John Paul II and Pope Benedict XVI can be found at www.justpeace.org/docu.htm.

Benedict XVI, Pope. *Caritas in Veritate* (Charity in Truth). Encyclical Letter, June 29, 2009.

Byers, David M., ed. *Justice in the Marketplace: Collected Statements of the Vatican and the U.S. Catholic Bishops on Economic Policy, 1891–1984.* Washington, DC: National Conference of Catholic Bishops, 1985. A comprehensive collection of documents.

Eagleson, J., and P. Scharper, eds. *Puebla and Beyond.* Maryknoll, NY: Orbis Books, 1980. A translation of final documents.

Economic Justice for All: Pastoral Letter on Catholic Social Teaching and the

---

23. Karl Barth, *The Word of God and the Word of Man*, trans. D. Horton (New York and Evanston: Harper and Row, 1957), 32. (Emphasis mine.)

U.S. Economy. Issued by the National Conference of Catholic Bishops, Nov. 18, 1986. Adapts the tradition of Catholic social teaching to United States' context. See also *Tenth Anniversary Edition of Economic Justice for All*, which includes *A Catholic Framework for Economic Life*, comprising ten points in both Spanish and English to summarize fundamental perspectives and facilitate discussion.

Francis, Pope. *Evangelii Gaudium* (The Joy of the Gospel). Apostolic Exhortation, November 24, 2013.

Gremillion, Joseph. *The Gospel of Peace and Justice: Catholic Social Teaching Since Pope John*. Maryknoll, NY: Orbis Books, 1976. An older collection of documents with historical introductions.

John Paul II, Pope. *Centesimus Annus* (On the Hundredth Anniversary of *Rerum Novarum*). Encyclical Letter, May 1, 1991.

————. *Laborem Exercens* (On Human Work) Encyclical Letter, September 14, 1981.

————. *Sollicitudo Rei Socialis* (On Social Concern). Encyclical Letter, December 30, 1987.

O'Brien, David J., and Thomas A. Shannon, eds. *Catholic Social Thought: The Documentary Heritage*. Maryknoll, NY: Orbis Books, 1992. Contains good introductions and brief commentaries. The older collections (by both Gremillion and Byers) remain helpful, since they cover statements not found elsewhere along with important introductions and comments.

Pontifical Council for Justice and Peace. *Compendium of the Social Doctrine of the Church*. Vatican City: Liberia Editrice Vaticana, 2004. Excellent collection of Church statements organized thematically with a fine index.

United States Catholic Conference. Publishing Services, 3211 Fourth St. NE, Washington, DC 20017–1194; www.usccb.org.

DISCUSSIONS AND SURVEYS OF CATHOLIC SOCIAL TEACHING

Burghardt, Walter J. *Justice: A Global Adventure*. Maryknoll, NY: Orbis Books, 2004. Pages 1–30, "Justice Analyzed," are a superb summary of biblical and theological foundations of social justice, while the rest of the book addresses significant contemporary issues. Section 5, "Justice Communicated," has a wealth of helpful material on various organizations dedicated to social justice, with excellent Web sites listed on pp. 262–67.

Coleman, John A., SJ, ed. *One Hundred Years of Catholic Social Thought: Celebration and Challenge.* Maryknoll, NY: Orbis Books, 1991. Especially helpful are: David J. O'Brien, "A Century of Catholic Social Teaching: Contexts and Comments;" John A. Coleman, "Neither Liberal or Socialist: The Originality of Catholic Social Teaching," Arbp. Rembert G. Weakland, OSB, "The Economic Pastoral Letter Revisited."

Curran, Charles E. *American Catholic Social Ethics: Twentieth Century Approaches.* Notre Dame: University of Notre Dame Press, 1982. An excellent survey focusing on individuals and movements.

—————. *Catholic Social Teaching, 1891–Present: A Historical, Theological, and Ethical Analysis.* Washington, DC: Georgetown University Press, 2002.

—————. "John Paul II's Use of Scripture in His Moral Teaching." *Horizons* 31 (2004): 118–34. A fine exposition with documentation.

—————. *The Social Mission of the Catholic Church: A Theological Perspective.* Washington, DC: Georgetown University Press, 2011.

Curran, Charles E., and Richard A. McCormick, eds. *Official Catholic Social Teaching.* Readings in Moral Theology 5. New York: Paulist Press, 1986.

Dwyer, Judith, ed. *The New Dictionary of Catholic Social Thought.* Collegeville, MN: Liturgical Press, 1994.

Himes, Kenneth, ed. *Modern Catholic Social Teaching: Commentaries and Interpretation.* Washington, DC: Georgetown University Press, 2005. Essays on aspects of Catholic social teaching as well as fine commentaries on the major papal encyclicals.

Massaro, Thomas. *Living Justice: Catholic Social Teaching in Action.* Franklin, WI: Sheed & Ward, 2000. Integrates Scripture and Church teaching with suggestions for application.

Schuck, Michael Joseph. *That They Be One: The Social Teaching of the Papal Encyclicals, 1740–1989.* Washington, DC: Georgetown University Press, 1991.

Schulteis, Michael J., Edward P. DeBerri, and Peter Henriot, eds. *Catholic Social Teaching: Our Best Kept Secret.* 4th ed. Maryknoll, NY: Orbis Books; Washington, DC: Center of Concern, 2007. A helpful survey ideal for classroom use.

RESOURCES FOR STUDIES OF BIBLICAL TEXTS

The number of commentaries is vast. Often the best place to begin is with one of the biblical dictionaries or one-volume commentaries listed below.

Carson, D. A. *New Testament Commentary Survey*. 6th ed. Grand Rapids, MI: Baker Academic, 2006.

Longman, Tremper. *Old Testament Commentary Survey*. Grand Rapids, MI: Baker Academic, 2007.

Commentaries in the various bibliographies will either be of special importance or published after these two surveys. Another most helpful resource for studying the influence of the Old Testament on the New is:

Beale, G. K., and D. A. Carson, eds. *Commentary on the New Testament Use of the Old Testament*. Grand Rapids, MI: Baker Academic, 2007.

STUDY BIBLES

Study Bibles provide an excellent resource because they contain introductory essays, introductions to particular books, and notes on particular texts.

Berlin, Adele, and Marc Z. Brettler, eds. *The Jewish Study Bible*. New York: Oxford University Press, 2004. An excellent commentary from a Jewish perspective with fine essays on different themes and on Jewish biblical interpretation.

Coogan, Michael D., Marc Z. Brettler, Carol A. Newsom, and Pheme Perkins, eds. *The New Oxford Annotated Bible with the Apocrypha*. Aug. 3rd ed., College ed. New Revised Standard Version. Oxford: Oxford University Press, 2007.

DeYoung, C. P., Wilda C. Gafney, Leticia Guardiola-Saenz, George Tinker, and Frank M. Yamada, eds. *The Peoples' Bible: New Revised Standard Version with the Apocrypha*. Minneapolis: Fortress Press, 2009. Through commentaries and introductions it seeks to give voice to those not part of the dominant cultures.

Halpur, Virginia, ed. *The College Study Bible*. Winona, MN: St. Mary's Press, 2006. Based on the Catholic translation found in the New American Bible.

Harrelson, Walter J., ed. *The New Interpreter's Study Bible*. Nashville: Abington Press, 2003.

Senior, Donald, ed. *The Catholic Study Bible*. 2nd ed. New York: Oxford University Press, 2006. Also based on the New American Bible.

ONE-VOLUME COMMENTARIES

These are commentaries on all the books of the Bible with extensive introductions and extended commentaries on individual sections and thematic essays.

Barton, John, and John Muddiman, eds. *Oxford Bible Commentary*. Oxford: Oxford University Press, 2007.

Blount, Brian, ed. *True to Our Native Land: An African American New Testament Commentary*. Minneapolis: Fortress Press, 2007. A commentary on each New Testament book, with articles on African American biblical interpretation and treatments of African American art.

Brown, Raymond E., Joseph A. Fitzmyer, and Roland E. Murphy, eds. *New Jerome Biblical Commentary*. Englewood Cliffs, NJ: Prentice Hall, 1990. An excellent resource with important essays and commentaries on each book of the Bible.

Dunn, James D. G., ed. *Eerdmans Commentary on the Bible*. Grand Rapids, MI: Eerdmans, 2003.

Farmer, William R., ed. *The International Bible Commentary: A Catholic and Ecumenical Commentary for the Twenty-First Century*. Collegeville, MN: Liturgical Press, 1998.

Karris, Robert J., ed. *Collegeville Bible Commentary*. Collegeville, MN: The Liturgical Press, 1997. Published originally as a collection of individual volumes; now gathered into one volume. Very helpful and readable.

Mays, James L., ed. *The HarperCollins Bible Commentary*. Rev. ed. San Francisco: HarperSanFrancisco, 1988.

Newsom, Carol A., and Sharon H. Ringe, eds. *Women's Bible Commentary*. Louisville, KY: Westminster John Knox Press, 1998.

OLD TESTAMENT INTRODUCTIONS

Boadt, Lawrence. *Reading the Old Testament: An Introduction*. 2nd ed. Revised and updated by Richard Clifford and Daniel Harrington. New York/Mahwah, NJ: Paulist Press, 2012. Long and standard introduction, updated after the author's death in 2010.

Carvalho, Corrine. *Encountering Ancient Voices: A Guide to Reading the Old Testament*. Winona, MN: St. Mary's Press, 2006.

Collins, John J. *An Introduction to the Hebrew Bible*. Minneapolis: Fortress Press, 2007.

BIBLICAL DICTIONARIES

Achtemeier, Paul J., ed. *The HarperCollins Bible Dictionary*. San Francisco: HarperSanFrancisco, 1996. Revised and updated in 2011 by HarperCollins.

Buttrick, George, ed. *The Interpreter's Dictionary of the Bible*. 4 vols. with supplementary volume. Nashville: Abingdon Press, 1962.

Freedman, D. N., ed. *Anchor Bible Dictionary*. 6 vols. New York: Doubleday, 1992. Most complete coverage of biblical material. Also available on CD–ROM.

————. ed. *Eerdmans Dictionary of the Bible*. Grand Rapids, MI: Eerdmans, 2000.

Stuhlmueller, Carroll, ed. *Collegeville Pastoral Dictionary of Biblical Theology*. Collegeville, MN: Liturgical Press, 1996. A helpful and accurate description of terms.

Sakenfeld, Katherine Doob, ed. *New Interpreter's Dictionary of the Bible*. 5 vols. Nashville: Abington Press, 2006–9.

STUDIES OF BIBLICAL ETHICS (WITH A FOCUS ON SOCIAL JUSTICE ISSUES)

The works of Houston and Pleins cover all the major issues and should be consulted whenever dealing with Old Testament topics.

Barton, John. *Ethics and the Old Testament*. Harrisburg, PA: Trinity Press International, 1998.

————. *Understanding Old Testament Ethics: Approaches and Explorations*. Louisville, KY: Westminster John Knox Press, 2003.

Berman, Joshua A. *Created Equal: How the Bible Broke with Ancient Political Thought*. New York/Oxford: Oxford University Press, 2008. An excellent study contrasting various perceptions of justice in the ancient world that argues for a fundamental egalitarian perspective in Israel.

Birch, Bruce C. *Let Justice Roll: The Old Testament, Ethics and the Christian Life*. Louisville, KY: Westminster John Knox Press, 1991. This work surveys the literature in canonical and historical order from Genesis through the Wisdom literature.

―――――. *What Does the Lord Require? The Old Testament Call to Social Witness*. Philadelphia: Westminster Press, 1985. More popular presentations of material that Birch later develops in *Let Justice Roll*.

Birch, Bruce C., and Larry L. Rasmussen. *The Predicament of the Prosperous*. Philadelphia: Westminster Press, 1978. This work arose from discussions in both academic and pastoral settings.

Brueggemann, Walter. *Journey to the Common Good*. Louisville, KY: Westminster John Knox Press, 2010. An insightful study of texts and themes.

Burnside, Jonathan. *God, Justice, and Society: Aspects of Law and Legality in the Bible*. New York: Oxford University Press, 2011. Burnside is Reader in Biblical Law at the School of Law, University of Bristol, England; this work is a comprehensive coverage of all aspects of biblical law organized around particular issues, for example, chapters 4, "Justice as a Calling," and 7, "Social Welfare."

Ceresko, Anthony B. *Introduction to the Old Testament: A Liberation Perspective*. Maryknoll, NY: Orbis Books, 1992. From 1991 to his early death in 2005, Ceresko taught seminarians in India and the Philippines.

Chan, Yiu Sing Lúcás. *Biblical Ethics in the 21st Century: Developments, Emerging Consensus and Future Directions*. New York/Mahwah, NJ: Paulist Press, 2013. An excellent survey of people and perspectives by an important young Chinese scholar.

Coomber, Matthew J. M. *Bible And Justice: Ancient Texts, Modern Challenges*. London/Oakville, CT: Equinox, 2011. A fine collection of essays by leading scholars.

Epsztein, Léon. *Social Justice in the Ancient Near East and the People of the Bible*. London: SCM Press, 1986. Good resource on the background of Israel's social legislation.

Felder, Cain H. "Toward a New Testament Hermeneutic for Justice," Howard University Lecture. *Journal of Religious Thought* 45 (1988): 10–28. An interesting study by a leading African American theologian.

Fitzmyer, J. A. "What Do The Scriptures Say About Justice?" In *Proceedings of the Jesuit Education 21 Conference*, edited by Martin Tripole, 98–112. Philadelphia: St. Joseph's University Press,

2000. With responses by biblical scholars Richard Clifford, Stanley Marrow, and Mark Smith.

Gill, Robin, ed. *Cambridge Companion to Christian Ethics*. 2nd. Ed. New York: Cambridge University Press, 2012. A collection of twenty essays by leading experts with important chapters on "The Old Testament and Christian Ethics" (John Rogerson), "The Gospels and Christian Ethics" (Allen Verhey), and "The Epistles and Christian Ethics" (Stephen C. Barton).

Green, Joel B., ed. *Dictionary of Scripture and Ethics*. Grand Rapids, MI: Baker Academic, 2011. A comprehensive coverage arranged alphabetically.

Haughey, John C., ed. *The Faith that Does Justice*. New York/Ramsey: Paulist Press, 1977. Though a bit dated, the essays by Donahue, "Biblical Perspectives on Justice," and Haughey, "Jesus as the Justice of God," offer a good introduction to important biblical themes and texts.

Hoppe, Leslie J. *There Shall Be No Poor Among You: Poverty in the Bible*. Nashville, TN: Abingdon Press, 2004. A treatment of the poor in all Old and New Testament literature. Ideal for classroom use.

Houston, Walter J. *Contending for Justice: Ideologies and Theologies of Social Justice in the Old Testament*. Library of Hebrew Bible/Old Testament Studies 428. London/New York: T & T Clark, 2006. An excellent study of texts and themes with an eye on contemporary problems.

Irani, K. D., and Morris Silver, eds. *Social Justice in the Ancient World*. Westport, CT: Greenwood Press, 1995. Individual essays on social justice in the wide context of the ancient world.

Johnson, Barbara. [*mshpt*] In *Theological Dictionary of the Old Testament*. Edited by G. Johannes Botterweck, H. Ringgren, and H.-J. Fabry. Grand Rapids, MI: Eerdmans, 2003. Vol 9, 86–98, and [*tsdq*] Ibid. Vol 12, 239–64.

Leclerc, Thomas. *Yahweh Is Exalted in Justice: Solidarity and Conflict in Isaiah*. Minneapolis: Fortress Press, 2001. A most thorough and informative study of justice in Isaiah with comments on the passages from Isaiah used in the lectionary.

Marshall, Chris. *The Little Book of Biblical Justice: A Fresh Approach to the Bible's Teaching on Justice*. Intercourse, PA: Good Books, 2005. An excellent work with many insights; would be ideal for a parish study group.

Mott, Stephen C. *Biblical Ethics and Social Change*. 2nd ed. New York: Oxford University Press, 2012. Organized thematically with coverage of both Testaments. Part 1 constitutes "A Biblical Theology of Social Involvement" and Part 2, "Paths to Justice." He views the Church as a "counter cultural" community committed to nonviolent implementation of social change.

Nardoni, Enrique. *Rise Up, O Judge: A Study of Justice in the Biblical World*. Peabody, MA: Hendrickson, 2004. A wide-ranging study with coverage from Mesopotamia through the New Testament with an extensive bibliography. Ideal for a seminary or graduate course.

Ogletree, Thomas W. *The Use of the Bible in Christian Ethics: A Constructive Essay*. Philadelphia: Fortress Press, 1983. A sophisticated attempt by an ethicist to bridge the gap between biblical studies and ethics. The chapter on "Covenant and Commandment" (47–85) is one of the best treatments of the implications of covenant for a theology of social justice.

Pedersen, Johannes. *Israel. Its Life and Culture (Vols. I–II)*. London: Oxford University Press, 1926. Reprinted in South Florida Studies in the History of Judaism 28. Atlanta: Scholars Press, 1991. A socio-anthropological treatment of ancient Israel.

Pleins, J. David. *The Social Visions of the Hebrew Bible: A Theological Introduction*. Louisville, KY: Westminster John Knox Press, 2001. A most comprehensive and scholarly study of social teaching of the Hebrew Bible.

Pontifical Biblical Commission. *Bible and Morality: Biblical Roots of Christian Conduct*. Vatican City: Libreria Editrice Vaticana, 2008. A helpful descriptive survey of biblical morality.

Reventlow, G., and Y. Hoffman, eds. *Justice and Righteousness: Biblical Themes and Their Influence*. JSOT Sup. 137. Sheffield: JSOT Press, 1992.

Rood, Cyril S. *Glimpses of a Strange Land: Studies in Old Testament Ethics*. Edinburgh: T & T Clark, 2001. A thorough and informative treatment organized topically, for example, "The Ten Commandments"; "Lending at Interest"; "The Poor."

Spohn, William C. *What Are They Saying about Scripture and Ethics?* 2nd ed. New York/Mahwah, NJ: Paulist Press, 1995. An excellent survey of the various ways Scripture is used in addressing ethical issues with guidelines for fruitful appropriation.

Westermann, Claus. *Creation*. Philadelphia: Fortress Press, 1974. This short volume (123 pages) is the best discussion of Creation.

Wolterstorff, Nicholas P. *Journey toward Justice: Personal Encounters in the Global South*. Grand Rapids: MI, Baker Academic, 2013. An important study by Professor Emeritus of Philosophical Theology at Yale. Wolterstorff argues strongly against the translation of *tsedaqah* as "righteousness." See also his *Justice in Love*. Grand Rapids: MI, Eerdmans, 2011.

CONTEMPORARY JEWISH STUDIES OF SOCIAL JUSTICE

Jewish scholars are the leading interpreters of the Hebrew Bible, but their works are most often directed to a wide audience of both non-Jewish and Jewish scholars and students. The works listed below manifest a concern to apply the Jewish traditions of the "written and oral Torah" primarily to Jewish life today.

Dorff, Rabbi Elliot. *The Way Into Tikkun Olam (Repairing the World)*. Woodstock, VT: Jewish Lights Publishers, 2006. An excellent introduction that explores the roots of the beliefs and laws that are the basis of the Jewish commitment to improve the world and examines the various motivations that the sacred texts provide for caring for others.

Dorff, Rabbi Elliot, with Reverend Cory Willson. *The Jewish Approach to Repairing the World (Tikkun Olam): A Brief Introduction for Christians*. Woodstock, VT: Jewish Lights Publishers, 2008. Good description of Jewish terms for social justice.

Jacobs, Jill. *There Shall Be No Needy: Pursuing Social Justice through Jewish Law and Tradition*. Woodstock, VT: Jewish Lights Publishers, 2009. The author recounts her journey toward applying her rabbinical training to issues of social justice.

Rose, Or N., Jo Ellen Green Kaiser, and Margie Klein, eds. *Righteous Indignation: A Jewish Call for Justice*. Woodstock, VT: Jewish Lights Publishers. 2008. See esp. part 4, "The Yoke of Oppression: Social and Economic Justice."

Schwarz, Sidney. *Judaism and Justice: The Jewish Passion to Repair the World*. Woodstock, VT: Jewish Lights Publishers, 2006.

Yanklowitz, Rabbi Shmuly. *Jewish Ethics and Social Justice*. Pompano Beach, FL: Derusha Publishing LLC, 2012. A study by an orthodox scholar drawing on multiple sources of Jewish tradition.

CHAPTER 2

CREATION AND EXODUS

Foundational Narratives

CREATION: A VISION OF THE PAST
THAT FORMS THE FUTURE

While the biblical literature evolved over centuries from diverse oral traditions to blocks of literature, and finally, named books, its canonical shape was fixed rather late. For example, Genesis 1—11 (Creation and primeval history), though "at the beginning" was appended to the national history (Exodus—Deuteronomy) only after the exile (586–36 BC), and the Torah receives its final shape only between 300 and 200 BC.

Though qualified by subsequent scholarship, the positions of Gerhard von Rad and Martin Noth still offer an excellent way to survey the development of the Old Testament. Von Rad argued that the Pentateuchal traditions developed from creedal formulae such as Deuteronomy 6:20–25 and 26:1–12 and Joshua 24:2–13, which provided the fundamental themes of Israel's faith, where a *theme* is understood as a basic act of God by which the people are constituted. When expanded into a narrative, these themes attract related themes and motifs. Noth underlined five such themes: (1) the guidance out of Egypt (Exodus); (2) the "guidance into arable land" (Joshua); (3) the promise to the patriarchs (Genesis 12—50); (4) the guidance (and testing) in the wilderness; and (5) the revelation at Sinai. Our focus will be on two of these themes: the exodus and covenant, but we begin with the Creation story, which is an important "overture" to the salvation history of Genesis through Joshua (Noth, "Major Themes," 46–62).

The final canonical shaping of the Pentateuch is important theologically. At its center stands the covenant of Sinai, which forms those liberated from Egypt into a nation with responsibilities and duties. God's *gift* of liberation, involves a *demand* for fidelity. The older story of the taking of the land, with its triumphalist tendencies has been supplanted by the beginning of the Deuteronomic history (Deuteronomy) with its warnings against recurring infidelity.

A generation of Catholics was nurtured on two perspectives that are no longer helpful for understanding Creation in the Bible. The first was that Genesis 1—3 (culminating in the fall and the expulsion of Adam and Eve) could be read as an independent block of material. This was undergirded by the use of these chapters primarily for the doctrine of original sin. The second was that the biblical Creation narratives dealt with cosmology. This latter view was supported by debates over evolution. As Claus Westermann has strongly argued, the whole primeval history (Gen 1—11) must be read as a unity, culminating in the tower of Babel (Westermann, *Creation*). Lawrence Boadt has described eloquently the power of these narratives:

> Its [Gen 1—11] strong images and rich language explore the depths of human experience at its most mysterious— the awesome wonder of creation, the joys of life, the agony of sin, the fear of death, the terrible human capacity for evil, the existence of God, and the questions about his patience and justice. In bold strokes, it makes us understand what God's *salvation* meant to Israel. (*Reading*, 87 [emphasis in original])

It is customary to see two major perspectives in the Creation account. The "preamble" or first account (Gen 1:1—2:4a) is attributed to the Priestly tradition (P), and is the later of the two accounts. The second account, which narrates the Creation of the man and the woman, their offspring, and the spread of civilization (Gen 2:4b— 4:26) is attributed to J (the Yahwist).

Contemporary reflection on social justice turns often to these accounts to ground human dignity in the Creation in God's image, to argue for the common claim of all humanity to the world's resources, and more frequently now, for reflection on ecological issues. I will now simply indicate elements in the text that are important.

The first account describes a primitive cosmology in rhythmic cadences identified by a division into "days," with the frequent refrain, that "it was good" (Gen 1:4, 10, 12, 18, 21, 25), culminating in the final day when God views all creation as "very good" (v. 31). Claus Westermann, whose extensive writings on Creation are the best resource for a proper biblical theology of Creation, notes that these narratives reveal the Priestly stress that all events have their origin in God's commanding Word. They prepare for the revelation on Sinai when God's Word forms the somewhat chaotic throng into a people (*Creation*, 42). He also notes that the author, by placing the separation of night and day through the Creation of "light" before the Creation of "space," stresses that human life is temporal and historical.

The goodness of creation is not something that men and women affirm but is a divine proclamation. By locating the Creation story as a preamble to the whole sacred history, the Priestly writer proclaims the goodness of all creation even though the narrative that unfolds depicts the catastrophic results of sin on both nature and human history (Westermann, *Genesis 1—11*, 60–64). The proper response to creation is praise and thanksgiving even amid suffering and catastrophe, since God has affirmed that nature and its power are "good." Two obvious implications arise from Genesis 1:1—2:4a: first, the response to creation is reverence and praise, not exploitation; and second, humanity shares solidarity with both the inanimate and animate world in owing its existence to the Word of God.

The Creation narrative of P reaches its summit in Genesis 1:26–27:

> Then God said, "Let us make humankind in our image, according to our likeness; and let them have dominion over the fish of the sea, and over the birds of the air, and over the cattle, and over all the wild animals of the earth, and over every creeping thing that creeps upon the earth."

> So God created humankind in his image,
>   in the image of God he created them;
>   male and female he created them. (Cf. also, Gen 5:1b–2; 9:6)

This proclamation is then followed by the blessing of man and woman, the command to be fruitful and multiply, and God's resting on the seventh day. Man and woman created in the image of God is one of the most frequently cited texts to undergird human dignity and human rights. Two major lines of interpretation have emerged from this powerful text. One locates the image of God among human qualities, for example, intellect or will, or other qualities described as "substantialist" and "functional," based on the meaning of the phrase in its biblical and historical contexts (Towner, "Clones of God," and Middleton, *The Liberating Image*, 17–24). Among the latter is the view that just as ancient Near Eastern kings erected "images" of themselves in subject territory, so humans are God's representatives, to be given the same honor due God. Claus Westermann argues that the phrase means that humans were created to be God's counterpart, humans analogous to God with whom God can speak and who will hear God's Word (*Creation*, 10). In either of these interpretations, all men and women prior to identification by race, social status, religion, or sex are worthy of respect and reverence.

People concerned about ecology have often criticized the term "have dominion" (see Gen 2:15, "to till and to keep") as the warrant for a utilitarian view of creation, or as justification for the exploitation of creation for human convenience. The Hebrew term is used in other places of the royal care that characterizes a king as God's vice regent (Pss 72:8; 110:2; cf. Ps 8:5–9). Like ancient kings, men and women are to be the mediators of prosperity and well-being (Westermann, *Genesis 1—11*, 51–53). Towner captures powerfully the power of these verses:

> In short, the Genesis assessment that we human beings are made in the image of God and that from a right relationship with God flows nurturing "dominion" in the world launches us aright....We are God's creatures and chosen partners in the work of the creation. We are given ever greater opportunity to be bearers of the divine image, that is, positive, responsible stewards in the world, until the day that God makes all things new. ("Clones," 410)

Reverential care for God's creation rather than exploitation is the mandate given humanity in this section of Genesis.

The second and older Creation story (2:4b—4:26) is more anthropomorphic and more dramatic. It may be composed of two originally different stories. One deals with the origin of the sexes. The original human one (*ha 'adam*) from the clay of the earth, is now differentiated into *'ish* ("man") and a complementary partner (*'ishsha*). In her groundbreaking discussion of this section, Phyllis Trible has stressed that this narrative, while stressing differentiation among humans, does not imply derivation or subordination of woman to man, but both "owe the origin to divine mystery" (Trible, *God*, 101–2). The other major theme, as Westermann stresses, is the spread of sin that runs through Genesis 1—11 (see also, 4:1–6; 6:1–4, 6–9; 11:1–10). The former motif has dominated the history of exegesis of the Creation account.

Two elements of the Creation of "man" and "woman" are important for contemporary reflection. First, as a story of mythic beginnings (akin to other ancient myths of "androgyny"), the narrative stresses the complementarity of male and female. The "human" is male and female united as "one flesh" (2:24), not understood simply as a description of marriage, but as a basic fact of prototypical human existence. On the anthropological level, this calls for recognition of the presence of "male" and "female" in every human. On the social level, it means that the human condition can never be defined or named in terms of the dominant characteristics or activity of one sex (Trible, *God*, 12–23, 72–105).

The narrative of the origin of the human family as a dialogue partner with God and living in mutual harmony with each other and with creation is followed by the "fall." Proper understanding of the "fall" or sin of the first parents also has implications for a theological grounding of social justice. Taking this narrative on its own terms requires a bracketing of its Pauline and post-Pauline interpretation (Rom 5:12–20; 2 Cor 11:3; 1 Tim 2:13–15), as well as of the Augustinian doctrine of "original sin." The narrative remains, however, a rich source for understanding human evil and alienation from God.

It explains the human potentiality for evil, no matter how gifted one may be. The human person, according to Genesis 2:4b—3:24, is created for life and knowledge. The ultimate test or temptation in this narrative is to "be like God" (3:5), knowing good and evil, which is "knowledge in a wide sense, inasmuch as it relates to the mastery of human existence" (Westermann, *Creation*, 92–93). "Knowing good and evil," also suggests defining what is good or evil, which characterizes every form of dictatorship. The temptation is always to an autonomy, which seeks knowledge and power apart from the limits of being human, or from life in community. Sin is overstepping the limits of the human condition by aspiring to divine power. It can take place through action (the woman) or through complicity (the man). Their desire to be like God, sadly, separates them from God.

After the fall, the narrative relates the trial and the punishment (3:8–24). The expected punishment of 3:3 ("you shall die") does not occur. Instead the harmony of their earlier status is destroyed. The desire for human autonomy leads to alienation and a breakdown of community—with nature and between man and woman. It is important to note that the subordinate position of woman (3:16–17), which reflects the de facto situation of women in ancient society, is not something that was to be part of the original blessing of creation but arises from human sinfulness. Alienation between the earth and humans (3:17–19) is likewise the result of sin. While the "work" of cultivating and caring for the earth is intrinsic to the human condition prior to sin, "toil" is its consequence.

The narratives of Genesis 4—11 capture the ambivalence of the human condition. As civilization grows through the multiplication of occupations (farmers and shepherds), through the invention of elements of culture (4:19–22), and weapons of war, sin is depicted as "crouched at the door" (4:7) and humans continually overstep their limits. As the generations unfold, the daughters of man (Gen 6:4) are united with beings identified as the sons of God (*bene ʿelohim*). Though obscure in meaning, it is another instance of the violation of the boundary between humanity and God. As in the original Creation account, while God saw that creation was very good, now "great was man's wickedness on earth" (Gen 6:5). The flood story therefore follows, in which the deity wipes out life on earth, which has become corrupt, and starts anew to repopulate it from the seed of an exceptionally righteous man, Noah.

This story culminates in the account of the covenant with Noah (9:1–17), the first one explicitly mentioned in Genesis. Though the promise and covenants with Abraham, which dominate the patriarchal history (Gen 12:1–9; 15:7–16; 17:1–27) are directed to the future people of Israel, this first covenant introduces an all-inclusive strain into the Bible. It requires nothing on humanity's part (unilateral), is extended to all creation (vv. 9–10), and its sign is a natural phenomenon (vv. 13–16). The covenant with Abraham presupposes his personal commitment to God, is extended only to his descendants, and its sign is circumcision (Gen 17). The covenant with Israel requires continuing loyalty (Exod 24:7–8), is restricted to the nation, and its sign is the Sabbath observance (Exod 31:16–17). The prescriptions of the Noachic covenant provide a vision of God's acceptance of Gentiles and have influenced the decision of James at the "Jerusalem Council" (Acts 15:19–20).

Yet humanity continues to overstep its bounds. This culminates in the tower of Babel, where humans attempt to invade the realm of God (Gen 11:1–9). Though a reprise of the attempt to be like God (cf. Gen 3:5), the narrative has political ramifications. Set in primeval time, it receives its final form after the Babylonian exile. The fate of Babylon, with its pretensions of world rule and its idolatrous self-exaltation, only to be split apart by the onslaught of Cyrus, is reflected in the tower of Babel. The spread of sin culminates in the idolatrous pretensions of national power, and its result is the splintering of the human family.

These early chapters of Genesis are also important for reflection on the somewhat controversial notion of "social sin." The term was first used by theologians and derived from reflection on certain official Church statements. Speaking of the economic, political, and social order in *Gaudium et Spes* (Pastoral Constitution on the Church in the Modern World), the Second Vatican Council stated that "the structure of human affairs is flawed by the consequences of sin," (no. 25). The 1971 Synod of Bishops noted that the present day situation of the world is marked by "the grave sin of injustice" (no. 29), and called for a renewal of heart "based on the recognition of sin in its individual and social manifestations" (no. 51).[1] In their pastoral letter on racism, *Brothers and Sisters to*

---

1. "Justice in the World: 1971 Synod of Bishops," in *Renewing the Earth: Catholic Documents on Peace, Justice, and Liberation*, ed. David J. O'Brien and Thomas A. Shannon (Garden City, NJ: Image Books, 1977), 384–408.

Us, the United States bishops describe racism as social sin "in that each one of us in varying degrees is responsible and all of us are in some measure accomplices."[2] The 1986 letter of the United States bishops on the economy, *Economic Justice for All*, said that in developing countries when "the elites" exclude masses of people from use of their own natural resources, this is a form of social sin (no. 77). Social sin came to be identified with structures of injustice, discrimination, or oppression that men and women participate in, either by direct action or by being passive accomplices.

Though Vatican and papal statements have cautioned that sin is primarily a freely chosen act of an individual, they have allowed for the term in an analogous or extended sense (see especially, the Apostolic Exhortation on Reconciliation and Penance, issued by Pope John Paul II in response to the 1983 Synod of Bishops, on December 11, 1984).[3] Actually the biblical notion of sin is primarily social and only gradually becomes individual. In the Genesis accounts, sin is a power that "lurks at the door" (Gen 4:7), and that spreads through humanity. The prophets indict the sins of groups rather than individuals, as in the denunciations of the nations or the indictments of "the house of Israel" (Amos 1:3—2:16). Those judged at the end of Matthew (25:31–46) for neglect of the little ones are "nations" not individuals. Paul conceives of sin as a power that threatens to rule over people's lives (Rom 5:12–21), and in the Gospel of John, Jesus is the Lamb who will take away the "sin of the world" (1:29, *not* "sins" as in the Latin translation: *qui tollis peccata mundi*).

The primeval history of Genesis 1—11 thus provides a rich resource for reflection on issues crucial to faith and justice. Men and women are God's representatives and conversation partners in the world, with a fundamental dignity that must be respected and fostered. They are to exist in interdependence and mutual support, and are to care for the world with respect, as for a gift received from God. Yet, the human condition is flawed by a drive to overstep the limits of the human situation, and to claim autonomous power. The result of this is violence (Cain and Abel) and the spread of evil and idolatry (the tower of Babel). These narratives anticipate the rhythm of divine gift, human

---

2. *Origins*, 9:24 (Nov. 29, 1979): 383–89.

3. *Origins*, 14:27 (Dec. 20, 1984): 434–58, esp. 441–42.

sin, and a divine restoration that permeates the Bible. They also function both as a normative description of the human condition before God and a critical principle against any power that distorts or usurps the dignity of humanity or God's claim over men and women.

The primeval history is followed by a sequence of narratives or "legends" under the aegis of promises to the ancestors of the people, primarily to Abraham and his descendants (Gen 12—50). The covenants and promises to Abraham, spanning his migration from Mesopotamia through the descent of his heirs to Egypt, anticipate the drama of the exodus—will God be faithful to his promises and how will people continue to respond? Despite the power of sin to destroy humanity and creation, people are called to live out of the promise of God's fidelity. Such a disposition is a prerequisite for the practice and theology of social justice.

EXODUS: THE BIRTH OF A NATION

As we approach the narratives of Exodus 1:1—15:21 as a paradigm of liberation, two cautions arise: the first, that a too generalized statement of its meaning absolves people from close attention to the rich theological dimensions of the text; the second, that the Exodus narrative is considered in isolation from other biblical themes. While liberation from oppression is a fundamental aspect of the Exodus narrative, it is not simply *freedom from* that is important but *freedom for* the formation of a community that lives under the covenant. As Michael Walzer says, the journey of Israel is to a "kind of bondage in freedom, the bondage of law, responsibility and obligation" (Walzer, *Exodus*, 56). Exodus and covenant, liberation and commitment must be taken together as part of one process.

The narrative falls roughly into the following divisions:

The oppression of the Hebrew people (1:1—2:22);

The preparation of Moses as the agent of liberation (2:23—7:7);

The plagues on Egypt, culminating in the death of Egypt's firstborn (7:8—13:16);

The crossing of the sea, the destruction of the Egyptian
armies, and the hymn of Miriam (13:17—15:21).

The description of Israel's bondage has become paradigmatic of
oppression. In fulfillment of the promise to Abraham and through no
action of their own, other than fulfilling God's command to be fruitful
and multiply, the people grow numerous and become a threat to a
dominant power. The initial response is one of massive forced labor.
Moses Maimonides described this as labor without limit or purpose
that exhausts and degrades the slave (Walzer, *Exodus*, 27). The second
major threat, the killing of the male children, is in effect genocide. The
people's identity will be slowly but surely destroyed. Theologically, it is
a challenge to the fidelity (justice) of God manifest in the promises to
Abraham.

Though it is customary to mark the beginning of the liberation
from the birth of Moses (Exod 2:1–20), the "revolt of the midwives"
(1:15–22) is an important paradigm of resistance to oppression. It is
described briefly: "But the midwives feared God; they did not do as the
king of Egypt commanded them, but they let the boys live" (1:17).
These women, the daughters of Eve, the mother of all the living, commissioned to bring forth life in the world, reject the murderous command of Pharaoh. They do this in light of a higher law ("fearing God,"
1:17, 21). Therefore, "God dealt well with the midwives, and the
people multiplied and became very strong" (see Exum, "Every
Daughter"). On the narrative level, they allow the promise to continue
and also prepare for the rescue of Moses from death (2:1–10).

The process of liberation continues with the "liberation" of the liberator. The agent of liberation must suffer the same fate as that of the
people (threat of death; life as an alien in an alien land [Exod 2:15;
3:22]). At the same time, the liberator must be equipped to meet the
threat (3:1–11) and be the agent of a higher power (4:10–11). Liberation is a power struggle, between humans and their oppressors, but
more fundamentally between God and the powers opposed to God.

The theophany at the burning bush and the call of Moses proclaim that liberation is fundamentally an act of God. God's action
begins in Exodus 2:24, "God heard their groaning, and remembered
his covenant," and is detailed in 3:7–12, which is a virtual summary of

the identity of Yahweh as the compassionate God who enters human history. Immediately after the revelation of the name, Yahweh says, "I have *observed* the misery of the people...; I have *heard* their cry....Indeed I *know* their sufferings, and I have *come down to deliver them*" (3:7–12, emphasis mine; see Luke 1:78, "By the tender mercy [compassion] of our God, the dawn from on high will break upon us").

The liberation itself unfolds through the sequence of ten plagues, divided into three triads culminating in the killing of the Egyptian first-born and the "passing over" of the firstborn of Israel. In the plagues, nature itself turns against the Egyptians, almost in revulsion for their oppression of God's people. As the plagues escalate, the issue again becomes the nature of God, and the usurpation of divine power. In Exodus 9:16–17a, God speaks through Moses to Pharaoh: "This is why I have let you live: to show you my power, and to make my name resound through all the earth. You are still exalting yourself against my people."

In the final plague, the Passover, (11:1—13:16) the P source (12:1–38) becomes prominent, demonstrating that the narrative had become "the cult legend" for the later celebration of Passover. Here the exodus receives the character of *anamnesis*, something to be re-presented and celebrated annually. Thus it continues to shape the identity of the people and reveal the nature of God.

Exodus is a paradigm of liberation—a power struggle in which the issues of oppression are progressively highlighted. Pharaoh begins with concern about the growth of an alien population, but the real issue is whether he will be their "god," or whether they will be free to worship the one who called their ancestors. Oppression and idolatry are never far apart.

Liberation most often does not originate from the most oppressed members of the community, but ultimately must be appropriated by them. Moses is nurtured at the center of Egypt's power, and is equipped to enter its world. Through his own conversion and prepa-ration by God, he becomes a prophet, one who speaks for God and for a people without a voice (cf. Deut 34:10, "Never since has there arisen a prophet...like Moses"). An enduring legacy of liberation theology is that the path to social justice always remains a struggle and that powerful people always oppose this struggle while others rise up to confront such power.

However, liberation is but one aspect of a true concept of freedom. Israel's journey is "from liberation to freedom," which is the ultimate theme of the wilderness wandering and the covenant at Sinai.

LIBERATION THEOLOGY

In the areas of social ethics, the biblical renewal had its most significant impact on the development of liberation theology (see Hennelly, *Liberation Theology*). Over the last four decades, liberation theology has become a mosaic of many movements, but there are fundamental and lasting perspectives, highlighted in a fine survey by Roger Haight.[4] Haight roots liberation theology in earlier movements such as the turn to experience in Karl Rahner, the rise of historical and political theology (Schillebeeckx, Metz, Tracy), and concern among Latin American theologians for "the dehumanized conditions of large numbers of people" and the challenge of theology (and the gospel) to respond to this condition. The *Encyclopedia Britannica* gives a general definition of liberation theology:

> In late 20th-century Roman Catholicism a movement centered in Latin America that sought to apply religious faith by aiding the poor and oppressed through involvement in political and civic affairs. It stressed both heightened awareness of the socioeconomic structures that caused social inequities and active participation in changing those structures.[5]

Ivan Petrella, a contemporary theorist of liberation theology, has called for its "reinvention" and argued one aspect of its original goals remains to be fulfilled: "its 'historical projects': models of political and economic organization that would replace an unjust status quo" (Petrella, *Future*, vii).

---

4. "Lessons From an Extraordinary Era: Catholic Theology Since Vatican II," *America* (March 17, 2008): 11–16.

5. Web edition, http://www.britannica.com/EBchecked/topic/339237/liberation-theology.

The Bible provided a rich storehouse of motifs and texts that enabled people to reflect on their lives in light of revelation, while challenging previously held positions. Not surprisingly, the exodus or the liberation of an oppressed people from Egypt became a prime symbol that spoke to people suffering contemporary forms of oppression. In the seminal work of Gustavo Gutiérrez, *liberation* has a threefold meaning: "political liberation, human liberation throughout history, and admission to communion with God" (Gutiérrez, *Theology*, 103). Despite the inaccurate criticism that liberation theology secularizes salvation and glosses over things such as sin and forgiveness, Gutiérrez sees these three forms of liberation as integrally related.

Liberation theology drew on the Old Testament for other major themes such as the prophetic attack on unbridled power and wealth, and the defense of the poor and oppressed, which developed into the somewhat controversial articulation of "the preferential option for the poor." Though inaccurately criticized by Catholic conservatives as choosing one group over the other, the option for the poor is articulated in the 1986 letter of the U.S. bishops, *Economic Justice for All*, as the duty to speak for the voiceless, to defend the defenseless, and to assess lifestyles, policies, and social institutions in terms of their impact on the poor. This "option for the poor" does not mean pitting one group against another, but rather, strengthening the whole community by assisting those who are the most vulnerable (no. 16).

Crucial to the hermeneutics of liberation theology is an analysis of the human experience and social location *of those who read the Bible*. This involves a dialogue between the biblical text and the experiences of readers, which are often related by a process of analogy. The process of analogy is itself justified by the theological perspective that God continually acts in human history in ways that are disclosed primarily in the Bible, and continued throughout human history.

Liberation theology itself changed and developed over four decades, and moved beyond its origin in Latin America. Even a cursory survey of current literature discloses a great number of works from Asia and Africa. Furthermore, although nurtured by Catholic theologians, liberation theology became the most ecumenical of theological disciplines with contributions by liberal and evangelical Protestant scholars, as well as by significant Jewish scholars. Feminist theology, which shares the same fundamental perspectives of liberation theology, continues to be one of the most vital theological movements in the contemporary churches. Liberation hermeneutics has provided a lens through which to read biblical texts that moves beyond Exodus and the prophets to embrace the whole of the biblical witness.

RESOURCE BIBLIOGRAPHY

ON CREATION

Anderson, Bernhard, ed. *Creation in the Old Testament.* Philadelphia: Fortress Press; London: S.P.C.K., 1984. A fine collection of classic and contemporary essays. See esp. G. Landes, "Creation and Liberation," 135–51 and B. Anderson, "Creation and Ecology," 152–71.

Boadt, Lawrence. *Reading the Old Testament: An Introduction.* 2nd ed. Revised and updated by Richard Clifford and Daniel Harrington. New York/Mahwah, NJ: Paulist Press, 2012.

Brown, William P. *The Seven Pillars of Creation.* New York: Oxford University Press, 2010. Study of seven major textual collections (Gen 1:1–2, 3; 2:4–3, 24; Job 38—41; Ps 104; Prov 8:22–31; Eccl 1:2–11, 12:1–7) and the emergence of the new creation in "Second Isaiah." An excellent cross-disciplinary study of biblical texts in dialogue with modern science, written in an appealing style for nonspecialists.

Clifford, Richard J. *Creation Accounts in the Ancient Near East and in the Bible.* Washington, DC: Catholic Biblical Association, 1994. An important collection of articles by leading scholars.

Dempsey, Carol J., and Mary Margaret Pazdan, eds. *Earth, Wind and Fire: Biblical and Theological Perspectives on Creation.* Collegeville, MN: Liturgical Press, 2004. A collection of essays by feminist scholars that joins biblical and theological reflection to contemporary ecological concerns.

Middleton, J. Richard. *The Liberating Image: The* Imago Dei *in Genesis 1.* Grand Rapids, MI: Brazos Press, 2005. A comprehensive study of *Imago Dei* in its biblical setting and ancient Near Eastern context with original insights on its contemporary importance.

Noth, Martin. "The Major Themes of the Tradition in the Pentateuch and their Origin." In *A History of the Pentateuchal Traditions*. Englewood Cliffs, NJ: Prentice Hall, 1972.

Towner, W. Sibley. "Clones of God Genesis 1:26–28 and the Image of God in the Hebrew Bible," *Interpretation* 59 (2005): 1–16. An excellent summary of different interpretations and discussion of the contemporary importance of Genesis 1:26–27.

Trible, Phyllis. *God and the Rhetoric of Sexuality*. Philadelphia: Fortress Press, 1978. By combining a "close reading" of the biblical text, rhetorical criticism, and feminist hermeneutics, Trible presents a landmark moment in the proper reading of Genesis 1—3.

Von Rad, Gerhard. *The Problem of the Hexateuch and Other Essays*. New York: McGraw Hill, 1966. A landmark study on the development of the Pentateuch.

Westermann, Claus. *Creation*. Philadelphia: Fortress Press, 1974. Westermann is an outstanding biblical theologian and this short volume is the best brief discussion of Creation.

——. *Genesis 1—11: A Commentary*. Vol. I. Minneapolis: Augsburg, 1984. Vol. II (1985), Gen 12—36; and Vol. III (1986), Gen 37—50. An invaluable reference commentary on Genesis. The commentaries in this series (*Biblischer Kommentar*) are notable for their coverage of subsequent theological interpretations of biblical passages, done with great ecumenical sensitivity.

——. *Genesis: A Practical Commentary*. Grand Rapids, MI: Eerdmans, 1987. Along with *Creation*, this offers a fine digest of Westermann's exegesis.

——. *Genesis: An Introduction*. Minneapolis: Fortress Press, 1991. This work contains the introductions to important sections taken from the three-volume commentary.

ON SOCIAL SIN

Henriot, Peter. "The Concept of Social Sin," *Catholic Mind* 71 (Oct 1973): 38–53.

——. "Social Sin and Conversion: A Theology of the Church's Social Involvement." *Chicago Studies* 11 (Summer 1972): 115–30. This and Henriot's "The Concept of Social Sin" are important seminal articles.

Himes, Kenneth. "Social Sin and the Role of the Individual," *Annual of the Society of Christian Ethics* (1986): 183–218.

Kerans, Patrick. *Sinful Social Structures.* New York: Paulist Press, 1974.

O'Keefe, M. *What Are They Saying About Social Sin?* New York: Paulist Press, 1990. A helpful overview.

EXODUS AND LIBERATION

Coats, George. *Moses: Heroic Man, Man of God.* Sheffield: JSOT Press, 1988. An academic study of the portrayal of Moses in Hebrew Bible.

Croatto, J. Severino. *Exodus: A Hermeneutics of Freedom.* Maryknoll, NY: Orbis Books, 1981. An influential study of Exodus as the basis of a theology of liberation.

Dykstra, Laurel. *Set Them Free: The Other Side of Exodus.* Maryknoll, NY: Orbis Books, 2004. "A book about biblical Egypt, global capitalism, liberation and oppression, and reading the Bible in the first world" (xiv).

Exum, Cheryl. "'You Shall Let Every Daughter Live' A Study of Exodus 1:8—2:10," *Semeia* 28 (1983): 63–82.

Fretheim, Terence E. *Exodus. Interpretation: A Bible for Teaching and Preaching.* Louisville, KY: John Knox Press, 1991. An excellent commentary, especially on Exodus 1—15, with sensitivity to issues of liberation and justice.

————. "The Plagues as Ecological Signs of Historical Disaster." *Journal of Biblical Literature* 110 (1991): 385–96. Fretheim argues that the plagues are signs that nature itself revolts against the moral injustice of Pharaoh's reign.

Langston, Scott. *Exodus Through the Centuries.* Blackwell Bible Commentaries. Malden: MA; Oxford: Blackwell, 2006. This work presents "reception history" of Exodus detailing "Jewish and Christian Uses," "Political and Social Uses," "Oppressive and Contradictory Uses," and finally "Artistic Uses."

Pixley, George V. *Exodus: A Liberation Perspective.* Maryknoll, NY: Orbis Books, 1987. A powerful, but somewhat simplistic, reading of the biblical text.

Selby, Gary. *Martin Luther King and the Rhetoric of Freedom: The Exodus Narrative in America's Struggle for Civil Rights.* Waco, TX: Baylor

University Press, 2008. Shows how the Exodus narrative helped to form the ideas of Martin Luther King, Jr., and the civil rights movement.

Walzer, Michael. *Exodus and Revolution*. New York: Basic Books, 1985. An interesting study of the biblical text and the subsequent impact of the Exodus narrative by a political theorist (author of *Spheres of Justice*. New York: Basic Books, 1983).

Wildavsky, Aaron. *Moses as a Political Leader*. Jerusalem: Shalem Center, 2005. An interesting study by an eminent political scientist.

LIBERATION THEOLOGY

Emphasis here is on bibliographical resources, surveys, and representative works; Jon Sobrino, one of the most original and prolific liberation theologians, writes from a New Testament perspective; significant works will be listed in the Resource Bibliography of chapter 7, "Jesus: Prophet of God's Reign."

Comblin, Joseph. *Called for Freedom: The Changing Context of Liberation Theology*. Maryknoll, NY: Orbis Books, 1998. A powerful assessment of achievements and problems of liberation theology by one of its leading exponents.

Ellacuria, Ignacio, and Jon Sobrino, eds. *Mysterium Liberationis: Fundamental Concepts of Liberation Theology*. Maryknoll, NY: Orbis Books, 1993.

Freire, Paulo. *Pedagogy of the Oppressed*. New York: Herder and Herder, 1972. Though it does not incorporate biblical material, this seminal work describes well both the structure of oppression and a way that education can free people from such structures.

Gutiérrez, Gustavo. *A Theology of Liberation*. 15th Anniv. ed. With a new introduction by the author. Maryknoll, NY: Orbis Books, 1988. When first published in 1971 (Spanish), it quickly became a landmark work for liberation theology and appropriation of biblical themes.

Haight, Roger. *An Alternative Vision: An Interpretation of Liberation Theology*. New York: Paulist Press, 1985. A good overview of the impact of liberation theology.

Hennelly, Alfred T. *Liberation Theology: A Documentary History*. Maryknoll, NY: Orbis Books, 1990.

McGovern, Arthur F. *Liberation Theology and Its Critics: Toward an Assessment*. Maryknoll, NY: Orbis Books, 1989.

Musto, Ronald G. *Liberation Theologies: A Research Guide*. New York: Garland, 1991.

Petrella, Ivan. *Beyond Liberation Theology: A Polemic*. London: SCM Press, 2008.

————. *The Future of Liberation Theology: An Argument and Manifesto*. Burlington, VT: Ashgate, 2004.

————, ed. *Latin American Liberation Theology: The Next Generation*. Maryknoll, NY: Orbis Books, 2005. A discussion of the newest generation of Latin American liberation theologians.

Rowland, Christopher, ed. *The Cambridge Companion to Liberation Theology*. 2nd ed. Cambridge/New York: Cambridge University Press, 2007.

Sugirtharajah, R. S., ed. *Voices from the Margin: Interpreting the Bible in the Third World*. Rev. ed. Maryknoll, NY: Orbis Books, 2006. An excellent collection on global impact and the development of liberation theology.

CHAPTER 3

COVENANT AND LAW

A Community Shaped by Justice

After the hymnic exaltation (Exod 15:1–21) of the release from slavery and the victory over the pursuing Egyptians, "Moses led Israel forward from the Red Sea, and they marched out to the desert of Shur" (15:22). In the sweep of salvation history, the people of Israel are on a journey to the land of promise from Exodus 13:17 through the Books of Exodus, Leviticus, Numbers, and Deuteronomy where Moses dies on Mt. Nebo, gazing into a land he will not enter (Deut 34:1–8). The long narrative thus becomes the context for interpreting how the liberated people are to live in community before God, which is the substance of the different law codes incorporated in this section. These represent traditions dating from the early nomadic origins of Israel to the latest postexilic redaction of the material. It is as if the Declaration of Independence, the Constitution, its Amendments, and the corpus of Supreme Court decisions were gathered in one book and all dated at the same time. In final canonical shape, these Israelite codes are the Torah that provides the founding narrative as well as the source of identity and guiding directives of the people.

Of fundamental importance is the bracketing of the sojourn at Sinai (Exod 19:1—Num 10:10) by stories of the rebellions of the people in the wilderness. Examples would be Exodus 16—17, the gift of manna and the water from the rock; Numbers 11:16–34, the revolt of the elders against Moses; and Numbers 16:1–40, the revolt of Dathan and Abiram. This is the root of the later ambivalence of "the wilderness" in Israel's traditions. It is the place of betrothal and first love (Sinai), and simultaneously the place of corporate disobedience.

The initial grumblings of the people center around a nostalgic remembrance of the "soft life" in Egypt, where slavery at least provided life's necessities (Exod 15:24; 16:3; 17:3). The challenge they face at Sinai is to be transformed from a "liberated" people to a free, responsible people. Walzer, citing Rousseau, states that Moses's great achievement was to transform a herd of "wretched fugitives" who lacked virtue and courage into a "free people." They are challenged to adopt a way of life that is not freedom from regulation but to accept a "bondage in freedom," consisting of freely chosen obligations (Walzer, *Exodus*, 53).

These initial soundings of the wilderness traditions are important for a proper liberation theology. Liberation, though beginning as a power struggle, is a process rather than an event. Freedom from external oppression brings with it the challenge of mature appropriation of freedom through adoption of a way of life that, as we will see, does not reproduce the very evils that have been overthrown. As Norbert Lohfink states so cogently, "Israel is brought out of Egypt to form a contrast society, a just and therefore blessed society, in opposition to all the corrupt societies of the world" (*Option*, 45). For this reason principally, liberation cannot be the center or sole focus of biblical revelation. St. Paul will tell the Galatians, "for freedom Christ has set us free" (Gal 5:1) and then lists a whole series of virtues that describe walking in the Spirit, or living in freedom (Gal 5:22–26). Too often the experience of oppression and the cry for liberation can produce a "moral holiday" for other virtues, where the perceived oppressor is so demonized that, as Paulo Freire noted, those oppressed take on the attitudes of the oppressors (*Pedagogy*, 29, 42).[1]

THE COVENANT AT SINAI

In the middle of the wilderness journey stands the long section on the covenant at Sinai (Exod 19—24). This provides the hermeneutical guidelines for interpreting elements of Israel's legal traditions and their relevance to concerns for social justice. Initially, we will highlight the nature of the biblical covenants, and follow with comments on the "ten

---

1. Often a revolution that deposes an oppressive government and is hailed by the people simply ends with a new dictatorial regime. A recent example existed in Zimbabwe when Robert Mugabe, who in 1978 was seen as a hoped-for liberator, sadly, became a ruthless despot.

words" (commandments) and on other law codes. Whatever the basis of justice in any society, its goals and ideals must ultimately be enshrined in law—understood as a way of life for people in community.

Michael Guinan offers a helpful description: "a covenant was an agreement or promise between two parties, solemnly professed before witnesses and made binding by an oath expressed verbally or by some symbolic action…" and suggests "obligation, in one of three forms: obligation taken upon one's self; obligation imposed on another; assuming of mutual obligations" (*Covenant*, 8–9). They are part of our ordinary lives, most visible in the celebration of marriage. Covenants are also founding acts, so constitutions of a nation are a form of covenant. Covenants also create new relationships and unions between individuals or groups and theologically between humans and God. Much of the discussion of biblical covenants has centered on their origins and literary structure, much in debt to the research of George Mendenhall (*Law and Covenant*).

Chief among the proposed background are the Hittite Suzerainty treaties. The Hittites were an Indo-European people who established an empire in east central Anatolia (modern-day central Turkey and the northern tip of Syria). Most of north and central Syria and modern-day Lebanon became vassal states of the Hittites. The apex of Hittite power was 1400–1200. They are mentioned in Genesis 15:20 and Exodus 23:28 as dwelling in Canaan, but this is doubtful. (See also Judg 1:26; 1 Kgs 10:29; 2 Kgs 7:6.) These treaties have a somewhat standard form: (1) *Preamble*, name and excellence of king: Exodus 19:3, God and Lord; (2) *Historical Prologue*: Exodus 19:1–4; (3) *Obligations of Vassal* (covenant stipulations): Exodus 19:5–6; (4) *Deposited in temple and read at important intervals* (not mentioned in Exodus, but see the renewal of the covenants in Josh 24; see 2 Kgs 22:8–10, discovery of book of law in temple); (5) *Witnesses* were listed, above all the gods involved (not really in Exod 19; but see Josh 24:22); (6) *Blessings and Curses*: Joshua 24:19; and (7) *Ratification*: Exodus 19:7; see Exodus 24; Joshua 24:15, 19. This research helps us to realize that covenants must have been an important aspect of Israel's life and, even before the codification of the laws, had formed its understanding of the divine-human relationship.

There are two major biblical types of covenant: First, a covenant with mutual obligations—a covenant that can be broken by the people (e.g., Exod 19 and Josh 24), but with a possibility of renewal (cf. Jer 31:31–34). Second, a "divine charter" covenant—a covenant that cannot be broken and that expresses God's unaltered choice of an individual who will bear the destiny of the people, for examples, see Genesis 9:8–17 (Noah), Genesis 17 (Abraham), and 2 Samuel 7:1–17 (dynastic promise to David); see also Psalm 89:1–13 (see "Covenant" by Mendenhall and Herion). Here the fidelity of God remains constant, even amid the failures of the covenant partner, and provides hope for the future.

Historical and formal considerations do not capture the theological importance of covenant. Walter Brueggemann states, "The Covenant that God made with Israel is perhaps the central and defining theological affirmation of the Old Testament," and Jon Levenson comments: "The momentous encounter with God at Sinai is, for the Torah, the defining and seminal moment in Israel's relationship with God."[2] Joseph Jensen has recently called attention to Pedersen's different understandings of covenant (*Ethical Dimensions*, 16–17). Less interested in historical parallels than in biblical anthropology, Pedersen roots covenant in the understanding of community that is held together by the blessing of God. It is held together by a common unity of will and is held together by *tsedaqah* (justice understood as proper relationships between God and people) and its result is *shalom*, "wholeness" in the community (*Israel*).

The preamble to the Sinai covenant crystallizes its importance:

> Moses went up the mountain to God. Then the LORD called to him and said, "Thus shall you say to the house of Jacob; tell the Israelites: You have seen for yourselves how I treated the Egyptians and how I bore you on eagle's wings and brought you to myself. Therefore, if you hearken to my voice and keep my covenant, you shall be my treasured possession, dearer to me than all other people, though all the earth is mine. You shall be to me a kingdom of priests, a holy nation. That is what you must tell the Israelites." (Exod 19:3–6)

---

2. Walter Brueggemann, *Reverberations of Faith: A Theological Handbook of Old Testament Themes* (Louisville, KY: Westminster John Knox Press, 2002), 37; Jon D. Levenson, "Torah" in *The Jewish Study Bible*, eds. Adele Berlin and Marc Zvi Brettler (New York: Oxford University Press, 2004), 145.

Covenant underscores the fundamental vision that God's gracious action in liberating or electing a people requires a free human response that will continue to shape the lives of individuals in community. It involves a free commitment to a new kind of "service." "Slavery is begun and sustained by coercion, while service is begun and sustained by covenant" (Walzer, *Exodus*, 74). Covenant is a founding act, creating alongside the old association of tribes a new nation composed of willing members. Covenant is the free commitment to be a person in relation to others; it is the direct opposite of autonomous existence. Theologically, being a covenant people (recall the Christian commitment) is radically to be a member of a community; religion is not merely vertical, "me and God," it is also radically horizontal. It is a community of mutually shared obligations, responsibilities, and gifts.

Covenant is the basis of community and its prescriptions form a community. Understanding that the Sinai and other covenants in the Bible begin with a recollection of what God *has done* for the people means that *what a people is called to do* in observing laws is a sign of fidelity and gratitude. This counters the often erroneous view that Judaism is a legalistic religion, and is the basis of James Sanders's understanding of "covenantal nomism" (Sanders, *Jesus*, 7).

JUSTICE IN THE TORAH

Following the initial revelation at Sinai, the response of the people, "everything that the Lord has spoken, we will do," is a set of fundamental divine "words," traditionally called the Decalogue (Exod 20:1–17; see Deut 5:1–21), which are both the initial stipulations of the covenant and embody its fundamental values.[3] However the commandments are numbered, they fall into two major sections, dealing directly with relation to God and to neighbor, and embody thematic groupings as dis-

---

3. The traditional lists of the "ten words" differ. The Hebrew Bible, Greek Orthodox, and Reformed traditions have two commandments in Exodus 20:2–6 (no other gods; no idols), and combine 20:17 (do not covet wife or property) into one commandment while the Catholic, Anglican, and Lutheran traditions list Exodus 20:2–6 as one commandment and divide 20:17 into two commandments. This creates some confusion among people schooled in different traditions, for example, the commandment to honor our parents (fourth for Catholics; fifth for most non-Catholics). We will follow the Catholic listing because it will be more familiar to most readers.

cussed by Walter Harrelson in his fine books (*The Ten Commandments and Human Rights; The Ten Commandments for Today*). The first three (Exod 20:3, 4, 7), deal with God's exclusive claim on Israel's faith and sound the rejection of idolatry that then pervades biblical faith both in the Old and New Testaments. The next two (Sabbath and family, Exod 20:8, 12), which belong together, are a gift recalling God's creative love, and "enable the family to share and deepen its relationship to God" (Harrelson, *Ten Commandments for Today*, 41). The following five "address issues that damage or even destroy life in community": destruction of human life, violation of sexual integrity, stealing, false witness against others, and rampant envy of the life and fortunes of others (ibid., 53). The two parts of the Decalogue "have to be held together as the one word of God...." Furthermore, "the relation to the neighbor is both a divine command and explicitly a matter of the relationship with God by being set as a part of the covenant with God" (Miller, "Place of the Decalogue," 233). Far from limiting human freedom, these commands make life in community possible, and protect vulnerable individuals.

Biblical law is both a major contribution to Judeo-Christian faith and a resource that demands immense dedication and study since it has spawned a rich corpus of commentary and interpretation in the Jewish tradition. We should also be aware that Torah (law) is wider than legal material, but describes also the founding narratives of Israel's faith that stretch from Genesis through Deuteronomy. We will focus on the distinctive understandings of justice that are revealed in specific law codes of Israel. Since examining the history and scope of the law codes is beyond the purpose of this chapter, I will focus my comments on the legal texts to those sections that deal with the powerless (often made concrete as the poor, the widow, the orphan, and the stranger in the land). In a magisterial study of law and justice in the Bible, Jonathan Burnside defines justice, as "deliverance from oppression and restoration of God's creative intent," which is rooted in "a divinely mandated social order" (*God, Justice*, 239) that provides a basis for a focus on laws dealing with suffering people.

The codes themselves comprise (1) the Decalogue, discussed above; (2) the "Covenant Code," (Exod 20:22—23:33), parts of which date from northern Israel in the ninth century BC and which reflect premonarchic rural life, though, like the rest of the Pentateuch, it receives its final shape after the exile; (3) the cult commands of the covenant renewal in Deuteronomy 34; (4) the "Holiness Code," (Lev 17—26), put together after the exile and often attributed to Priestly circles. It is also similar to the thought of Ezekiel; (5) the "Deuteronomic Code," (Deut 12—26), which embodies traditions from the seventh century BC, and perhaps from Josiah's reform, but which was incorporated into the full blown "Deuteronomic history," only after the exile. Much of the Book of Leviticus consists of cultic legislation for temple personnel, and though located in the wilderness, it clearly presupposes a functioning cult and temple.

While the content of concern for the poor and marginalized is similar, the foundation and motivation is different. In Israel, care for such persons is part of the "contrast society," which is through the laws of Israel (Lohfink, *Option*). Also in Israel such concern functions more as a critical principle against the misuse of power, while in some of the surrounding cultures, it is a way in which those in power dampen revolutionary tendencies of the people and thus maintain a divinely sanctioned hierarchy of power. Also, as Paul Hanson notes, in Israel responsibility for the well-being of such people devolves on the covenant community as a whole and not simply on the king (*People*, 70–86).

COVENANT AND THE LIFE OF THE POOR

One of the purposes of these reflections is to highlight those parts of the Old Testament where the plight of the powerless and marginal people is singled out along with calls to give them justice. In recent years, concern for these people often referred to as the *personae miserae* ("people socially marginalized or vulnerable": the poor, the widow, the orphan, and the stranger in the land) has been the subject of an increasing number of important studies (Baker, *Tight Fists*; Berman, *Created Equal*; and Hamilton, *Social Justice*). Concern for these groups that appears in the calls for justice is anchored in the Law and prophets of ancient of Israel:

> You shall not wrong or oppress a resident alien, for you
> were aliens in the land of Egypt. You shall not abuse any

widow or orphan. If you do abuse them, when they cry out to me, I will surely heed their cry. (Exod 22:21–23)

For the LORD your God is God of gods and Lord of lords, the great God, mighty and awesome, who is not partial and takes no bribe, who executes justice for the orphan and the widow, and who loves the strangers, providing them with food and clothing. You shall also love the stranger, for you were strangers in the land of Egypt. (Deut 10:17–19)

You shall not deprive a resident alien or an orphan of justice; you shall not take a widow's garment in pledge. Remember that you were a slave in Egypt and the LORD your God redeemed you from there; therefore I command you to do this.

When you reap your harvest in your field and forget a sheaf in the field, you shall not go back to get it; it shall be left for the alien, the orphan, and the widow, so that the LORD your God may bless you in all your undertakings. When you beat your olive trees, do not strip what is left; it shall be for the alien, the orphan, and the widow.

When you gather the grapes of your vineyard, do not glean what is left; it shall be for the alien, the orphan, and the widow. Remember that you were a slave in the land of Egypt; therefore I am commanding you to do this. (Deut 24:17–22, see also 26:13; 27:19)

When summoning people to conversion, the prophets recall this concern for these suffering groups. In the temple sermon of Jeremiah, written most likely by editors during or shortly after the exile, the prophet summons the community to repentance:

For if you truly amend your ways and your doings, if you truly act justly one with another, if you do not oppress the alien, the orphan, and the widow, or shed innocent blood in this place, and if you do not go after other gods to your own hurt, then I will dwell with you in this place, in the land that I gave of old to your ancestors forever and ever. (Jer 7:5–7)

And Zechariah, an early postexilic century prophet (c. 518 BC), does not allow people to forget the covenant traditions when he proclaims:

> Thus says the LORD of hosts: Render true judgments, show kindness and mercy to one another; do not oppress the widow, the orphan, the alien, or the poor; and do not devise evil in your hearts against one another. (Zech 7:9–10)

A recently discovered inscription on an ostracon at Khirbet Qeiyafa in July 2008 is further evidence that concern for groups of socially marginalized people was part of the "genetic stamp" of Israel.[4] It may be the earliest example of Hebrew writing and is dated to the reigns of David or Solomon, and according to the latest reconstruction reads:

> you shall not do [it], but worship the [Lord].
> Judge the sla[ve] and the wid[ow] / Judge the orph[an]
> [and] the stranger. [Pl]ead for the infant / plead for the po[or and]
> the widow. Rehabilitate [the poor] at the hands of the king.
> Protect the po[or and] the slave / [supp]ort the stranger.

Achenbach notes that the Hebrew (*shpt*) behind the verb *judge* in the second line is used in the biblical writings "to establish a legal order within ancient Israelite society with particular respect to the protection of the *personae miserae*," who are the same groups who are to be treated justly in the laws and the prophets.[5] In analyzing other terms and on the basis of the location of the ostracon at the "city gate," Achenbach then argues for contact between Egyptian scribal wisdom and early Israelite legal practice and concludes that "the ethical teachings of the prophets in their oracles of woes against the *qatsinim* and *sarim*

---

4. Virtually every aspect of this discovery has been a source of debate and discussion. See Reinhard Achenbach, "The Protection of *Personae Miserae* in Ancient Israelite Law and Wisdom and in the Ostracon from Khirbet Qeiyafa," *Semitica* 54 (2012): 91–123. Achenbach discusses all the major reconstructions of the inscriptions and their relation to biblical texts. He directs readers to the Web site of the Hebrew University of Jerusalem for a chronicle of the discovery: http://qeiyafa.huji.ac.il/ostracon.asp.

5. Ibid., 107.

["rulers" and "administrators," see Isa 1:23; 22:3; Mic 3:1] of the royal administration served to remind them of their own ancient knowledge of legal justice."[6] When one asks for an enduring mandate of biblical faith, concern for the poor and vulnerable stretches from Khirbet Qeiyafa through the Law and prophets, the Gospels and Letters of Paul until the Book of Revelation.

Such concern for "the poor" raises many problems regarding their identity (for example, economically poor, or spiritually poor) and about the social location of statements concerning them. Since the biblical vocabulary for the poor is much richer than ours, at the risk of seeming overly technical, I will indicate some of the various usages. There are five principal terms for the poor: (1) 'ani (plural 'aniyyim) meaning "bent down" or "afflicted," which the Greek Old Testament most often translates as ptōchos ("beggar" or "destitute person"), and which is the prime New Testament term for "the poor"; (2) 'anaw (plural 'anawm), which is derived from the same root as 'ani and often confused by copyists, and is translated most often as tapeinos and praüs ("humble" and "lowly"); (3) 'ebyon (term "Ebionites" derives from this), from root meaning "lack" or "need," or "wretched, miserable," (used sixty-one times in the Old Testament, especially in the Psalms where it appears twenty-three times); (4) dal from a root that means "be bent over," "bend down," "miserable"; (5) rash, which is "poor" in a derogatory sense with overtones of a lazy person responsible for his or her own poverty, and is found only in the Wisdom literature (for example, Prov 10:4; 13:23; 14:20; 19:7; 28:3).

The importance of the terminology is twofold. First, it shows that poverty was not itself a value. Even etymologically, the poor are bent down, wretched, and beggars. While the Bible has great concern for "the poor," poverty itself is an evil. Second, the terminology (as well as actual use) is a caution against misuse of the phrase "spiritually poor." Though later literature (the Psalms and Dead Sea Scrolls) often equates the poor with the humble or meek, and though the poor are those people open to God, in contrast to idolatrous or blind rich people, the foundational meaning of these terms is an economic condition. Certain contemporary usages of "spiritual poverty," which allow it to be used

---

6. Ibid., 125.

of wealthy people who are unhappy even amid prosperity, are not faithful to the biblical tradition. "Poverty of spirit" when understood as complete trust in God captures an important aspect of biblical faith, but is rooted in the concept of physical need.

The "poor" in the Bible are almost without exception *powerless* people who experience economic and social deprivation. For example, in both Isaiah and the Psalms, the poor are often victims of the injustice of the rich and powerful. Isaiah tells us that the elders and princes "devour" the poor and grind their faces in the dust (Isa 3:14–15); they turn aside the needy from injustice to rob the poor of their rights (Isa 10:2); wicked people "ruin" the poor with lying words (Isa 32:7). In the Psalms, the poor, often called "the downtrodden," are contrasted not simply to the rich, but also to the wicked and the powerful (Pss 10:2–10; 72: 4, 12–14). Today poverty is most often not simply an economic issue, but arises when one group can exploit or oppress another.

In all the law codes, the poor have a special claim on the community and its leaders; they are "just" because they do not follow the evil ways of the rich and powerful. Both the king and the whole people are obliged to seek justice, which involves being on the side of the poor and the powerless. This perspective informs all of Israel's traditions at all stages in its history. Great wealth and power are both a danger and an evil. Often they are associated with idolatry and oppressions (cf. Ps 10). The biblical responses to poverty are not simply acts of charity and compassion but involve diagnosis and criticism of its agents and causes, and cooperation in the empowerment of the marginalized.

Concern for the powerless emerges first as part of the "Covenant Code" (see above). For our purposes, the first important section is Exodus 22:21–27. Here God says, "You shall not wrong or oppress a resident alien, for you were aliens in the land of Egypt" (v. 21, note the motivation of a contrast society). The following verse proscribes abuse of the widow and the orphan, with the promise that God will heed their cry and "kill with the sword" their oppressors. The section concludes with the prohibition of lending to the poor at interest, and on restoring a neighbor's coat taken in surety for a loan. Here also the motivation is God in his role as the protector of the poor: "And if your neighbor cries out to me, I will listen, for I am compassionate" (Exod 22:27).

The next section contains a series of laws on the proper administration of justice. One of the first states: "You shall not side with the majority so as to pervert justice, nor shall you be partial to the poor in a lawsuit" (Exod 23:2–3). The prohibition of "partiality" to the poor in the specific context of a lawsuit does not contradict the concern for the marginalized as an enduring social commitment, since Exodus 23:6 immediately says that "you shall not pervert the justice due to your poor in their lawsuits" (there is no corresponding statement on the rich or powerful), and 23:9 repeats the protection of the alien. In verses 10–11, a more cultic setting, the code mandates a sabbatical year of leaving land fallow "so that the poor…may eat."

The second major block of legal material that deals with the poor comes from the Deuteronomic legislation of Deuteronomy 12—26. Norbert Lohfink points out that the ideal in the Covenant Code of a contrast society without oppression and poverty was in fact not realized, and locates Deuteronomy in this context ("Poverty in the Laws"). While retaining an ideal that "There will…be no one in need among you, because the LORD is sure to bless you" (Deut 15:4, cf. Acts 4:34), Deuteronomy realistically states: "there will never cease to be some in need on the earth," and commands, "open your hand to the poor and needy neighbor in your land" (Deut 15:11). More strongly than the other codes, Deuteronomy commands justice and compassion for the powerless (Deut 15:1–18; 24:10–15; 26:11–12). The historical significance of Deuteronomy is evidence for a continuing concern in Israel's law for the *personae miserae*, which attempts to institutionalize the covenant ideal through law and practice. The significance of Deuteronomy in its present canonical location is that it is cast in the form of farewell speeches from Moses to the people on the brink of the promised land. The land is God's gift on condition of fidelity to the covenant (Deut 12:1: "These are the statutes and ordinances that you must diligently observe in the land the LORD, the God of your ancestors, has given you to occupy"). When read *after the exile*, it can be seen as a warning against an infidelity that allows the kind of society to develop, and that is in opposition to the exodus event and the Sinai covenant (cf. Berman, *Created Equal*, 6).

The Holiness Code (Lev 17—26) contains provisions similar to Deuteronomy. In 19:9–10 and 23:22, gleanings from the harvest are to be left for "the poor and the alien," though as Lohfink points out, specific mention is not made of "the widow and the orphan," who now seem to be subsumed under "the poor." The Holiness Code spells out other detailed provisions for the poor, very often those who have come suddenly upon hard times (Lev 25:35–42; 47–52). Leviticus is also more concerned with the details of repayment of debts and cultic offerings made by the poor (Lev 12:8; cf. also Luke 2:24). The significance of Leviticus is twofold. First, though it is primarily a cultic code concerned with the holiness of the people and the means to assure that holiness, it manifests a practical concern for the poor in the land. As John Gammie has shown in his excellent study, there is no tension between Israel's concern to be a holy people consecrated to God and a people concerned about justice (*Holiness*). Second, and perhaps less positive, Leviticus seems to represent a relaxation of some of the earlier provisions for the poor. Lohfink argues that the stipulations of the Jubilee (Lev 25:8–17, 23–25; 27:16–25), where debts are canceled every fiftieth year, would hardly benefit the majority of people who lived in poverty and represent a step back from the sabbatical year legislation of Deuteronomy. The Holiness Code may also reflect the radically changed postexilic political situation when the monarchy was extinct and people had limited ability to enshrine the ideals of the covenant in law. This period also represents the beginning of apocalyptic thought, when many groups projected the hope of God's justice and a society free of oppression and poverty to a new heaven and a new earth that would be ushered in by cosmic cataclysm.

REMISSION OF DEBTS AND
FREEDOM FROM SERVITUDE

A series of laws found in the different collections deal directly with Sabbath regulations. Issues of debt, debt servitude, impoverishment, and release from debt, are found in Exodus 21:1–10 and 23:10–12. Laws on the Sabbath rest are found in Leviticus 25 and Deuteronomy 15:1–18. While multiple historical and literary problems pervade these texts, our purpose is to highlight the fundamental social values that lie behind them. The Sabbath rest that is at the basis of the above legislation has a double focus. In Exodus 20:8–11, the focus of the Sabbath rest is a perpetual sign of God's creative work and in Deuteronomy 5:15 "that one should remember the deliverance from Egypt," and "the sabbatical principle" becomes one of the primary manifestations of God's provision for justice and compassion in the community (Miller, *Ten Commandments*, 130, 134).

The first application of the sabbatical principal in the book of the covenant deals with the rest given to the land (Exod 20:9–11) and the release of slaves (Exod 21:1–10). Both recognize the sovereignty of God over nature and the human family. Neither the land nor a fellow human is to be totally under human domination. In evaluating subsequent laws dealing with "slavery," a more accurate translation would be "servitude," since the biblical slavery especially of other Israelites most often is a form of "indentured service" and is very different from later chattel slavery, especially as practiced in North and South America, primarily in its directives for humane treatment and possibility of release after a limited time.

The earliest instance of the sabbatical principle (canonically and most likely historically) occurs in the Covenant Code:

> For six years you shall sow your land and gather in its yield; but the seventh year you shall let it rest and lie fallow, so that the poor of your people may eat; and what they leave the wild animals may eat. You shall do the same with your vineyard, and with your olive orchard.
>
> Six days you shall do your work, but on the seventh day you shall rest, so that your ox and your donkey may have relief, and your homeborn slave and the resident alien may be refreshed. (Exod 23:10–12)

Similar provisions follow in the Holiness Code of Leviticus:

> Speak to the people of Israel and say to them: When you enter the land that I am giving you, the land shall observe a sabbath for the LORD. Six years you shall sow your field, and six years you shall prune your vineyard, and gather in their yield; but in the seventh year there shall be a sabbath of complete rest for the land, a sabbath for the LORD: you shall not sow your field or prune your vineyard. You shall not

reap the aftergrowth of your harvest or gather the grapes of your unpruned vine: it shall be a year of complete rest for the land. You may eat what the land yields during its sab-bath—you, your male and female slaves, your hired and your bound laborers who live with you; for your livestock also, and for the wild animals in your land all its yield shall be for food. (Lev 25:2–7)

However, the rest of Leviticus 25 contains elaborate provisions for the Jubilee year:

Then you shall have the trumpet sounded loud; on the tenth day of the seventh month—on the day of atone-ment—you shall have the trumpet sounded throughout all your land. And you shall hallow the fiftieth year and you shall proclaim liberty throughout the land to all its inhabi-tants. It shall be a jubilee for you: you shall return every one of you, to your property and every one of you to your fam-ily. That fiftieth year shall be a jubilee for you: you shall not sow, or reap the aftergrowth, or harvest the unpruned vines. (Lev 25: 9–11)

These provisions include return of hereditary property, legislation for a relative to redeem indebted property, concern for the poor tenant, and prohibitions of exacting interest from your countrymen (Lev 25:35–36) and the mitigation of slavery, as a memorial of their own lib-eration from Egypt:

I am the LORD your God, who brought you out of the land of Egypt, to give you the land of Canaan, to be your God.
If any who are dependent on you become so impoverished that they sell themselves to you, you shall not make them serve as slaves. They shall remain with you as hired or bound laborers. They shall serve with you until the year of the jubilee. Then they and their children with them shall be free from your authority; they shall go back to their own family and return to their ancestral property. For they are my ser-vants, whom I brought out of the land of Egypt; they shall not

be sold as slaves are sold. You shall not rule over them with harshness, but shall fear your God. (Lev 25:38–43)

After further, often complex, provisions on debt release, the chapter concludes:

For to me the people of Israel are servants; they are my servants whom I brought out from the land of Egypt: I am the LORD your God. (Lev 25:55)

These multiple provisions are built on major foundations of Israel's faith: creation, Sabbath rest, and the deliverance from Egypt. Even amid changing circumstances, these remain the beacons on the path to justice. These same provisions of the sabbatical principle appear in Deuteronomy 15:7–12, but with an important addition (*italicized* below):

If there is among you anyone in need, a member of your community in any of your towns within the land that the LORD your God is giving you, do not be hard-hearted or tight-fisted toward your needy neighbor. You should rather open your hand, willingly lending enough to meet the need, whatever it may be. Be careful that you do not entertain a mean thought, thinking, "The seventh year, the year of remission, is near," and therefore view your needy neighbor with hostility and give nothing; your neighbor might cry to the LORD against you, and you would incur guilt. Give liberally and be ungrudging when you do so, for on this account the LORD your God will bless you in all your work and in all that you undertake. *Since there will never cease to be some in need on the earth*, I therefore command you, "Open your hand to the poor and needy neighbor in your land."[7]

Moshe Weinfeld, a leading interpreter of Deuteronomy, notes the importance of these changes: "Deuteronomy indeed draws upon the

---

7. This phrase, "Since there will never cease to be some in need on the earth," is quoted by Jesus in response to the complaints of the disciples about the waste of costly oil when the woman anoints him before his passion (see Matt 26:6–12), but it is often misused to affirm the inevitability of poverty ("the poor you will always have with you,") without alluding to the full context in Deuteronomy.

previous traditions of the Pentateuch, but was revised according to the principles of the Hezekianic-Josianic reforms....They appear however in Deuteronomy in a new form, adjusted to the principles of centralization of cult as well as to the social-humane tendency which is characteristic of Deuteronomy" ("Deuteronomy," *ABD*, 2:149).

IMPORTANCE OF SABBATICAL AND JUBILEE LEGISLATION

A legion of problems surrounds these important texts, most dramatically whether they describe practices that actually existed as described. The two works of Robert North span the debate, and in the latter one, he offers an exhaustive survey of research. Yet whatever their historical setting, the texts echo throughout the Bible, especially in Isaiah 61:1–2: "The spirit of the Lord GOD is upon me, because the LORD has anointed me; he has sent me to bring glad tidings to the lowly, to heal the brokenhearted, to proclaim liberty to the captives, and release to the prisoners; to proclaim the year of LORD's favor." Sharon Ringe notes that this passage that echoes the Jubilee legislation "celebrated God's commitment to justice and concern for the poor and suffering and the requirement that people confess their faith in God by that same commitment and concern," and as these verses form the initial proclamation of Jesus in Luke 4:18, has further shown their "influence and importance for New Testament Christology" (*Jesus*, 32.).

These somewhat arcane and archaic directives seem to have little to say in our complex economic world. However, these two focal points underscore issues that are a concern today. The directives to let the land lay fallow because it is the gift of God, shows a respect for God's creation that has been dramatically lost in recent decades. The provision for release from debt servitude recalls the people's own release from Egyptian servitude and counters the existence of a permanent underclass in Israel's history.

Two prophetic figures from recent history have captured the deepest meaning of the Sabbath itself and of sabbatical and Jubilee legislation.

With his usual profound eloquence Abraham Joshua Heschel has reflected on the Sabbath rest not simply as an institution but as a way of life:

> To set apart one day a week for freedom, a day on which we would not use the instruments which have been so easily turned into weapons of destruction, a day for being with ourselves, a day of detachment from the vulgar, or independence of external obligation, a day on which we stop worshipping the idols of technical civilization, a day on which we use no money, a day of armistice in the economic struggle with our fellow men and the forces of nature—is there any institution that holds out a greater hope for man's progress than the Sabbath? (*The Sabbath*, 28)

In anticipating the Great Jubilee of the year 2000, Pope John Paul captured the spirit of the biblical Jubilee:

> The period of the Jubilee introduces us to the vigorous language which the divine pedagogy of salvation uses to lead man to conversion and penance. The human race is facing forms of slavery which are new and more subtle than those of the past; and for too many people freedom remains a word without meaning. Some nations, especially the poorer ones, are oppressed by a debt so huge that repayment is practically impossible. It is clear, therefore, that there can be no real progress without effective cooperation between the peoples of every language, race, nationality and religion. The abuses of power which result in some dominating others must stop: such abuses are sinful and unjust. Whoever is concerned to accumulate treasure only on earth (cf. Matt 6:19) "is not rich in the sight of God" (Luke 12:21, *Incarnationis Mysterium*, Nos. 2 and 12).

National debt and rampant financial speculations are dramatic instances of "abuse of power" that mostly impact the poor and vulnerable and create forms of servitude far less benign than the biblical version.

Despite an inadequate survey of Israel's legal texts, certain observations may stimulate continued engagement. The events of salvation history, especially the leading out from Egypt and the covenant at Sinai are thus the foundations in Israel of a society that seeks justice and manifests concern for the marginalized. This concern is incorporated in law and custom, which take different shapes in different historical circumstances, stretching over five centuries. As founding documents not only of the historical people of Israel, but of the Christian church, they offer a vision of life in society before God that is to inform religious belief and social practice. The laws of Israel have two great values. First, they show that religious belief must be translated into law and custom, which guide life in community and protect the vulnerable. Paul Hanson states this well in describing *torah* as "faith coming to expression in communal forms and structures" (*People*, 41). Since biblical values should find expression in communal forms and structures in our contemporary, pluralistic society, the Church and its episcopal leadership rightly strive to infuse the legislative process with a vision of social justice.

Second, although these traditions do not offer concrete directives for our complex socioeconomic world, they offer a vision of a "contrast society," not ruled by power and greed, but rather where the treatment of the marginalized becomes the touchstone of "right relationship" to God. Christians today must ask soberly how our lives provide a contrast society, and whether, when we think of our "right relation" to God, the concerns of the marginalized in our own time have been really made concrete in our attitudes and style of life.

RESOURCE BIBLIOGRAPHY

Baker, David L. *Tight Fists or Open Hands: Wealth and Poverty in the Old Testament.* Grand Rapids, MI: Eerdmans, 2009. A comprehensive study dealing with Old Testament laws on wealth, poverty, and different forms of servitude.

Berman, Joshua A. *Created Equal: How the Bible Broke With Ancient Political Thought.* New York/Oxford: Oxford University Press, 2008. An original study that argues that "Deuteronomy inaugurates a new social, political, and religious order—the first to be founded on egalitarian ideals..." (6–7).

Bovati, Pietro. *Re-establishing Justice: Legal Terms, Concepts and Procedures in the Hebrew Bible.* Trans. Michael J. Smith. *JSOT* suppl. Ser. 105. Sheffield: JSOT Press, 1994. A comprehensive and foundational study.

Brueggemann, Walter. *A Social Reading of the Old Testament: Prophetic Approaches to Communal Life.* Minneapolis: Fortress Press, 1994. Especially important are chapter 2, "Covenant as Subversive Paradigm," and chapter 3, "Covenant as Social Possibility."

Burnside, Jonathan. *God, Justice, and Society: Aspects of Law and Legality in the Bible.* New York: Oxford University Press, 2011. Burnside is Reader in Biblical Law at the School of Law, University of Bristol, England; this work is a comprehensive coverage of all aspects of biblical law organized around particular issues, for example, chapter 4, "Justice as a Calling."

Chan, Yiu Sing Lúcás. *The Ten Commandments and the Beatitudes: Biblical Studies for Real Life.* Lanham, MD: Roman and Littlefield, 2012. A combination of fine scholarship on each commandment and beatitude, with pastoral sensitivity by a young Catholic Chinese scholar.

Chirichigno, Gregory C. *Debt-Slavery in Israel and the Ancient Near East.* Sheffield: JSOT Press, 1993.

Doorly, William J. *The Laws of Yahweh: A Handbook of Biblical Law.* New York/Mahwah, NJ: Paulist Press, 2002. Includes very helpful information on the various law codes with a detailed listing of the contents of each.

Freire, Paulo. *Pedagogy of the Oppressed.* New York: Herder and Herder, 1972.

Gammie, John G. *Holiness in Israel.* Minneapolis: Fortress Press, 1989. This is the best study in English on holiness. Gammie surveys holiness in the priestly, prophetic, wisdom, and apocalyptic traditions and writes with great sensitivity to contemporary religious and social concerns.

Guinan, Michael. *Covenant in the Old Testament.* Chicago: Franciscan Herald Press, 1975. A fine brief introduction.

Hamilton, Jeffries M. *Social Justice and the Case of Deuteronomy 15.* SBLDS 15. Atlanta: Scholars Press, 1992.

Hanson, Paul D. *The People Called: The Growth of Community in the Bible.* San Francisco: Harper and Row, 1986. This is a complete biblical theology seen through the lens of different understandings of community in the historical evolution of Israel (through the New Testament). Community for Hanson always involves a triad of worship, compassion, and righteousness (justice).

Harrelson, Walter. *The Ten Commandments and Human Rights*. Philadelphia: Fortress Press, 1980. An excellent study based on solid scholarship that highlights contemporary importance of Decalogue.

————. *The Ten Commandments for Today*. Louisville, KY: Westminster John Knox Press, 2006. A digest and updating of earlier work, excellent for classroom use.

Heschel, Abraham Joshua. *The Sabbath: Its Meaning for Modern Man*. New York: Farrar, Strauss and Giroux, 1951. A profound reflection on the meaning of sabbatical for contemporary life; more relevant than ever sixty years after publication.

Horsley, Richard A. *Covenant Economics: A Biblical Vision of Justice for All*. Louisville, KY: Westminster John Knox Press, 2009. An interesting and important approach that locates the covenant in the social and economic worlds of ancient Israel and early Christianity.

Jensen, Joseph. *Ethical Dimensions of the Prophets*. Collegeville, MN: Liturgical Press, 2006.

Lohfink, Norbert. *Option for the Poor: The Basic Principle of Liberation Theology in Light of the Bible*. N. Richland Hills, TX: Bibal Press, 1995. Treats both legal and prophetic texts, but is listed here because it offers fundamental perspectives on issues of justice for the poor; short and written in a lively style. Available also as *La opcion por los pobres*. Mexico, D.F: Universidad Iberoamericana, 1998.

————. "Poverty in the Laws of the Ancient Near East and the Bible." *Theological Studies* 52 (1991): 34–50. An excellent study of laws dealing with the poor in Israel's evolving legal traditions.

McCarthy, Dennis J. *Old Testament Covenant: A Survey of Current Opinions*. Atlanta: John Knox Press, 1972. The best survey of opinions on covenant.

Mendenhall, George. *Law and Covenant in Israel and the Ancient Near East*. Pittsburgh: Biblical Colloquium, 1955. A landmark study of the covenant. See also "Covenant" (with Gary Herion, *ABD*, 1:1179–1202). Mendenhall (b. 1916) is also famous for his theory of the emergence of ancient Israel; see *The Tenth Generation: The Origins of the Biblical Tradition*. Baltimore: Johns Hopkins University Press, 1973.

Miller, Patrick D. *The Ten Commandments*. Louisville, KY: Westminster John Knox Press, 2005. A magisterial study that elucidates the meaning of each command and shows the trajectory of its influence throughout the Old Testament. See also his shorter treatment, "The Place of the Decalogue in the Old Testament and Its Law." *Interpretation* 43, no. 3 (1989): 229–42.

North, Robert. *The Biblical Jubilee...After Fifty Years*. Analecta biblica 145. Rome: Biblical Institute Press, 2007. An excellent survey of research of the previous half-century with revision of the author's original views.

————. *Sociology of the Biblical Jubilee*. Analecta biblica 4. Rome: Biblical Institute Press, 1954. An early study that shaped the debate for decades.

Pedersen, Johannes. *Israel: Its Life and Culture, Volume 1*. South Florida Studies in the History of Judaism 28. Atlanta: Scholars Press, 1991. Orig. Oxford University Press, 1926. "Peace and Covenant," 263–310.

Ringe, Sharon. *Jesus, Liberation and the Biblical Jubilee: Images for Ethics and Christology*. Philadelphia: Fortress Press, 1985. Though the focus of this study is on the New Testament, Ringe provides a fine description of the Jubilee legislation.

Sanders, E. P. *Jesus and Judaism*. Philadelphia: Fortress Press, 1985. Sanders is especially sensitive to the Jewish background and context of Jesus' teaching, see esp. 123–245. See also Sanders, *The Historical Figure of Jesus*. New York: Penguin, 1993.

Walzer, Michael. *Exodus and Revolution*. New York: Basic Books, 1985. A very interesting study of the biblical text and the subsequent impact of Exodus narrative by a political theorist (author of *Spheres of Justice*. New York: Basic Books, 1983).

Weinfeld, Moshe. *The Place of the Law in the Religion of Ancient Israel*. Leiden/Boston: Brill, 2004.

————. *Social Justice in Ancient Israel and in the Ancient Near East*. Minneapolis: Fortress Press; Jerusalem: Magnes, 1995. Weinfeld is the leading expert on Israel's legal traditions and author of the Anchor Bible Commentary on Deuteronomy 1—11.

CHAPTER 4

PROPHETIC VOICES

Justice Renewed

PROPHETS: MEDIATORS BETWEEN GOD AND HUMANITY

When a people forgets its origins or loses sight of its ideals, figures arise who often speak a strident message to summon it to return to God. In Israel's history, the prophetic movement represents such a phenomenon. The Hebrew word for prophet, *nabi*, is probably not of Hebrew origin, perhaps a loanword from Akkadian (*nabu*) translated as "to call, proclaim, or announce," and also used for a "diviner," which implies contact with divinity and expression of it. The Greek etymology of the term *pro-phēmi* suggests "speaking on behalf of another." This has a dual sense. The prophet speaks on behalf of God and he or she is a "forth teller," who also speaks on behalf of those who have no one to speak for them, specifically the powerless and poor in the land. The prophet is an intermediary between God and humans, who also voices human words to God.

The prophets of Israel have inspired generations of people interested in social justice, perhaps most notably Martin Luther King, Jr., who constantly cited and invoked the prophets. Like all topics treated in this work, prophecy is a verdant forest of historical and literary issues. Biblical scholars have examined all aspects of prophecy in ancient Israel: its nature and origin, historical setting and role in various historical periods, formation and structure of prophetic writings, comparison with prophetic movements in world religions, and theological message.

Though Moses was never called a prophet in the Pentateuch, and was only alluded it to in Hosea 12:13: "By a prophet the LORD brought

Israel up from Egypt, and by a prophet he was guarded," he became the archetype of a prophet as liberator, and one who spoke to God face-to-face, handed on God's law, and interceded for the people.[1]

The call of Moses as it unfolds in Exodus is the prototype for subsequent calls, and also reveals the nature of God. It begins with a divine confrontation between God and Moses at the burning bush (Exod 3:1–4a), followed by introductory words that identify the one calling (3:4b–9), then includes a commission to the one called (3:10) that evokes an objection or hesitation (3:11), which is followed by divine reassurance and a sign (3:12). The nature of the God who calls unfolds in a series of vivid actions: "I have *observed* the misery of my people who are in Egypt; I have *heard* their cry....I *know* their sufferings, and I have *come down to deliver* them from the Egyptians, and *to bring them up* out of that land to a good and broad land" (Exod 3:7–8 [emphasis mine]). This pattern of a compassionate God who intervenes in history informs the whole of biblical thought.

While Moses is an archetype, different forms of the mission of a prophet unfold throughout Israel's history, and we will highlight the work of a number of prophets who are of special importance for issues of social justice. No one has captured the distinctive character of the prophets more than the great Jewish theologian, Abraham Joshua Heschel (1907—72), whose study of prophets is now a classic.[2]

While the inner life of the prophets is minimally available in the biblical text, Heschel's journey through the prophetic texts is such a powerful and eloquent statement that no summary can substitute for engaging the whole text, so a few excerpts must suffice. Fundamental to Heschel's theology is that the prophet communicates "the divine pathos" that is the great paradox of biblical faith, "a longing God's pursuit of humanity."[3]

This *divine pathos* is the key to inspired prophecy. God is involved in the life of man. A personal relationship binds him to Israel; there is

---

1. Moshe Greenberg, "Moses," in *Encyclopaedia Judaica* (New York: McMillan, 1972), XII, col. 387–88.

2. Descended from a distinguished line of Hasidic teachers and formed by the best of rabbinic and secular education, Heschel combined profound scholarship with his own prophetic commitment as a leader in the civil rights movement who marched with Martin Luther King, Jr., at Selma (much to the chagrin of some of his faculty colleagues).

3. *God in Search of Man: A Philosophy of Judaism* (New York: Octagon Books, 1972), 136.

an interweaving of the Divine in the affairs of the nation. The divine commandments are not mere recommendations for man, but express divine concern, which, realized or repudiated, is of personal importance to him (Heschel, *Prophets*, vol. 1, 14). He launches the two-volume work in vivid descriptions of "what manner of man is the prophet" (ibid., 3–26):

> *"Sensitivity to evil":*
> Instead of dealing with the timeless issues of being and becoming, of matter and form, of definitions and demonstrations, he is thrown into orations about widows and orphans, about the corruption of judges and affairs of the market place. Instead of showing us a way through the elegant mansions of the mind, the prophets take us to the slums....To us injustice is injurious to the welfare of the people; to the prophets it is a deathblow to existence: to us, an episode; to them, a catastrophe, and a threat to the world. Their breathless impatience with injustice may strike us as hysteria....The prophet is a man who feels fiercely. God has thrust a burden upon his soul, and he is bowed and stunned at man's fierce greed. Frightful is the agony of man; no human voice can convey its full terror. Prophecy is the voice that God has lent to the silent agony, a voice to the plundered poor, to the profaned riches of the world. It is a form of living, a crossing point of God and man. God is raging in the prophet's words. (3)
> *"The prophetic message comes to us as 'one octave too high'":*
> We and the prophet have no language in common. To us the moral state of society, for all its stains and spots, seems fair and trim; to the prophet it is dreadful. So many deeds of charity are done, so much decency radiates day and night; yet to the prophet satiety of the conscience is prudery and flight from responsibility. (9)
> *"The prophet is an iconoclast":*
> The prophet challenges "the apparently holy, revered, and awesome. Beliefs cherished as certainties, institutions endowed with supreme sanctity, he exposes as scandalous pretensions." Yet the message is not simply one of indict-

ment and doom but of compassion. The words of the
prophet are stern, sour, stinging. But behind his austerity is
love and compassion for mankind (cf Ezek 18:23). Indeed,
every prediction of disaster is in itself an exhortation to
repentance. The prophet is sent not only to upbraid, but
also to "strengthen the weak hands and make firm the fee-
ble knees" (Isa 35:3). Almost every prophet brings consolation, promise, and the hope of reconciliation along with
censure and castigation. He begins with a message of doom;
he concludes with a message of hope. (12)

While Heschel's descriptions are drawn mainly from the works of
the "writing prophets" (Isaiah through Malachi) who provide the major
focus for concerns about social justice, their mission is foreshadowed
in the conflicts between prophet and king in the Books of Kings (part
of the *Nevi'im*, or major prophets in the Jewish canon).

PROPHETS AGAINST ROYAL POWER

Kingship is a powerful strain of biblical faith with echoes of the
"golden age" of David and Solomon, and divine kingship, yet its origin
is fraught with ambivalence. The foundation of the monarchy spans
1 Samuel 8—12, but with two different valuations: negative in 1 Samuel
8; 10:17–27, and chapter 12, while positive in other chapters. In
response to their request for a monarch, Samuel warns the people of
the dangers of a king—dominating power and control over their possessions, yet they still persist in their desire, and Samuel anoints Saul
and pronounces him "king over His [God's] own people (10:1–2). The
epitome of the royal theology is reached in the dynastic oracle of 2 Samuel
7:11–16, where God will assure David that his throne will last forever
and "I will be a father to him, and he shall be a son to me" (v. 14, see
also Ps 89).

In the anti-monarchic strain, desire for a king is rejection of God:

"Thus says the LORD, the God of Israel, 'I brought up Israel
out of Egypt, and I rescued you from the hand of the

70

Egyptians and from the hand of all the kingdoms that were oppressing you.' But today you have rejected your God, who saves you from all your calamities and your distresses; and you have said, 'No! but set a king over us.'" (1 Sam 10:18–19)

Such ambivalence permeates the Deuteronomistic editing of the historical books, which rejects virtually every king of Israel often with a formula such as "He [Nadab] did what was evil in the sight of the LORD, walking in the way of his ancestor and in the sin he caused Israel to commit" (1 Kgs 15:26). Two narratives of the prophet against king are especially important for understanding aspects of social justice in Israel.

Second Samuel tells of the rise to power of David (1:1—8:18) followed by the "court history" (9:1—20:26), with an appendix of various items, including the death and last words of David (chapters 21—24). Central motifs in the second section are the wars of David, his sinfulness, and divisions within his family. The sin of David, his conflict with Nathan, the prophet, stands at the center of a book that combines the ethos of Homeric epics and Greek tragedy (2 Sam 11:1—12:17).

In the midst of the wars with the Ammonites, David rises from his afternoon nap and sees from his rooftop Bathsheba, "a very beautiful woman" bathing. Though she is the wife of "Uriah the Hittite," David sends messengers "to fetch her" and "he lay with her." When she sends word to David, "I am pregnant," he panics, summons Uriah from the battlefield and tries to entice him by gifts and getting him drunk to have intercourse with Bathsheba to cover up his adultery. Since Uriah observes the rules of the holy war (1 Sam 21:4–5), he refuses and David arranges for him to be cut down in the next battle.

Though seemingly a simple indictment of adultery and murder, deeper issues are embedded in this narrative. A king, who should lead his people in war, is taking an afternoon nap; a woman is sexually abused by a powerful male; a non-Israelite soldier observes the law; David involves others in his murderous scheme; the rights of a resident alien are violated; David seems unscathed by his actions; he marries Bathsheba and she bears a son.

The story shifts dramatically when "the Lord sent Nathan [the prophet] to David" (2 Sam 12:1–17). Nathan begins by telling a touching and seemingly simple parable of two men, one rich, the other poor, but a story replete with concerns for justice. The contrast is dramatic. While the rich man had flocks and herds in great numbers, the poor man "has one little ewe lamb that he had bought. He nourished her, and she grew up with him and his children. She shared the little food he had and drank from his cup and slept in his bosom. She was like a daughter to him" (2 Sam 12:3). A traveler, a rich man, visits, but the poor man must observe the customs of hospitality by offering a meal, and then the rich man takes the poor man's lamb and slaughters it for a meal.

David, now king, but once a poor shepherd, flew into a rage and said that the rich man deserves to die (vv. 5–6); the seducer is now seduced by Nathan's parable. Like a judge at the gate the prophet says, "You are the man," and the narrative will go on to recount the consequences of David's sin. But what is the sin of David, and why did David react so strongly? As king, David is obliged to uphold justice and to have special concern for the vulnerable and poor (Pss 72, 89). Only when David is seduced into the world of the parable and can see his own actions reflected can he understand that his sin was one of rank injustice and the brutal use of power, especially since, in the world of the Bible, adultery is primarily a sin of injustice, as it remains today, when people break the marriage covenant.

NABOTH'S VINEYARD: A LEGACY BETRAYED

A major segment of the Elijah cycle describes the degradation of monarchy in the reign of Ahab of Israel (1 Kgs 16:29—22:40). Married to a Syrian princess, Jezebel, Ahab adopted the idolatrous worship of Baal, which Elijah opposed in the unforgettable narrative of the contest of the prophets on Mount Carmel, which evoked the murderous designs of Jezebel against the prophet (1 Kgs 18:11—19:2). After various accounts of the wars of Ahab, Elijah returns from exile, in direct opposition to the royal designs. Ahab desires a vineyard of Naboth's that is next to his palace, but when Naboth refuses, Ahab and Jezebel engage in juridical murder to gain possession of the land.

Injustice and violation of the covenant haunt the narrative. Naboth's immediate response ("the Lord forbid") and claim that the land is "ancestral inheritance" echoes the command in Leviticus that the land is fundamentally God's land that humans hold as tenants (Lev 25:18–24). When Ahab sulks and is upbraided by Jezebel—"now it is time to show yourself king over Israel" (1 Kgs 21:7, *JSB*)—Jezebel then arranges for a juridical murder by trumping up charges against Naboth for cursing God; he is stoned to death and Ahab takes "possession" of the vineyard. Along with the violation of injunctions against murder, stealing, and false witness in the Decalogue, Jezebel's forced perjury by the false witnesses violates the commands of Deuteronomy 19:15–20 for truthful witnesses in a capital trial. The frequent use of the word *possession*, which in Hebrew can suggest forced possession (21:15, 16, 18, 19), echoes the perversion of kingship that Samuel predicted (1 Sam 10).

Ahab's secure possession recoils when "the word of the LORD came to Elijah the Tishbite," and he confronts the king with the charge, "would you murder and take possession?" (1 Kgs 21:17, 19). The prophet quickly pronounces horrible retribution on Ahab where the dogs "that lapped up Naboth's blood will lap up your blood," and Jezebel and Ahab's son will be devoured by dogs. This royal couple worships an unholy trinity of injustice: idolatry, greed, and the arrogance of power, a triad still served among the powerful of the twenty-first century.

CONCERN FOR THE POOR AND MARGINALIZED

The prophetic heritage is described in different ways: writing prophets with named books; major prophets (Isaiah, Jeremiah, Ezekiel) and minor prophets (for example, Amos, Hosea, and others); preexilic, exilic, and postexilic prophets. Running through all of these is a concern for those same marginal groups—the poor, the widow, the orphan, and the stranger in the land—that we saw in the legal corpus. Our primary aim is to highlight the vivid descriptions and imaginative language of the prophets that challenge both our imaginations and our values.

More than any topic covered in this work, engagement with the prophets must be in the form of snapshots. The powerful language and images of the prophets are some of the most striking in the Bible, and merit reading again and again.

AMOS OF TEKOA

Amos, from Tekoa in the South (1:1), was among shepherds (really a breeder of livestock) and also a "tender of mulberry figs" (7:14). Recent research rejects the view of Amos as a "righteous peasant" and envisions him rather as a small vine grower or landowner. His career spans the reigns of Uzziah of Judah (783–742 BC) and Jeroboam II (son of Joash) of Israel (786–746, see 2 Kgs 14:23–29). In his words, the Lord "roars from Zion" against the "top of Carmel." He prophesied at Bethel, the northern sanctuary near the border of Israel and Judah (7:10–17). He was opposed by the "court prophet," Amaziah, and then arrested for sedition.

During this time, however, the Northern Kingdom experienced material prosperity. Under the reign of Solomon, a more prosperous upper class had emerged that created a class with a vested interest in the accumulation of land and goods as capital. The old emphasis on the land as the inheritance of every Israelite disappeared (see above, 1 Kgs 21, the story of Naboth's vineyard). James Mays describes this as "the shift of the primary social good, land, from the function of support to that of capital; the reorientation of social goals from personal values to personal profit; to subordination of judicial process to the interests of the entrepreneur" ("Justice," 9).

Amos is truly the "Person of the Year" in unmasking social evil. After the standard form of oracles against foreign nations, his indictments of Israel include: selling fellow Israelites, "the righteous," into slavery (2:6–8; 8:6); abuse of the poor (8:4); "father and son go in to the same girl" (2:7, may be sexual in nature; cult prostitution); garments taken in pledge (2:8, in violation of Exod 22:16; Deut 24:17); the strongholds of the powerful become places where violence and robbery are planned (3:9–10); conspicuous consumption by the idle rich (3:15); ostentatious living by rich, upper-class women at the expense of the poor (4:1); distortion of justice (5:7); rejection of anyone who speaks of justice against them (5:10); "trample upon the poor," (5:11, cf. also 2:7; 8:6); and excessive taxation to force people to give up their property; use of money to buy useless property; perversion of justice (5:12–14); use of religion as a pretext to avoid doing justice (5:24, cf. also 4:4–5); ostentatious lifestyle of the upper classes (6:1–7); and abuse of the poor combined with perfunctory and utilitarian view of religious practice (8:4–6). As Lawrence Boadt notes:

> Although Amos never mentions the Ten Commandments by name his charges reflect them in every chapter. The people violate all the demands that God has made upon them in the great covenant on Mount Sinai. His words touch moral failure in every level of society: law, leadership, economic life and even worship. (*Reading*, 278)

In response, Amos delivers oracles of judgment and a call to conversion. People of the covenant who abused the covenant will be destroyed (3:1–15); war and natural disaster will come upon the people who did not heed previous warnings (4:1–13); the city will be delivered up to foreign powers; the upper classes (4:1–3; 6:1–14), king (7:10–11), and the priests (7:16–17) will all be punished; and the misuse of religion will be unmasked and punished (5:13–23). Yet he utters a fundamental call for conversion that crystallizes the ethics of the prophets, "Seek good and not evil…establish justice in the gate" (5:14–15), and the words so dear to Martin Luther King, Jr., "let justice roll down like waters, and righteousness like an ever-flowing stream" (5:24). In the world of the Bible, water was the source of life and a gift from God; social justice will bring about this gift.

HOSEA

The prophet Hosea was the only canonical prophet who was a native of the Northern Kingdom and also prophesied there. His ministry, roughly contemporaneous with Amos, extended from around the mid-eighth century to the fall of Samaria in 721 BC. While reflecting the same historical situation as Amos, Hosea does not catalog social abuses but is most concerned with the alliances of King Jeroboam (786–746) with Assyria and with the influences of idolatrous religion on Israelite faith. He draws explicitly on the historical traditions of

Israel and especially on the call to fidelity in the covenant. Though a bit overstated, "Amos was a prophet who put forward God's demand for justice, so Hosea is the prophet who puts forward God's plea for *chesed* [mercy or loving kindness]" (Jensen, *Ethical Dimensions*, 109).

The book falls into two rough divisions: chapters 1—3, Hosea's marriage and its meaning; chapters 4—14, random oracles against Israel's infidelity, calls for conversion, and concluding words of hope. The initial chapters are most likely an allegory where Israel's infidelity is embodied in a narrative of the adultery of Gomer, Hosea's wife, and the call to again "lure her and lead her into the desert and speak to her heart" (2:14). Here, God will renew the marriage covenant in "right and justice, in love and in mercy, and in fidelity" (2:19-20) that will lead to true knowledge of the LORD. While not as explicit as other prophets in exposing injustice, Hosea underscores the fundamental causes of injustice: reliance on the false gods of political power and alliances, and forgetfulness of the covenant gifts and call for fidelity. For her part, Israel must repent and sow justice (*tsedaqah*) in order to reap the fruits of *chesed* (10:12). The people must hold fast to loyalty and justice (12:6).

ISAIAH OF JERUSALEM

In an exceptional recent commentary, Walter Brueggemann compares Isaiah to "a mighty oratorio whereby Israel sings its story of faith" (*Isaiah, 1—39*, 16-18). Sounding through this oratorio are passages of beautiful poetry that shape the hope in God for people suffering external threat and even exile. In Judaism, it is "perhaps the best loved of the prophetic books," and more prophetic readings chanted in synagogue services are taken from it than from any other book (Sommer, in *JSB*, 780). The scroll of Isaiah is the longest text among the Dead Sea Scrolls, and among Christians, Isaiah has been called "the Fifth Gospel."[4]

The canonical Book of Isaiah is divided into three sections, each of which reflects a different historical period. The first section (1—39) contains sayings and recollections of Isaiah of Jerusalem described below; the second (40—55), called Deutero or Second Isaiah, reflects

---

4. John F. A. Sawyer, *The Fifth Gospel: Isaiah in the History of Christianity* (New York: Cambridge University Press, 1996).

the exile and the return; the final chapters (56—66) are in a postexilic setting. Yet contemporary research stresses that editors have created themes and motifs that pervade the whole work such as the holiness and sovereignty of Zion; concern for *tsedaqah* and *mishpat* and the closely related term, *yeshua*; salvation; and constant calls for conversion.[5]

Isaiah is active during a tumultuous time in Israel's history. His "prophetic vocation" (6:1–13) dated in the year king Uzziah died (742 BC), occurs through a vision in the temple where he is overwhelmed by God's holiness, protests his unworthiness, and is commissioned to "make the mind of this people dull, and stop their ears, and shut their eyes" (6:10; see also Mark 4:12, and parallels). He lived and worked in and around Jerusalem and draws heavily on royal (Davidic) traditions and the temple liturgy. The literary quality of his work, his contacts with the wisdom traditions, and his personal contacts with royalty suggest that he was of the upper class. He married a woman who was a prophetess and had two sons with symbolic names (8:1–3), and he prophesied during the reigns of Jotham (742–735), Ahaz (735–715), and Hezekiah (715–687). His activity seems to end around 701. A later noncanonical writing, *The Martyrdom of Isaiah* (c. first century BC) recounts his martyrdom as being sawed in half at the instigation of a false prophet.

Events in the Northern Kingdom of Israel and the rise of Assyrian power under Tiglath Pileser III (745–727 BC) influence his message. In addition to his attacks on injustice and corruption (see below), his constant concern is for the fidelity and trust in the holiness of God that he feels is compromised by foreign alliances. He warns the kings against joining the alliance with Israel in what has been called the Syro-Ephraimite War (734–733, see 2 Kgs 16:1–20), which ultimately brought about the destruction of the Northern Kingdom (721 BC), the exile of the people, and the reduction of Judea into vassalage to Assyria that brought into its wake idolatrous practice and social injustice. During the reign of Hezekiah, Isaiah warned against revolting against Assyrian power; his warnings were not heeded (cf. 30:1–2; 31:1–3). In 701, Hezekiah revolted against Assyria; the revolt was crushed and Hezekiah pays a huge indemnity.

---

5. We will treat Isaiah 40—66 in a later section since these sections show the influence of the destruction of the Davidic monarchy and the exile. (See Leclerc, *Yahweh Is Exalted*, 18–24, for an excellent discussion of the divisions of Isaiah).

Isaiah of Jerusalem has a number of the most strident charges against injustice found in the Bible, along with passionate cries for conversion. In language resonant of the concerns in the Covenant Code for the marginal groups, Isaiah begins with ringing denunciations of injustice calling the people "Ah, sinful nation, people laden with iniquity, offspring who do evil, children who deal corruptly, who have forsaken the LORD, who have despised the Holy One of Israel, who are utterly estranged!" (1:4–5). He then castigates reliance on cultic observance and continued prayer: "When you stretch out your hands, I will hide my eyes from you; even though you make many prayers, I will not listen" (1:15), while proclaiming true devotion to God: "Wash yourselves; make yourselves clean; remove the evil of your doings from before my eyes; cease to do evil, learn to do good; seek justice, rescue the oppressed, defend the orphan, plead for the widow," (1:16–17, cf. also 1:23), with a promise of divine forgiveness, "though your sins are like scarlet, they shall be like snow; though they are red like crimson, they shall become like wool" (1:18).

Playing on the image of the people as God's vineyard, Isaiah conducts a court case against them for the perversion of justice:

> The LORD enters into judgment
>   with the elders and princes of his people:
> It is you who have devoured the vineyard;
>   the spoil of the poor is in your houses.
> What do you mean by crushing my people,
>   by grinding the face of the poor? says the Lord GOD of hosts.
>
> (3:14–15)

The vivid imagery of "devouring," "crushing," and "grinding" shows the depth of the indictment, which is then followed by a long and bitter denunciation of the lifestyle of the rich women: "the daughters of Zion are haughty / and walk with outstretched necks, / glancing wantonly with their eyes, / mincing along as they go, / tinkling with their feet" (3:16), with vivid descriptions of their "signet rings and nose rings; the festal robes, the mantles, the cloaks, and the handbags" (3:21–22)—all of which will be turned against them on the day of judgment.

The later allegory of God's love song for the vineyard, which is "the house of Israel," is perhaps the harshest indictment (5:1–10). After planting and caring for it, in place of grapes it yielded wild grapes so God will destroy it, and this section concludes with a powerful play on words: "He looked for judgment (*mishpat*) but bloodshed (*mishpach*) for justice (*tsedaqah*) but hark, the outcry, (*tse 'akah*)" (5:7, *au. trans.*). The attack on the poor and marginalized is manifest not only in the gap between the ostentatious rich and the poor and the violence against them, but equally in the perversion of justice where people might seek some redress:

> Ah, you who make iniquitous decrees,
> > who write oppressive statutes,
> to turn aside the needy from justice
> > and to rob the poor of my people of their right,
> that widows may be your spoil,
> > and that you may make the orphans your prey!
>
> (10:1–2)

While these denunciations are a stimulus for conversion, Isaiah looks to God's gift of a time when "for out of Zion shall go forth instruction, / and the word of the LORD from Jerusalem" and the people "shall beat their swords into plowshares / and their spears into pruning hooks; / nation shall not lift up sword against nation, / neither shall they learn war any more" (2:3–4). These hopes will take root in a Davidic king in images that echo through every celebration of Christmas:

> The people who walked in darkness
> > have seen a great light;
> those who lived in a land of deep darkness—
> > on them light has shined.
> You have multiplied the nation,
> > you have increased its joy;
> they rejoice before you
> > as with joy at the harvest,
> > as people exult when dividing plunder.
>
> (9:2–3)

For a child has been born for us,
    a son given to us;
authority rests upon his shoulders;
    and he is named
Wonderful Counselor, Mighty God,
    Everlasting Father, Prince of Peace.
His authority shall grow continually,
    and there shall be endless peace
for the throne of David and his kingdom.
    He will establish and uphold it
with justice and with righteousness
    from this time onward and forevermore.
The zeal of the LORD of hosts will do this.

(9:6–7)

This hope culminates in a reign that will be sustained by *tsedaqah* and *mishpat* (justice and judgment), which, as we have noted, is a hendiadys (a double expression conveying a single idea) best understood as "social justice." For Isaiah, in oversimplified terms, injustice toward the suffering and marginal people is the cancer that will destroy Judah; social justice is the cure. Again, as we look at contemporary capitalist economies, as in the saying attributed to Mark Twain: "history does not repeat itself, it often rhymes."

MICAH OF MORESHETH

Micah (c. 725–701 BC) is from Moresheth, a village in Judah about twenty-one miles south of Jerusalem. Where Isaiah writes with poetic beauty, hobnobs with royalty, and knows firsthand the lifestyle of the oppressive rich, Micah views the world through the eyes of a village elder, and castigates prophets, priests, and judges with bitter invective:

Hear, you leaders of Jacob,
rulers of the house of Israel!
Is it not your duty to know what is right (*mishpat*),

you who hate what is good, and love evil?
You who tear their skin from them,
and their flesh from their bones;

They eat the flesh of my people,
and flay their skin from them,
and break their bones;
They chop them in pieces like flesh in a kettle,
and like meat in a caldron.

(3:1–3)

He addresses directly "rulers of the house of Israel! / You who abhor what is just, / and pervert all that is right; / Who build up Zion with bloodshed, / and Jerusalem with wickedness!" for they are venal and easily bribed (3:9–10). Like Isaiah and Amos before him, he criticizes sacrificial worship when divorced from ethical concern (Amos 5:21–24; Isa 12–17), but while indicting evil, he offers the remedy in a summary of the fundamental demand of the covenant:

"Will the LORD be pleased with thousands of rams,
   with ten thousands of rivers of oil?
Shall I give my firstborn for my transgression,
   the fruit of my body for the sin of my soul?"
He has told you, O mortal, what is good;
   and what does the LORD require of you
but to do justice, and to love kindness,
   and to walk humbly with your God?

(6:7–8)

Micah also voices the hope for a faithful remnant (2:12; 5:7–8) that will return after the coming destruction as well as hope for a restored Zion and monarchy.

JEREMIAH: A CALL TO REFORM AND
THE END OF THE SOUTHERN KINGDOM

For many people the name *Jeremiah* is synonymous with Old Testament prophecy. His dates correspond roughly to the last half-

81

century of the independence of the people of Israel (640–587 BC). Jeremiah is the most biographical of the prophets. He was born the son of Hilkiah, a priest at Anathoth, and was called to be a prophet in the thirteenth year of the reign of Josiah, 627 BC (1:2, 4). In his account of the call, Jeremiah lays stress on his young age, perhaps in his teens— the approximate age of the "boy" Samuel—when he was serving Eli at Shiloh, and the call to be Yahweh's prophet came to him (1 Sam 2:11, 18, 21, 26; 3:1, 8). Jeremiah's call, fearful and resisted, is to be a prophet to the nations, and his life's work is "to pluck up and to break down...to build and to plant" (Jer 1:10). Jeremiah is the most personal of all the prophets and the only one explicitly commanded not to marry (16:2).

He first prophesied in Anathoth (north of Jerusalem), provoking the anger of the villagers and his family (11:21; 12:6), and then moved to Jerusalem, a one-hour walk from home. He lived in exciting and tragic times. He supported the reform and renewal of worship by Josiah (2 Kgs 23), and criticized the Judean policy of alliance with Egypt against Assyria (Jer 2:14–19, 36–37). After the fall of Nineveh in 612 BC to the Babylonians, Egypt, a vassal state to Assyria, tried to assist the floundering empire and was opposed by Josiah who died in 609 BC at the battle of Megiddo. Josiah was heralded in the Deuteronomic history as a good king, and Chronicles records that Jeremiah uttered a lament for Josiah (2 Chr 35:25).

Jeremiah's career continued during the reign of Jehoiakim (608–598 BC), and later in Zedekiah's reign (597–587 BC). Repeatedly, he warned the king from revolting against Babylon (Jer 27:12–15). The revolt broke out, yet the king kept consulting him, either by messengers (37:3–10) or personally (37:17–20). The ministers wanted Jeremiah dead but did not dare kill him. Charging him with desertion to the enemy, they jailed him in a pit-house where he would starve to death (37:11–16), but the king moved him to a better prison, "the court of the guard," where he received food until the fall of Jerusalem (586 BC) (37:21). The Chaldeans freed Jeremiah from prison, committing him to the care of their Judean governor, Gedaliah, son of Ahikam (39:14). After the latter's assassination, the remnants decided against Jeremiah's oracle to flee to Egypt, taking along the prophet and his secretary, Baruch. Several oracles date from this Egyptian period

(43:8—44:30; 46:13–26). Although his death is not reported, later Jewish and Christian sources tell of his martyrdom in Egypt by other Jewish exiles.

Though the subject of considerable editing, the Books of Jeremiah and Lamentations (attributed to him) contain some of the most beautiful, poignant, and poetic language in the Bible, and have inspired artists such as Michelangelo and Rembrandt to picture him as the "sorrowful prophet" with head bowed resting on his right arm, lamenting the destruction of Jerusalem. More than any other biblical writer, Jeremiah evokes the sheer terror of military conquest from the victim's point of view:

> "My anguish, my anguish! I writhe in pain!
>   Oh, the walls of my heart!
> My heart is beating wildly;
>   I cannot keep silent;
> for I hear the sound of the trumpet,
>   the alarm of war."
>
> (4:19)[6]

Even as he was active in the Southern Kingdom, Jeremiah adopts traditions associated with Moses and the covenant. The center of his theology is trust in God and fidelity to the covenant even as the world around him seems to be dissolving. His comments on social justice, while not as extensive as earlier prophets, are equally powerful. He casts scorn on the people for their idolatry and trust in foreign gods: "As you have forsaken me and served strange gods in your own land, so shall you serve strangers in a land that is not your own" (5:19), and castigates false prophets, "They have spoken falsely of the LORD, / and have said, 'He will do nothing. / No evil will come upon us, / and we shall not see sword or famine.' / The prophets are nothing but wind, / for the word is not in them" (5:12–13).

---

6. Leonard Bernstein wrote a symphony in his honor that premiered during World War II (March 29, 1944) in New York City at Carnegie Hall with three movements of prophecy, profanation, and lamentation. "Music Critics Prize Won by Bernstein," *New York Times* (May 16, 1944), 19.

SEEK JUSTICE THAT YOU MAY LIVE

Later in the same section, he underscores their social iniquities:

For scoundrels are found among my people;
    they take over the goods of others.
Like fowlers they set a trap;
    they catch human beings.
Like a cage full of birds,
    their houses are full of treachery;
therefore they have become great and rich,
    they have grown fat and sleek.
They know no limits in deeds of wickedness;
    they do not judge with justice
the cause of the orphan, to make it prosper,
    and they do not defend the rights of the needy.

(5:26–28)

During the final years before Jerusalem falls to Babylon, Jeremiah indicts the various leaders of the city. First are commands to the king and his servants:

Thus says the LORD: Act with justice and righteousness, and deliver from the hand of the oppressor anyone who has been robbed. And do no wrong or violence to the alien, the orphan, and the widow, or shed innocent blood in this place. (22:3)

Clearly, here, justice for the marginal groups is the touchstone of divinely sanctioned leadership. This is followed by one of Jeremiah's oracles that has had immense significance on contemporary theological reflection on social justice. Josiah was succeeded by his son Jehoahaz, who was exiled to Egypt, but favored, like his father, a policy of alliance with Babylon. After three months, Necho then replaced him with Jehoiakim (608–598 BC), who was pro-Egyptian. Jeremiah then attacks him for betraying the values of his father (Josiah):

Woe to him who builds his house by unrighteousness,
    and his upper rooms by injustice;

who makes his neighbors work for nothing,
    and does not give them their wages;
who says, "I will build myself a spacious house
    with large upper rooms,"
and who cuts out windows for it,
    paneling it with cedar,
    and painting it with vermilion.
Are you a king
    because you compete in cedar?
Did not your father eat and drink
    and do justice and righteousness?
    Then it was well with him.
He judged ["dispensed justice to," NABRE] the cause of the
      poor and needy;
    then it was well.
Is not this to know me?
    says the LORD.

(22:13–16)

Josiah embodies the ideal of a Davidic king (cf. Ps 72) while his son distorts this ideal. In contrast to exploitation of workers and conspicuous consumption, true justice consists in dispensing justice (that is taking up the cause of) the weak and the poor. Such action is equated with true knowledge of God.

Jeremiah's words gave rise to the famous and disputed statement from the 1971 Synod of Bishops, *Justice in the World*: "Action on behalf of justice and participation in the transformation of the world fully appear to us as a constitutive dimension of the preaching of the Gospel" (no. 6).[7]

---

7. This statement inspired subsequent generations who refused to see a gap between social action and the commitment of faith, but has proved problematic among conservative Catholic circles. Presently, synods of bishops issue no independent statements, but the pope issues a post-synodal document on the issues considered by the synod. For reactions to this statement, see Charles M. Murphy, "Action for Justice as Constitutive of the Preaching of the Gospel: What Did the 1971 Synod of the Bishops Mean?" *Theological Studies* 44 (1983): 298–311, and "Charity, Not Justice as Constitutive of the Church's Mission," *Theological Studies* 68 (2007): 274–86.

The second oracle of woe is against other rulers in the city:

> Woe to the shepherds who destroy and scatter the sheep of
> my pasture! says the LORD. Therefore thus says the LORD,
> the God of Israel, concerning the shepherds who shepherd
> my people: It is you who have scattered my flock, and have
> driven them away, and you have not attended to them.
> (23:1–2)

This is followed by an indictment of false prophets and priests
who proclaim a message of peace and security:

> Do not listen to the words of the prophets who prophesy to
> you; they are deluding you. They speak visions of their own
> minds, not from the mouth of the LORD. They keep saying
> to those who despise the word of the LORD, "It shall be well
> with you"; and to all who stubbornly follow their own stub-
> born hearts, they say, "No calamity shall come upon you."
> (23:16–17)

Jeremiah is often seen as a prophet of doom and gloom, but sends
the people in exile a message of hope, urging them to settle in Babylon
with the hope of restoration by God (29:1–27), which is then followed
by the "book of consolation" (30:1—31:40) with its proclamation of
forgiveness and restoration to both Judah and Israel and the promise
of a new covenant (31:31–33):

> The days are surely coming, says the LORD, when I will
> make a new covenant with the house of Israel and the house
> of Judah. It will not be like the covenant that I made with
> their ancestors when I took them by the hand to bring them
> out of the land of Egypt—a covenant that they broke,
> though I was their husband, says the LORD. But this is the
> covenant that I will make with the house of Israel after those
> days, says the LORD: I will put my law within them, and I
> will write it on their hearts; and I will be their God, and they
> shall be my people.

This new covenant law will be a renewal of the Sinai covenant but will now be an interior guide for the people (written "on their hearts"). All the concerns in the Sinai covenant for the poor and the marginalized are now to be interiorized in the lives of the community. What is new is not the content of the covenant but how it is learned. Later, Jewish mystical thought (for example, Lurianic Kabbalah) will argue that all people have a "divine spark" within them, so Torah need not be taught.

THREE PROPHETS OF EXILE

Jeremiah is a bridge between the preexilic and postexilic prophets since, despite his warnings about political intrigue with Egypt against Babylon, Jerusalem fell to the Babylonian empire first in 597 BC, when the city was captured, the temple looted, and the king and leading citizens were deported to Babylon, among whom was Ezekiel. The Babylonian king Nebuchadnezzer appointed one of Josiah's sons, Zedekiah, as king, who continued to oppose and rebel against Babylon, which brought fierce retaliation (2 Kgs 24—25) that resulted in the destruction of the temple and the deportation of the population to Babylon while some fled to Egypt, taking Jeremiah along. The exile would last until 538 BC when the Jews were allowed to return by the Persian ruler, Cyrus.[8]

A remarkable thing about the exile is that from it emerged three of the most profound and eloquent prophets in Israel's history: Ezekiel, priest and prophet, who was active in its early years (until c. 573 BC), and the poetic visionaries of Second (and Third) Isaiah, who were active near the end of the exile (538 BC). The period after the exile would also witness the codification of the Torah by the Priestly editors as well as the collection of the Psalms and the rise of other forms of religious expression, such as "tales of the diaspora" (Tobit and Daniel) and apocalyptic treatises.

---

8. See Leclerc, *Prophets*, 235–39, for a fine summary of the events surrounding the fall of Jerusalem.

EZEKIEL

My somewhat limited focus on issues of social justice does not allow full consideration of the immense importance of Ezekiel. Marvin Sweeney comments that he "presents some of the most theologically challenging and dynamic material among the prophets of the bible, and some of its most intricate and bizarre passages....With striking images and extended metaphors" (*JSB*, 104). The work begins with an ornate temple vision and prophetic commissioning (1:1—7:27) and ends with an equally powerful image of the restored temple (40:1—48:35), then moves from stern judgment to consolation and hope. Not only are the oracles of Ezekiel powerful, his message is communicated by symbolic actions: eating a scroll on which were written words of lamentation and woe (2:8–10); digging a hole in the city wall and carrying his baggage outside (12:1–6); not mourning for his wife (24:15–23). Like his older contemporary, Jeremiah, Ezekiel warned against the power of Babylon, and was exiled there with prominent citizens of Jerusalem in 597 BC and witnessed the destruction of the city and temple in 587 BC.

The book manifests clear divisions beginning with a series of oracles of judgment against Judah and Jerusalem (chapters 1—24), and concluding with visions of hope and restoration (chapters 24—48). The prophet's sense of awe at the holiness of God and his horror of idolatry (chapters 8, 16, and 23, written in the temple city of Babylon that was replete with idols) is the implicit foundation of a theology of social justice. "The temple and hence the land had been polluted by Israel's economic injustice, violence, and idolatry" (Gordon Matties, *NISB*, 1154). When people forsake a proper relationship with God (injustice), then ruin follows. Ezekiel stands in the prophetic heritage by condemning abuses of the law and speaking on behalf of the marginal groups, "Father and mother are treated with contempt in you; the alien residing within you suffers extortion; the orphan and the widow are wronged in you" (22:7), then follows with ringing denunciations of priests, nobles, and prophets who cover the sins of the nobles with "white wash" and extends the denunciations to "the people of the land" (that is all Israel): "The people of the land have practiced extortion and committed robbery; they have oppressed the poor and needy, and have extorted from the alien without redress" ("without justice," *mishpat* in Hebrew) (22:29).

Ezekiel continues his indictment of leaders in accusations against the false shepherds (chapters 34) who take care of themselves while neglecting the poor and vulnerable (the weak, the sick, the injured, and those who strayed, vv. 1–6). The Word of the Lord proclaims:

> I myself will be the shepherd of my sheep, and I will make them lie down, says the Lord GOD. I will seek the lost, and I will bring back the strayed, and I will bind up the injured, and I will strengthen the weak, but the fat and the strong I will destroy. I will feed them with justice [*mishpat*]. (34:15–16)

The kinds of service the shepherds failed to give suffering people provides a background to the service of the hidden Christ, provided by the "just" in Matthew 25:31–46.

Ezekiel, then, is a sober reminder that not even social disaster and personal suffering excuses a people from fidelity to God's law. Concern for justice and the marginalized remains an essential part of a faithful response to God's gifts and hope of future salvation.

SECOND ISAIAH (ISA 40—55)

The ornate and beautiful poetry of Isaiah 40—66 (Deutero-Isaiah) that arose from the heart and soul of an exiled people is itself testimony to the power of hope and trust in God to overcome tragedy. It has also inspired the great oratorios of Handel's *Messiah* and has been a treasure trove for early Christian writers who want to root their understanding of the Christ event in their Jewish heritage. Still, when a people has lost its political independence and power to challenge and form its own living conditions, prophets cannot have the same power or influence they possessed prior to the exile.

The Prophet heralds the return from exile with the powerful call: "Comfort, give comfort to my people, says your God. Speak tenderly to Jerusalem, and proclaim to her that her service is at an end" (40:1–2), and describes the return as a new exodus evoking the history of God's saving action. Yet as Leclerc notes, there is little emphasis on issues of social justice. The standard hendiadys for social justice (*tsedaqah we mishpat*) does not appear in these chapters, and there is no concern for the usual marginal groups (Leclerc, *Yahweh Is Exalted*, 92). Second Isaiah's acrimony is most directed against the idolatry witnessed in Babylon when he compares idols being carried in procession in contrast to the God who carries his people.

> Bel bows down, Nebo stoops,
>   their idols are on beasts and cattle;
> these things you carry are loaded
>   as burdens on weary animals.
> They stoop, they bow down together;
>   they cannot save the burden,
>   but themselves go into captivity.
>
> Listen to me, O house of Jacob,
>   all the remnant of the house of Israel,
> who have been borne by me from your birth,
>   carried from the womb;
> even to your old age I am he,
>   even when you turn gray I will carry you.
> I have made, and I will bear;
>   I will carry and will save.
>
> (46:1–4)

Perhaps most known from Deutero-Isaiah are the four Servant Songs (Isa 42:1–9; 49:1–7; 50:4–11; 52:13—53:12). Justice (*mishpat*) appears in each Servant Song but with different nuances in each context.[9] Though the identity of the Servant is highly disputed (for example, the people as a whole; a prophet; a royal figure), the person and mission of the Servant have had immense influence on the Christology of the New Testament. The mission of the Servant is described:

> Here is my servant, whom I uphold,
>   my chosen, in whom my soul delights;

---

9. See Leclerc, *Yahweh Is Exalted*, 94–130, for a thorough discussion of justice in Second Isaiah.

I have put my spirit upon him;
    he will bring forth justice to the nations.
He will not cry or lift up his voice,
    or make it heard in the street;
a bruised reed he will not break,
    and a dimly burning wick he will not quench;
    he will faithfully bring forth justice.
He will not grow faint or be crushed
    until he has established justice in the earth;
    and the coastlands wait for his teaching.

(42:1–4)

The mission of the Servant is to bring about "the victory of justice" and God has formed him "as a covenant to the people, a light to the nations" (42:6). This mission of the Servant captures a central theme of Second Isaiah. Like the prophets, the Servant is given a mission to proclaim justice (mentioned three times) even amid the non-Jewish nations. Like Moses, a servant of God (Exod 4:10), he is to proclaim Torah understood as a way of life in fidelity to the covenant. In contrast to the often strident proclamations of the preexilic prophets, this Servant will be gentle (not crying out or shouting). His call is to be a "light to the nations"—resonant of the promise to Abraham that "in you all the nations of the world will be blessed" (Gen 12:3), and a foreshadowing of the pilgrimage of the nations to Zion at the end of Isaiah (66:12–13): "The people will become the tool through which the nations will know that God is mighty, just and reliable" (Sweeney, *JSB*, 867).

This note of universalism even amid exile will characterize one strain of Second Temple Judaism. Matthew adapts almost verbatim this section of Isaiah to the mission of Jesus (12:18–21). Along with enlightenment (with overtones of true teaching and wisdom, cf. Isa 51:4), the Servant will "bring out prisoners" which, Walter Brueggemann suggests, may be the release of those imprisoned for debt, in fidelity to the "poor law" of Deuteronomy 15:1–11 (*Isaiah 40—66*, 4).

Second Isaiah does not contain the explicit concerns with justice and injustice of the earlier prophets, however, the person and mission of the Servant embodies the vocation and suffering of those committed to justice. Joseph Jensen summarizes this well:

91

[H]e establishes the Lord's judgment (*mishpat*) and *torah* throughout the earth (42:4), toils and spends his strength and undergoes sufferings in the mission entrusted to him (49:4; 50:6), and an "open ear" for hearing (obeying) and (unlike Israel) does not rebel or turn back (50:5), submits meekly to harsh treatment (53:7); sinless himself, he patiently gives his life for the sins of others (53:4–5; 10—12)....The Servant actively pursues a mission of establishing God's rule. (*Ethical Dimensions*, 157)

THIRD ISAIAH (ISA 56—66)

Like the book as a whole, Third Isaiah is a collection of oracles from different periods, and in its final form, mirrors a setting and theology after the return from exile. Its message is very different from Second Isaiah, as well summarized by Thomas Leclerc:

Chapters 56 to 66 reveal a deeply divided community, rife with social injustice and disorder, power politics, despair and hopelessness. Moreover some prophecies are critical of the Temple-building project and the official, Temple centered cult (Isa 66:1–3). However other texts not only validate the cult but argue for its expansion to include foreigners and others prohibited from the Temple (56:3–5). (*Introduction*, 361)

The word-pair of *tsedaqah* and *mishpat* that was absent in Second Isaiah returns as does a strong concern for social justice—which shows the perdurance of this prophetic message and the need to repeat the message even as the Prophet repeats the joyous news of God's favor.

Early in these chapters, the Prophet proclaims a program for the returned exiles: "Thus says the LORD: / maintain justice (*mishpat*), and do what is right (*tsedaqah*), / for soon my salvation will come, / and my deliverance be revealed." (56:1). The salvation and deliverance that follow upon seeking social justice will be available to all peoples as all people bring their gifts to the holy mountain (Zion) "for my house shall be called a house of prayer / for all peoples" (56:7). At the same time, the Prophet castigates, like his predecessors, leaders who abuse their offices, the sentinels are blind; the shepherds are drunk and bent on greed. The author cries out: "Therefore justice (*mishpat*) is far from us, / and righteousness (*tsedaqah*) does not reach us" (59:9); "We wait for justice, but there is none" (59:11); "Justice is turned back" (59:14) and the Lord is sorrowed because there is no justice (59:16).

The attack on false worship continues with a proclamation of what constitutes true religion, that is, the right relation to God and neighbor (justice). True piety "would engender justice toward the weak, compassion toward the downtrodden, and charity toward the poor" (Sommer, *JSB*, 899) as proclaimed eloquently in the well-known description of true worship in Isaiah 58:1–8. In response to the complaint of the people that God does not hear their prayers and see their fasting "as if they were a nation that practiced righteousness," and claim to be seeking "righteous judgments" (58:2), the Prophet first upbraids them for invoking religious observance as an excuse to oppress their workers (58:3), and declares the nature of true worship:

> Is not this the fast that I choose:
>   to loose the bonds of injustice,
>   to undo the thongs of the yoke,
> to let the oppressed go free,
>   and to break every yoke?
> Is it not to share your bread with the hungry,
>   and bring the homeless poor into your house;
> when you see the naked, to cover them,
>   and not to hide yourself from your own kin?
>
> (58:6–7)

As in other prophets, when people take to heart the denunciation of evil, words of hope and consolation pour forth:

> Then your light shall break forth like the dawn,
>   and your healing shall spring up quickly;
> your vindicator shall go before you,
>   the glory of the LORD shall be your rear guard.

Then you shall call, and the LORD will answer;
  you shall cry for help, and he will say, Here I am.

(58:8–9)

THE ENDURING IMPORTANCE OF THE PROPHETS

For many decades, the social teaching of Israel was virtually iden-tified with the prophetic message. This was a danger when prophetic religion was often contrasted to a religion of law or was seen as a crit-icism of all legal texts and cultic activity. The reduction of the religion of Israel to prophetic ethics often fostered an undercurrent of anti-Semitism, since post-biblical Judaism was and remains heavily cen-tered on the Torah. The attitude developed among some Christian scholars that Judaism after the prophets was a decline into legalism. Also, the somewhat naïve interpretation of the prophets as anti-cultic was often seen as justification for the reduction of religious life to social activism or a neglect of communal liturgical life. But recent research on the prophets has underscored a number of things that are of impor-tance in assessing the prophetic texts.

First, the prophets are generally "conservative" in the best sense of the word. Their fundamental vision harkens back to the originating experiences of Israel to counter corrupting influences of urbanization and centralized power that developed under the monarchy, especially after the split between the Northern Kingdom (Israel) and the Southern Kingdom (Judah) after the death of Solomon (922 BC). Their works are also a collection of traditions, some going back to the origi-nally named prophets, additions by disciples and later editors. Much recent research has attempted to describe these levels of tradition.

Second, the prophets are not opposed to cultic worship, but to its corruption. Jeremiah was the son of a priest; Isaiah used cultic imagery; Ezekiel was a priest, associated with the Jerusalem temple. At the same time, the prophets urged that cultic worship be accompanied by a conversion of the heart.

Third, though the prophets criticize the misuse of power by those in authority, their message is reformist rather than revolutionary. They do not envision a community without a king, or without laws and statutes. During the bulk of the postexilic period, especially after the codification of the law under Ezra and Nehemiah, when the people lack their own kings and live under the successive rule of the Persians, the successors of Alexander the Great, and finally the Romans, prophecy as a movement within Judaism virtually ceases. Biblical prophecy required a shared heritage of values by the rulers and the ruled, even when those in power did not live up to these values. When a people have no control over their destiny and are subject to brutal power, prophecy can take the form only of protest or hope for a new age (apocalyptic) not a call to national reform.

Finally, attention to their language is an enduring legacy, especially in our age of colorless imagination, when suffering and poverty are reduced to statistics and euphemism covers crime. The images used by the prophets to describe injustice shock our imaginations, for example, "grinding the poor in the dust" (Isa 3:15); they "eat the flesh of my people, / flay their skin off them, / break their bones in pieces, / and chop them up like meat in a kettle, / like flesh in a caldron" (Mic 3:3). Such images can shock us out of our complacency and allow us to view the plight of the poor and marginalized with similar eyes. Today massive injustice appears in Brooks Brothers' suits. The prestigious *Financial Times* noted that one of the leaders of the Wall Street collapse of 2008 "breached his fiduciary responsibility." Amos would have said this differently! Naming evil without circumlocution or evasion is indispensable for any quest for social justice.

The purpose of this brief tour through select prophets has been to view their works through the lens of their social concern. But other important aspects of their thought suffered: stress on the utter holiness of God, and calls for true worship; powerful exhortations and images of conversion or return to God (*teshuva*); and the need to care for God's creation. Reading the Scriptures in their canonical order we can affirm that the prophetic concern for the poor and marginalized is a continuation of the Creation of all men and women "in the image of God, according to his likeness." The ultimate scourge of poverty and exploitation are their assaults on human dignity.

My hope is that this chapter has underscored a pervasive and important strain of biblical revelation that extends from the Sinai covenant through the prophets and was meant to form the conscience and conduct of generations, then and now. But no work can be a substitute for a deep engagement with the biblical texts themselves. As God commanded Ezekiel, "eat this scroll" (Ezek 3:1).

TYPICAL SINS ENUMERATED BY THE PROPHETS

Prepared by Rev. Lawrence Boadt, CSP (1942–2010)

1. Worshipped False Gods	Hosea 11:2; 4:13
2. Made Idols	Hosea 4:12; Jeremiah 5:7
3. False Oaths	Hosea 10:4; 4:2; Jeremiah 5:7
4. Fail to Keep the Sabbath	Ezekiel 18
5. Disrespect for Parents	Isaiah 3:5
6. Murder	Hosea 6:9; 4:2
7. Violence	Amos 3:10; Isaiah 5:7; Micah 3:2; Habakkuk 1:2–3
8. Oppression of the Poor	Amos 4:1; Micah 2:2; Isaiah 3:14; Zephaniah 3:1
9. Adultery	Hosea 7:4; 4:2; Jeremiah 5:7
10. Prostitution	Hosea 1:3; 4:14
11. Dishonest Weights	Micah 6:11; Proverbs 20:10
12. Lying	Hosea 4:2; Micah 2:11
13. Robbery	Hosea 7:1; 4:2; Amos 3:12; Micah 2:2; Habakkuk 2
14. Dishonest Cheating of Property	Hosea 12:8; Micah 6:11; Amos 8:5; Isaiah 5:8ff
15. Exorbitant Usury	Isaiah 5:8; Micah 7:3
16. Luxurious Concern	Amos 6:4; 4:1ff; Isaiah 3:6ff; 5:11; 31:8f
17. Greed	Hosea 7:14
18. Insolence on the Tongue	Hosea 7:16
19. Hatred	Hosea 9:7f; Amos 5:10

20. Leaders' Treachery	Hosea 7:3; Micah 3:1, 9
21. No Fidelity to Covenant	Hosea 4:1
22. Drunkenness	Hosea 4:11, 18; Isaiah 5:11
23. Corrupt Judges	Amos 2:6ff; Isaiah 1:26; 5:23; 10:1ff; Micah 3:9ff; Habakkuk 1:4
24. Rejecting God and His Law	Isaiah 5:24
25. False Prophets	Jeremiah 23; 28; Micah 3:11
26. Take Bribes	Amos 5:12
27. Cannibalism	Micah 3:3
28. Creates Starvation of Poor	Micah 3:5
29. Dishonest Priests	Micah 3:11

RESOURCE BIBLIOGRAPHY

Achtemeier, Paul J., and James L. Mays, eds. *Interpreting the Prophets.* Philadelphia: Fortress Press, 1987. A series of articles originally published in *Interpretation.* They treat mainly literary and historical problems, with the essays on Jeremiah by Brueggemann and Holladay especially helpful, as is "Resources for Studying the Prophets" by J. Limburg.

Berlin, Adele, and Marc Z. Brettler, eds. *The Jewish Study Bible.* New York: Oxford University Press, 2004. An excellent commentary from a Jewish perspective with fine essays on different themes and on Jewish biblical interpretation.

Blenkinsopp, Joseph. *A History of Prophecy in Israel.* Rev. ed. Louisville, KY: Westminster John Knox Press, 1996. One of the best standard introductions to all aspects of the prophets.

Boadt, Lawrence. *Reading the Old Testament: An Introduction.* 2nd ed. Revised and updated by Richard Clifford and Daniel Harrington. New York/Mahwah, NJ: Paulist Press, 2012.

Boda, Mark J., and J. Gordon McConville, eds. *Dictionary of Old Testament Prophets.* Downers Grove, IL: Intervarsity Press, 2012. A collection of 115 articles covering all the prophets in their historical, cultural, and literary backgrounds.

Brueggemann, Walter. *Isaiah 1—39 and Isaiah 40—66.* Westminster Bible Companion, 2 vols. Louisville, KY: Westminster John Knox Press, 1998. Among biblical scholars, Brueggemann is exceptional in finding concerns for social justice in the Old Testament writings.

————. *The Prophetic Imagination.* 2nd ed. Minneapolis: Fortress Press, 2001. A very influential and readable interpretation of the prophets.

Coote, Robert. *Amos Among the Prophets. Composition and Theology.* Philadelphia: Fortress Press, 1981. A challenging view of Amos with a strong emphasis on his social teaching.

Cuéllar, Gregory Lee. *Voices of Marginality: Exile and Return in Second Isaiah 40—55 and the Mexican Immigrant Experience.* New York: Peter Lang, 2008. In using postmodern and postcolonial resources, Lee correlates experiences of immigrants with Israel's exiles.

Dempsey, Carol J. *Hope Amid the Ruins: The Ethics Of Israel's Prophets.* Louis, MO: Chalice Press, 2000.

Domeris, William. *Touching the Heart of God: The Social Construction of Poverty among Biblical Peasants.* New York/London: T & T Clark, 2007. An excellent discussion of the nature of poverty in the Old Testament and the structures of injustice and forms of oppression suffered by various groups, with powerful application to our world, "Combating poverty means leveling the playing field, even if this is apparently unjust to those who have for centuries been exploiting the poor" (177).

Doorly, William J. *Prophet of Justice: Understanding the Book of Amos.* New York/Mahwah, NJ: Paulist Press, 1989.

Furman, Frida K. "The Prophetic Tradition and Social Transformation." In *Prophetic Visions and Economic Realities: Protestants, Jews and Catholics Confront the Bishops' Letter on the Economy*, edited by C. Strain, 103–14. Grand Rapids, MI: Eerdmans, 1989. A good survey of the ways the prophetic traditions have been used.

Gossai, Hemchand. *Justice, Righteousness, and the Social Critique of the Eighth-Century Prophets.* American University Studies: Series 7, Theology and Religion 141. New York: Peter Lang, 1993.

Heschel, Abraham. *The Prophets.* 2 vols. New York: Harper and Row, 1962. A very original reading of the prophets with strong emphasis on their religious experience. Reissued in 2001 as a one-volume edition by Perennial Classics (HarperCollins).

Jensen, Joseph. *Ethical Dimensions of the Prophets*. Collegeville, MN: Liturgical Press, 2006. One of the best books on the prophets, reflecting the scholarship of recent decades.

Leclerc, Thomas L. *Introduction to the Prophets: Their Stories, Sayings, and Scrolls*. Mahwah, NJ: Paulist Press, 2007. Excellent coverage and ideal for classroom use.

————. *Yahweh Is Exalted in Justice: Solidarity and Conflict in Isaiah*. Minneapolis: Fortress Press, 2001. Most thorough and informative study of justice in Isaiah with comments on the passages from Isaiah used in the lectionary.

Limburg, James. *The Prophets and the Powerless*. Atlanta: John Knox Press, 1977. A helpful and readable study.

Mays, James L. "Justice: Perspectives from the Prophetic Tradition." In *Prophecy in Israel*, edited by D. Petersen (see below). A concise summary of prophetic concern for justice, also in *Interpretation* 37 (1983): 5–17.

Page, Hugh R., Jr., and Randall C. Bailey, eds. *The Africana Bible: Reading Israel's Scriptures from Africa and the African Diaspora*. Minneapolis: Fortress Press, 2009. The usual exegetical tools and features that one would expect are complemented—in fact, integrated—into an "Africana" perspective.

Petersen, David L., ed. *Prophecy in Israel: Search for an Identity*. Philadelphia: Fortress Press, 1987. A collection of classic (by Hermann Gunkel, Sigmund Mowinckel, and Max Weber) and recent articles on prophets. The introduction by Petersen is a good statement of contemporary research on the prophets.

Reid, David P. *What Are They Saying About the Prophets?* New York/Mahwah, NJ: Paulist Press, 1980. A good survey of research but not a great deal on justice and the prophets. Good bibliography.

Sawyer, John F. *The Fifth Gospel: Isaiah in the History of Christianity*. New York: Cambridge University Press, 1996.

Schipper, Jeremy, and Candida R. Moss, eds. *Disability Studies and Biblical Literature*. New York: Macmillan, 2011. People with disabilities are clearly among the vulnerable today, which has generated a new area of disability studies. This work and that of Yong below provide good introductions.

Schuller, Eileen. *Post-exilic Prophets*. A Michael Glazier Book. Collegeville, MN: Liturgical Press, 1988. Good on historical setting and theology of postexilic prophets.

Sklba, Richard J. *Pre-Exilic Prophecy: Words of Warning, Dreams of Hopes, Sprituality of the Pre-Exilic Prophets*. Message of Biblical Spirituality 3. Collegeville, MN: Liturgical Press, 1990. A fine study of prophets organized thematically. The section on "Voices for the Poor" is very helpful.

Wilson, Robert. *Prophecy and Society in Ancient Israel*. Philadelphia: Fortress Press, 1980. A scholarly and important study on the social setting of the prophets.

Yong, Amos. *The Bible, Disability, and the Church: A New Vision of the People of God*. Michigan: William B. Eerdmans Publishing Company, 2011.

Zucker, David. *Israel's Prophets: An Introduction for Christians and Jews*. New York/Mahwah, NJ: Paulist Press, 1994.

CHAPTER 5

THE PSALMS

Justice Heralded in Liturgy and Worship

Psalms (from the Greek term for "hymn") is the first book in the third section of the Hebrew canon, the writings (*ketuvim*), and has been described as "the hymn book of the Second Temple," but many psalms contain traditions from the earliest days of Israel's history. Though not all are "hymns" in the formal sense, most scholars feel that they were used in liturgical settings both for group and personal prayer.[1] As with hymns used in worship today, they capture the faith of generations past. Today, on Sunday, people may sing Luther's stirring hymn, "A Mighty Fortress Is Our God," along with "Amazing Grace," and often conclude with a psalm set to music by Gelineau. Rooted in the Jewish heritage of prayer, the psalms have been at the center of group and individual raising of hearts and minds to God. Prayer has often been called "*conversatio cum Deo*" mistranslated as "conversing with God," but the Latin term really means "delaying in the presence of God," or "hanging out" with God. The psalms present the most extensive conversation with God found in the Bible.

---

1. While scholars group the psalms into different formal or generic categories, for example, Laments or Prayers (the largest category); Hymns or Songs of Praise; Songs of Thanksgiving; Royal Psalms; Songs of Zion; Liturgies; Wisdom and Torah Psalms (see James Limburg, "Psalms, Book of," *ABD*, 4, esp. 531–36), there is much overlap and the setting of a particular psalm is often difficult to describe.

ENGAGING THE PSALMS

The psalms present a symphony of Israel's faith, played in a new key. Psalm 1 sets the initial tone for the whole collection. Reminiscent of the "two ways" theology of Deuteronomy 30:19: "I have set before you life and death, blessings and curses. Choose life so that you and your descendants may live," the Psalmist contrasts the way of the wicked with the way of the just, "but their delight is in the law of the LORD, / and on his law they meditate day and night" and "for the LORD watches over the way of the righteous, / but the way of the wicked will perish" (Ps 1:2, 6).[2] The law (*torah*) that brings joy is the whole revelation of God in the saving history of the people. Beautiful meditations on human and natural creation are celebrated in Psalms 8 and 104; a poetic retelling of the covenants with Abraham, the liberation from Egypt, the journey and covenant in the wilderness are found in Psalms 78 and 105; the giving of the law to Moses along with the rhythm of infidelity and calls for conversion are in Psalm 25; a job description for a just king who cares for the poor and marginalized is in Psalm 72, as well as in Psalm 89 that expresses the heights of Zion's royal theology (cf. Wenham, *Psalms as Torah*).

The psalms run the gamut of human experience. We hear the cries of the poor in Psalms 34, 40, and 70, and of scorn heaped on the oppressive rich and powerful in Psalms 10 and 49. The psalms draw us into the majesty of God (95—100), who is also compassionate and long suffering (86 and 103). In the psalms, we hear the laments of those who suffer and question God (22; 44; 88), and words of hope for those who trust in God (34); our sensitivities are shocked by pleas for the destruction of enemies (9; 18; 137). "The Psalter is the poetry of suffering and justice" (Pleins, *The Psalms*, 1).

No book, and certainly not a chapter, can do justice to this splendid collection, so we will limit our engagement to a reflection on the poor in the psalms, with special attention to the laments, and the related question of images of biblical justice that populate the psalms.

---

2. In both the NRSV and the NABRE, *tsedaqah* is usually translated as "righteous," and *mishpat* as "justice." The translation used for this work is the NRSV, but the use of "righteous" should be understood as described in chapter 1, 9–13.

We will conclude with the difficult question of biblical violence using certain psalms as our touchstone.[3]

A JUST GOD WHO SEEKS JUSTICE

All the nuances of *tsedaqah* and *mishpat* appear. God who is a lover of justice: "For the LORD is righteous; / he loves righteous deeds; / the upright shall behold his face" (Ps 11:7, see also 33:5); who is faithful to his promises: "But the LORD sits enthroned forever, / he has established his throne for judgment. / He judges the world with righteousness; / he judges the peoples with equity" (9:7–8); who is merciful and compassionate: "Gracious is the LORD, and righteous; / our God is merciful" (116:5); who is just while condemning the sin of a people and calling them to conversion (51:6); yet who is present as a warrior protecting his people (24:8).

The Psalter is also a tour through the distortions of the human heart—what St. Augustine will later describe and Martin Luther adopt as *homo incurvatus in se* ("humanity turned in on itself, and turned away from God"). God hates those who worship worthless idols (31:7) and who were ensnared by them, even sacrificing their own children to them (38; 106:36, 38), and has scorn for the arrogant and proud (10:4; 18:28; 31:18). Pilloried are social evils that destroy community, such as bribery, false witness, and deceptive friends (15:5; 26:10; 27:12; 35:12; 63:12; 69:4, 20–22, 28–29; 70:3–4). Paradigmatic evildoers are those who conspire against the poor (see esp. 10:1–11; 37:7–17) and who are driven by greed (53:4–5; 55:11–12; 58:2–3). Even this cursory overview shows that the fundamental precepts of the Decalogue and the commands to love God and one's neighbors continually inform the worship of the community. The psalms do not evidence a gulf between personal morality and social commitments, but rather see the two as interconnected.

---

3. For additional references to justice in the psalms, see "Justice in the Psalms" at the conclusion to this chapter.

THE POOR IN THE PSALMS

We have seen that one characteristic of biblical justice is a concern for four groups of suffering and marginal people: the poor, the widow, the orphan, and the stranger [or non-Israelite] in the land. Their defining characteristic is their lack of power and vulnerability in the face of oppression. From an estimated count in the NRSV translation of the psalms, *poor* appears in twenty-four verses along with related terms such as *the lowly* (three verses), *the needy* (twenty verses), *widow* (five verses), and *the orphan* (eight verses)—all often in the same psalm, where they function virtually as synonyms. But the meaning and identification of the poor has evoked significant discussion.

An important contribution to the debate has been Albert Gelin's book *The Poor of Yahweh* (1964). Gelin described three strains in biblical thought: poverty as an evil that should not exist in Israel, and criticism of the exploitation of the poor found mainly in the prophets; condemnation of the poor man as a sinner (for example, Prov 19:1, 22; 28:6); and poverty as humble openness to God, often described as poverty of the spirit. Gelin sees this third aspect as most characteristic of the psalms, a view that subsequent research has countered. In his excellent survey, David Pleins covers similar ground but stresses that the meaning of the poor, their oppression, and God's concern for them, can be found in examining the larger context of the meaning of justice in the psalms. Our perspective is that powerlessness and material poverty remain the prime analogue of the term *poor,* a perspective underscored by Leslie Hoppe that, while there is evidence in some psalms for poverty as a virtue, "using the psalms to support spiritualization of poverty and the poor is an unauthentic way to appropriate these ancient prayers today. It is still necessary to hear the cries of the poor as articulated in the psalms. These are cries for justice" (*There Shall Be No Poor,* 122). We will now comment on select psalms that provide a prism through which to reflect on social justice in the psalms.

PSALMS 9 AND 10

Though listed as a distinct psalm in the Hebrew and in most contemporary versions, Psalm 10 is really a continuation of Psalm 9 and is so listed in the Septuagint and in older Catholic versions (giving rise to the often confusing numbering of subsequent psalms). Its unity is underscored by the acrostic composition where every second line begins with a different letter of the Hebrew alphabet. Yet the mood differs sharply: Psalm 9 is a joyous hymn of thanksgiving, while Psalm 10 is the lament of one suffering from abusive power. Psalm 9, perhaps sung as part of a great annual festival, celebrates God, "who judges the world with righteousness; / he judges the peoples with equity," and who is "a stronghold for the oppressed, / a stronghold in times of trouble" (vv. 8–9) and brings victory for the people so that "the needy shall not always be forgotten, / nor the hope of the poor perish forever" (v. 18).

The mood shifts immediately in the initial verses of Psalm 10:

> Why, O LORD, do you stand far off?
>   Why do you hide yourself in times of trouble?
> In arrogance the wicked persecute the poor—
>   let them be caught in the schemes they have devised.
>
> For the wicked boast of the desires of their heart,
>   those greedy for gain curse and renounce the LORD."
>
> (vv. 1–3)

These read like a legal brief against those opposed to God's thoughts and actions:

> They "curse and renounce [or revile) the Lord" (10:3), conduct that is strictly forbidden in the Torah and regarded as a capital offense (1 Kings 21:10–14). They ride roughshod over other people, wounding them by the malicious, hurting words to which they are only ever ready to give voice and by their brutal actions against those powerless to protect themselves. Their actions are vividly portrayed in two metaphors and a simile in vv. 8 and 9; they are brigands or outlaws pursuing unsuspecting victims, like a lion prancing on its prey, and they are hunters trapping prey in their nets. It seems clear that in the psalmist's eyes it is the refusal of such people to accept the authority of God which leads to

their refusal to recognize the rights of other people.
(Davidson, *Vitality*, 45)

Yet the psalm ends (as does Ps 9) with a message of hope:

> O LORD, you will hear the desire of the meek [Heb. "poor"];
>   you will strengthen their heart, you will incline your ear
> to do justice for the orphan and the oppressed,
>   so that those from earth may strike terror no more.

> (vv. 17–19)

The justice of God resounds through the psalm, where God, a judge
(also protector) of justice, in fidelity to his nature and promises, comes to
the aid of the oppressed and hears the cries of the afflicted (see Isa 5:7).
Throughout, the Psalmist identifies with those suffering in various forms:
oppression (Heb. *dak*, 9:9; 10:18); the afflicted, the poor, and the
oppressed (9:10; 10:2, 9, 12, 17); and the needy (*'ebyon*, 9:18). These are
a virtual glossary of expressions found in the Prophet's over concern for
the *personae miserae* and are often translated differently. "Yet whatever the
precise circumstances, these words point to those who feel crushed by
life, who recognize their own need, and who seek close refuge in God.
They are the opposite of and often the victims of the arrogant wicked"
(Davidson, *Vitality*, 44). Psalms 9 and 10 present a liturgical summary of
the Torah and Prophets on the deepest meaning of social justice.

PSALM 37

This psalm, an acrostic poem, is fundamentally a wisdom psalm
that wrestles with the problem of the prosperity of evildoers and the
suffering of the just, and the challenge they face in trusting in God: "Do
not fret because of the wicked; / do not be envious of wrongdoers"
(37:1). The Dead Sea Scrolls contain a commentary on this psalm that
applies to their own situation, and verse 11: "But the meek [or poor]
shall inherit the land, / and delight themselves in abundant prosperity"
(also vv. 9, 29) is echoed by Matthew 5:5: "Blessed are the meek, for
they will inherit the land."

The evil, who prosper in their way, appear in similar garb as in other psalms. They plot against the just people, gnash their teeth at them (Ps 37:12), mock them or vent their anger against them. They attack the poor and the needy (v. 14; cf. also Ps 9:12). They have the goods of this world in abundance (v. 12) yet are unwilling even to pay their debts (v. 16). They use their success to inspire terror (v. 35), and they dominate the landscape like gigantic trees.

Unlike psalms with a more prophetic edge against the powerful, here the Psalmist urges trust in God's future: "Commit your way to the LORD; / trust in him, and he will act" (v. 5). In contrast to the vices of the wicked, "The mouths of the righteous utter wisdom, / and their tongues speak justice. / The law of their God is in their hearts; / their steps do not slip" (vv. 30–31), in contrast to the "wicked," "for they will soon fade like the grass, / and wither like the green herb" (v. 2).

The advice of the Psalmist may seem naïve as will its hope for destruction of the wicked. But again, Robert Davidson offers great insight into its profound meaning: "It, [the psalm], points to an attitude of faith which can face life, recognize its anomalies, yet retain a lively hope based on the conviction that whatever may happen the Lord does deliver. He does provide refuge (v. 39) or a stronghold for those prepared to address themselves to his protection" (*Vitality*, 127). In terms of social justice, this psalm provides encouragement and hope to those who face the overwhelming power of evil, while maintaining trust in God and keeping alive future hope. People like Nelson Mandela and others who suffered through the dark night of apartheid in South Africa embody the ethos of this psalm.

PSALMS 49 AND 73

These wisdom psalms offer scathing criticisms of wealth that exceed even the cautions of the Wisdom literature, and foreshadow the often harsh statements in subsequent biblical writings, for example, the Gospel of Luke (12:13–21). Interestingly, Psalm 49, though a wisdom reflection, was performed "to the music of a lyre" (perhaps much like the folk songs of the 1960s):

I will incline my ear to a proverb;
I will solve my riddle to the music of the harp.

Why should I fear in times of trouble,
    when the iniquity of my persecutors surrounds me,
those who trust in their wealth
    and boast of the abundance of their riches?

(vv. 4–6)

In conclusion, the Psalmist reflects on the fragility of life and human achievement and the continuity of vanity of wealth:

Do not be afraid when some become rich,
    when the wealth of their houses increases.
For when they die they will carry nothing away;
    their wealth will not go down after them.
Though in their lifetime they count themselves happy
    —for you are praised when you do well for yourself—
they will go to the company of their ancestors,
    who will never again see the light.
Mortals cannot abide in their pomp;
    they are like the animals that perish.

(vv. 16–20)

In even more scathing images, Psalm 73 speaks not only of the folly of the rich but of their arrogance and power. With overtones of a lament and a crisis of faith, the underlying question of the Psalmist is why the just suffer and the wicked prosper:

For I was envious of the arrogant;
    I saw the prosperity of the wicked.

For they have no pain;
    their bodies are sound and sleek.
They are not in trouble as others are;
    they are not plagued like other people.
Therefore pride is their necklace;
    violence covers them like a garment.
Their eyes swell out with fatness;
    their hearts overflow with follies.

They scoff and speak with malice;
    loftily they threaten oppression.
They set their mouths against heaven,
    and their tongues range over the earth.

(vv. 3–9)

While these plaints may seem today as passive acquiescence to injustice, they serve a critical function, as David Pleins notes, "the text draws the connection, known more clearly from the prophets, to an amassing of wealth that is dangerously bound up with social injustices in ancient Israel" (*Social Visions*, 435). Such a view of wealth counters the connection often promoted among wealth and prestige and virtue. Today, no matter how poor people might be, if they have a sense of respect and dignity, and a sense of God's presence, they need not envy nor emulate the pretensions of the rich.

PSALM 72

While the above psalms stress the sufferings of the poor and marginalized, and warn of the dangers of wealth, Psalm 72 is a royal psalm that expresses the highest ideals of kingship. Attributed to Solomon, it concludes the second book of the Psalter and may have been used as a royal coronation ode. The first hoped-for gift for the king is justice and his task is to assure justice:

Give the king your justice, O God,
    and your righteousness to a king's son.
May he judge your people with righteousness [*tsedaqah*],
    and your poor with justice [*mishpat*].
May the mountains yield prosperity for the people,
    and the hills, in righteousness.
May he defend the cause of the poor of the people,
    give deliverance to the needy,
    and crush the oppressor.

(vv. 1–4)

This charge to the king, phrased in the familiar word pair (hendiadys) found in Isaiah, is repeated in clear concern for the socially marginalized:

> For he delivers the needy when they call,
>> the poor and those who have no helper.
> He has pity on the weak and the needy,
>> and saves the lives of the needy.
> From oppression and violence he redeems their life;
>> and precious is their blood in his sight.

(vv. 12–14)

And just as the psalm begins with a prayer that God grant justice to the king, it ends with a clear paean of praise to God as the source of the justice that the king will enact: "Blessed be the LORD, the God of Israel, who alone does wonderful deeds. Blessed be his glorious name forever; may all the earth be filled with the Lord's glory. Amen and amen" (vv. 18–19). The glory that is hoped for is the reign of justice and concern for the poor and oppressed. One must reflect on how this psalm should be applied in today's Church to divinely invoked leadership.

LAMENTING INJUSTICE

The psalms of lament comprise roughly half of all the psalms. The Psalter begins with a series of five laments of the individual (Pss 3—7) and the bulk of Book I (Pss 1—41) consists of further individual laments. Perhaps the best known lament for Christian readers is Psalm 22, quoted frequently in the passion narrative and recorded as the prayer of Jesus at his death (Mark 15:34). Though in a certain sense all the laments touch on the question of the justice of God—how God can act in fidelity to his promises—some treat explicitly the question of injustice in the world. They are generally divided into communal and individual laments and follow a fairly set form:

1. An *address* to God (Ps 13:1, "O LORD"; 22:1, "My God, my God");

110

2. A *complaint* in three forms, with the subject "I" (13:2a; 22:2, 6, 14–15, 17a), "thou" (13:1; 22:1), or "they" (13:2c; 22:7–8, 12–13, 16, 17b–18);

3. A *request for help* (13:3–4; 22:11, 19–21);

4. An *affirmation of trust* (13:5; 22:3–5, 9–10);

5. A *vow to praise God* when the crisis is past (13:6; 22:22–31).[4]

Claus Westermann has stressed that such laments before God are found throughout biblical literature. He states "in the Old Testament, from beginning to end, the 'call of distress,' the 'cry out of the depths,' that is, the lament, is an inevitable part of what happens between God and man," and further depicts Exodus 1—15 as a long lament by an oppressed people and a plea for God's help.[5] The subsequent narratives of murmuring in the wilderness are also a form of lament. The lament moves between abandonment and hope and affirms before God that the world is "out of joint," and confronts most dramatically the question of theodicy, how a just and loving God can permit such social and individual evil.

Walter Brueggemann describes the laments as a complaint that make the shrill insistence that (1) things are not right in the present arrangement; (2) they need not stay this way and can be changed; (3) the speaker will not accept them in this way, for the present arrangement is intolerable; and (4) it is God's obligation to change things ("Costly Loss," 105). By examining select psalms, mainly those that repeat the cries of the poor, we will now integrate some of the insights of Westermann and Brueggemann, and apply them to the quest for social justice.

The pleas of "the poor and needy," appear strongly in the brief lament of Psalm 12, which begins with a cry, "Help, LORD, for no one loyal remains" (v. 1, NABRE) and after, moves quickly to God's saving help, "'because they rob the weak, and the needy groan, / I will now arise,' says the LORD" (v. 6). Psalm 14 (repeated almost verbatim in Psalm

---

4. Limburg, "Psalms," *ABD*, 5:532.

5. Claus Westermann, "Role of Lament in the Theology of the Old Testament," *Interpretation* 28, no. 1 (1974): 20–38.

53), though perhaps not formally a lament, begins with things out of joint: "Fools say in their hearts, / 'There is no God.' / Their deeds are loathsome and corrupt; / not one does what is right" (v. 1). They crush the hopes of the poor, but the poor have God as their refuge, and then God is implicitly invoked at the end of the psalm, "Oh, that from Zion might come / the deliverance of Israel!" (v. 7).

A virtual cry of despair, "Why, God, have you cast us off forever?" (v. 1) introduces Psalm 74, a communal lament, and proceeds through a litany of sufferings, probably reflecting the destruction of the temple in 587 BC, but then the Psalmist calls on God to remember his power manifest in creation and covenant, "Look to your covenant, / for the land is filled with gloom / the pastures, with violence. / Let not the oppressed turn back in shame; / may the poor and needy praise your name" (v. 20).

Psalm 109, one of the most poignant laments, begins:

Do not be silent, O God of my praise.
For wicked and deceitful mouths are opened against me,
    speaking against me with lying tongues.

(vv. 1–2)

The Psalm goes on to indict the persecutor:

For he did not remember to show kindness,
    but pursued the poor and needy
    and the brokenhearted to their death.

(v. 16)

But the Psalmist cries out to God:

But you, O LORD my Lord,
    act on my behalf for your name's sake;
    because your steadfast love is good, deliver me.
For I am poor and needy,
    and my heart is pierced within me.

(vv. 21–22)

It concludes with a hope that is rooted in the very nature of God:

> For he stands at the right hand of the needy,
> to save them from those who would condemn them to death.
>
> (v. 31)

Though the "poor and needy" (*'ani* and *'ebyon*) is often interpreted to refer to the general condition of human helplessness, in these psalms, it is based on objective material deprivation and victimization by stronger forces. The plea is for justice in both the sense of God's fidelity to his promises and in rescue for those suffering. David Pleins states this eloquently, "If only in a rhetorical sense the Psalms preserve for us the universal cry of the poor. In this sense, they do hold out poverty and justice as key issues for their community and any group that seeks to take up the Psalter to frame its liturgical life" (*Social Visions*, 429).

The laments offer even deeper challenges to our world today. Through their cries and desperation and even challenge to God, they affirm that suffering and injustice should not afflict God's people. Here is no naïve theology of the value of suffering. Again Brueggemann writes with great insight, "When the lament form is censured, justice questions cannot be asked and eventually become invisible and illegitimate. Instead, we learn to settle for questions of 'meaning' and we reduce the issues to resolutions of love" (Brueggemann, *The Psalms*, 107). The lament becomes the weapon of the weak and poor against the arrogant power of the oppressive rich and exposes their claims to respect and approval. Laments belie any facile theology that suffering is a sign of divine rejection, that it is therapeutic, or is sent by God as a test. Lament is the ultimate form of truth-telling in the quest for justice. In the United States, the all too frequent memorial services for people, especially children, massacred by gun violence are a form of national lament.

VIOLENCE: THE SHADOW SIDE OF PRAISE

Approval of violent actions and violent attitudes present for many today a stumbling block in appropriating biblical revelation. Both

Jewish and Christian Scriptures sanction violence and both call for its elimination. Given the vast and important studies of both violence in the Bible and counter-voices of peace and reconciliation, my reflections are more than usually inadequate, so the resources listed here are more important than ever.

John Collins begins his fine discussion with a quote from Mieke Bal that "the Bible, of all books is the most dangerous one, the one that has been endowed with the power to kill" (*Bible Justify*, 1). Collins goes on to discuss neuralgic issues such as the *herem*, the command to slaughter the inhabitants of a conquered city, and the praise given to Phineas when he killed a Midianite woman to fulfill the command against intermarriage (Num 25:10–15). He presents a succinct and excellent survey of the kinds of violence sanctioned with exposition of the historical setting. An important strain of early biblical thought is God as "the divine warrior," who rescues a people from near extinction. Apocalyptic thought with images of a final victory of God's power over evil extends this perspective.

Collins then surveys attempts to mitigate the misuse of these traditions, by use of allegory in Philo and early Christianity (for example, enemies are evil passions), statements in the Bible itself against violence, and an honest admission that not everything in the Bible is worthy of admiration, not to mention imitation, and that the Bible withholds certitude when dealing with such difficult issues.

The situation in the psalms is often more acute since the prayers for vengeance and destruction of enemies are often strikingly vivid and more personal, especially in the "imprecatory psalms." Again, a contemporary work by Erich Zenger (*A God of Vengeance*) grapples with the many pleas for triumph over or destruction of enemies (Pss 5:5–7; 41:11–12; 58:1–12; 79:10–12; 94:1–2, 22–23; 137:7–9). Unlike some authors, Zenger does not feel that these should be excised from all prayer and worship and offers careful attention to translation issues of these psalms. He does not want even the offense of these psalms to be lost, but stresses that "they appeal to a God who, as the God of justice, considers, decides and punishes, not out of a pleasure in punishment, but in order to restore and defend the damaged order of law" (*God*, 71). Praying these psalms by oppressed people makes clear the destructive elements in life, and exposes webs of violence that oppress the weak. They also put the petitioners in touch with that violence they share with the "enemies," and create a horror of violence itself.

These psalms raise dramatically the issue of theodicy in its literal sense (*theos* + *dike* = justice); how God can be seen as just, that is, faithful, to promises made to the people. When we think of these psalms as prayers for the abolition of enemies, we realize that the enemies triumphed either in the destruction of the first temple, the destruction of the second temple (AD 70), and/or of Jerusalem itself in AD 125. During the long history of anti-Semitism and its horrible effects culminating in the Shoah, these psalms were prayed in longing for God's help. But the continuing life of Judaism through the centuries is a sign that perhaps the deepest meaning of these psalms is that people cry out to a God who seems absent, and never lose hope in the face of unspeakable evil.

While the works discussed above join a cadre of authors grappling with these difficult texts along with others who stress that the Bible itself presents stronger alternate visions of peace and nonviolence, I would add that behind much of the discussion lies a lurking literalism and inaccurate theory of inspiration. In grappling with these issues, the Dogmatic Constitution on Divine Revelation (*Dei Verbum*) of the Second Vatican Council offered a significant hermeneutical guideline: "The books of Scripture must be acknowledged as teaching solidly, faithfully and without error that truth which God wanted put into the sacred writings for the sake of our salvation" (no. 11). In effect, this warrants a principle of *Sachkritik* (content criticism), where certain texts and traditions can no longer offer a proper vision of life before God (that is, salvation). Also, as noted initially, theological use of Scripture involves an awareness of diverse trends in the Bible and trajectories of interpretations. In both early Christianity and Rabbinic Judaism, there are clear rejections of violence, a rejection that must continue if our world is to survive.

JUSTICE IN THE PSALMS

Prepared by Lawrence Boadt, CSP

The following list contains particular verses, but read carefully, the following complete Psalms: 10, 37, 72, and 89.

God is a Just God: Psalms 7:18; 11:7; 22:32; 33:5; 35:24; 36:7; 40:10–11; 48:11–12

The Way of the Just: Psalms 1:1–6; 15:2–5

God Protects the Just: Psalms 5:9, 13; 7:9, 11–12; 9:5; 36:11; 37:17–18

God Hears the Just; He is the Refuge of the Just: Psalms 13:1–4; 14:6; 16:1; 17:1–3; 27:5; 30:3, 11; 34:16, 18; 37:30–40; 40:14–15; 46:2; 57:2; 61:4–5; 62:7–9; 64:11; 71:1–3

The Lord Judges Fairly: Psalms 11:5; 26:1–2; 33:13–15; 50:6–7; 58:11–12; 62:12; 71:15

The Lord Forgives the Penitent: Psalms 32:1; 37:24; 38:19; 51:11, 19; 65:4; 69:6–12

God Hates Evildoers Who Plot against the Just: Psalms 5:6; 6:9; 14:3–4; 26:4; 28:4; 37:7–9; 50:17–18; the Greedy: 10:3; 49:7; 53:4–5; 55:11–12; 57:5–7; 58:2–3

The Lord Blesses Those of Clean Hands: Psalms 18:21, 25; 19:13; 24:4; 26:6; 51:4, 9

God Remembers the Poor and Afflicted: Psalms 9:13, 14, 19; 10:14, 18; 22:25; 25:9; 35:10; 40:18; 41:2–4; 68:6–7; 69:34; 72:1–4, 12–13; 146:1–10

God Hates the Arrogant and Proud: Psalms 10:4; 18:28; 20:7; 31:18; 36:12; 40:4; 54:5; 59:13; 73:4; 94:2; 101:5; 119:51

God Punishes Idolatry: Psalms 31:6; 44:21; 78:58; 96:5; 97:7; 106:36, 38; 115:4

The Evil of Bribery; False Witnesses; False Friends: Psalms 15:5; 26:10; 27:12; 35:12; 63:12; 69:4

False Friends: Psalms 69:20–22, 28–29; 70:3–4

Power of Speech for Evil or Good: Psalms 10:7; 12:3; 24:4; 31:9; 35:20; 36:2–5; 37:30; 41:7–9; 50:19–20; 52:5; 55:22; 59:13; 62:5; 63:4–7

RESOURCE BIBLIOGRAPHY

The quantity and quality of literature on the psalms are immense. I will list certain commentaries and select articles that were helpful in probing issues of social justice.

Brown, Sally A., and Patrick D Miller, eds. *Lament: Reclaiming Practices in Pulpit, Pew and Public Square.* Louisville, KY: Westminster John Knox Press, 2005.

Brueggemann, Walter. *The Psalms and the Life of Faith.* Edited by Patrick D. Miller. Minneapolis: Fortress Press, 1985. See especially "The Costly Loss of Lament," 98–111.

Cottrill, Amy C. *Language, Power, and Identity in the Lament Psalms of the Individual.* Leiden: Brill, 2008. An original, scholarly study of individual laments underscoring both the value and problems with this form.

Davidson, Robert. *The Vitality of Worship: A Commentary on the Book of Psalms.* Grand Rapids, MI: Eerdmans; Edinburgh: Handsel Press, 1998. An outstanding commentary with thorough expositions, multiple cross-references, and applications of psalms to contemporary life.

Gelin, Albert. *The Poor of Yahweh.* Collegeville, MN: Liturgical Press, 1964. A classic work on the poor in the Bible, especially in the psalms, but with a tendency toward "spiritualization" of poverty.

Gillingham, Susan. *Psalms through the Centuries.* Oxford: Blackwell, 2007.

Hoppe, Leslie J. *There Shall be No Poor Among You: Poverty in the Bible.* Nashville, TN: Abingdon Press, 2004. An excellent discussion of poor in the Psalms.

Houston, Walter J. *Contending for Justice: Ideologies and Theologies of Social Justice in the Old Testament.* Library of Hebrew Bible/Old Testament Studies 428. London/New York: T & T Clark, 2006. An excellent study of texts and themes and their relation to contemporary problems. This work and that of Pleins (*Social Visions*) constitute two of the best studies of social justice and the Old Testament.

Jenkins, Michael. *In the House of the Lord: Inhabiting the Psalms of Lament.* Collegeville, MN: Liturgical Press, 1988. A pastoral and liturgical reflection on lament psalms.

McCann, J. Clinton. "The Hope of the Poor: The Psalms in Worship and our Search for Justice." In *Touching the Altar: The Old Testament for Christian Worship*, edited by Carol M. Bechtel, 155–78. Grand Rapids, MI: Eerdmans, 2008. The articles of McCann listed here are among the best treatments of justice in the psalms.

————. "The Psalms as Instruction." *Interpretation* 46 (1992): 117–28. Discussion of teaching in the various genres, for example, "The laments challenge us to locate our pain and the pain of the world, a particularly important task, given the kind of world we live in" (125).

————. "Righteousness, Justice and Peace: A Contemporary Theology of the Psalms." *Horizons in Biblical Theology* 23 (2001): 111–31.

Mays, James Luther. *Preaching and Teaching the Psalms*. Louisville, KY: Westminster John Knox Press, 1995.

————. *Psalms: Interpretation: A Commentary for Teaching and Preaching*. Louisville, KY: Westminster John Knox Press, 1994.

Pleins, J. David. *The Psalms: Songs of Tragedy, Hope, and Justice*. Maryknoll, NY: Orbis Books, 1993. This book refers to the Psalter as "poetry of suffering and justice," and powerfully develops this idea from particular psalms.

————. *The Social Visions of the Hebrew Bible: A Theological Introduction*. Louisville, KY: Westminster John Knox Press, 2001.

Wenham, Gordon. *Psalms as Torah: Reading Biblical Song Ethically*. Grand Rapids, MI: Baker Academic, 2012. Describes how the psalms form conscience and practice, and embody a distinct form of ethical teaching. See especially chapter 8, "Virtues and Vices in the Psalter."

Westermann, Claus. *Praise and Lament in the Psalms*. Atlanta: John Knox Press, 1981. See also "The Role of Lament in the Theology of the Old Testament." *Interpretation* 28 (1974): 20–38.

Westermeyer, Paul. *Let Justice Sing: Hymnody and Justice*. Collegeville, MN: Liturgical Press, 1998. This work discusses the psalms that deal with justice.

RESOURCES FOR THE QUESTION OF VIOLENCE

Chilton, Bruce. *Abraham's Curse: The Roots of Violence in Judaism, Christianity, and Islam*. New York: Doubleday, 2008. Focuses on the ideology of self-sacrifice and martyrdom as a root cause of violence.

Collins, John J. *Does the Bible Justify Violence?* Facet Books. Minneapolis: Fortress Press, 2004. Enlarged version of an often reprinted article "The Zeal of Phineas: The Bible and the Legitimation of Violence." *Journal of Biblical Literature* 122 (2003): 1–21.

Day, John. *Crying for Justice: What the Psalms Teach Us about Mercy and Vengeance in an Age of Terrorism.* Grand Rapids, MI: Kregel, 2007.

Ellens, J. Harold, ed. *The Destructive Power of Religion: Violence in Judaism, Christianity and Islam.* 4 vols. Westport, CT: Praeger, 2004. Ellens is a psychologist and research scholar in the Origins of Judaism and Christianity in the Department of Near Eastern Studies, University of Michigan. The volumes cover multiple aspects of violence and contain important articles on the Bible. There is a fine review by Daniel Smith-Christopher, in *Reviews in Religion & Theology* 12, no. 2 (2005): 196–202.

Fretheim, Terrence E. "God and Violence in the Old Testament." *Word and Work* 24 (2004): 18–28. An excellent survey of important works with creative suggestions on dealing with violence.

Kimball, Charles. *When Religion Becomes Evil: Five Warning Signs.* New York: HarperCollins, 2008. Kimball writes frequently on contemporary manifestations of religiously grounded violence.

Leiter, David A. *Neglected Voices: Peace in the Old Testament.* Scottsdale, PA: Herald Press, 2007. An original approach to issues of peace with an ample bibliography.

Niditch, Susan. *War in the Hebrew Bible: A Study in the Ethics of Violence.* New York: Oxford University Press, 1993. After a survey of various causes of violence, the author covers major texts on "the ban" with creative proposals for interpretation.

Polner, Murray, and Naomi Goodman, eds. *The Challenge of Shalom: The Jewish Tradition of Peace and Justice.* Philadelphia, PA: New Society Publishers, 1994. See especially Maurice Freedman, "Hasidism and the Love of Enemies," 40–48.

Seibert, Eric A. *The Violence of Scripture: Overcoming the Old Testament's Troubling Legacy.* Minneapolis: Fortress Press, 2012. The author approaches difficult texts with different "reading strategies," and offers reflections on the authority of Scripture.

Zenger, Erich. *A God of Vengeance: Understanding the Psalms of Divine Wrath.* Louisville, KY: Westminster John Knox Press, 1994. One of the best discussions of these difficult psalms.

CHAPTER 6

WISDOM AND APOCALYPTIC JUSTICE

THE WORDS OF THE WISE

As mentioned earlier, my reflections are inevitably superficial, a charge especially pertinent when engaging the vast and fruitful traditions of Israel's Wisdom literature. The term can refer to a collection of books found in the third part of the Jewish canon ("the writings") "or it can refer to a movement in the ancient world associated with 'teachers' or sages, and it can also suggest a particular understanding of reality which presents some contrasts with other biblical books" (Roland E. Murphy, "Wisdom in the Old Testament," *ABD*, 5:920–31). The term *wisdom* (Heb. *hokma*; Gk. *sophia*) itself is multivalent: embracing skill or know-how; advice for everyday living, garnered from experience; guidelines for proper action; an attribute and partner of God before and at Creation; and knowledge gained from experience or by divine revelation—to mention the major nuances. Its teachings are handed on mostly by short maxims or proverbs, and the teachers of wisdom range from sages and professional scribes to temple priests. Though associated with particular bodies of literature, it permeates law, prophecy, and the psalms. Negatively, the point of view of much of the literature is that of privileged groups and its perspectives on women reflect the worst aspects of a patriarchal culture.

As a body of literature, Wisdom reaches back to pre-Israelite traditions (for example, Prov 22:17—24:22 reflect a classic Egyptian Wisdom text, *The Instruction of Amenemope*), and extends well into the New Testament, where much of the teaching of Jesus adopts the forms of Old Testament Wisdom literature. Later Wisdom literature also overlaps with themes found in the moral teaching of the Hellenistic world, especially the focus on balance and moderation. Though not citing the narrative traditions of Israel with any great frequency, the Wisdom literature represents its grand themes played in a different, and not always consistent, key: a Creator God, who discloses a way of life (*torah*); warnings against evil and injustice (prophets); and ways of being in God's presence and concern for the poor (psalms).

As with the psalms, the power of Wisdom literature arises also from its rhetorical and literary quality. The sayings appear most often as two phrases or two-line verses, most frequently antithetical, where one contrasts the other, or synthetic, where the second enforces the first. For example:

ANTITHETICAL

The mind of one who has understanding seeks knowledge,
    but the mouths of fools feed on folly.
All the days of the poor are hard,
    but a cheerful heart has a continual feast.

(Prov 15:14–15)

The mind of the righteous ponders how to answer,
    but the mouth of the wicked pours out evil.
The LORD is far from the wicked,
    but he hears the prayer of the righteous.

(Prov 15:28–29)

SYNTHETIC

Those with good sense are slow to anger,
    and it is their glory to overlook an offense.

(Prov 19:11)

A worthless witness mocks at justice,
    and the mouth of the wicked devours iniquity.

(Prov 19:28)

Wisdom literature embodies what the literary critic William Wimsatt once called the "concrete universal," where a work of literature or art presents "an object which in its mysterious and special way is both highly general and highly particular."[1] Vivid and surprising images and metaphors, often tinged with irony, bedeck its sayings, but they touch on universal human experience, even over the centuries since their origin:

> Like a thornbush brandished by the hand of a drunkard
> is a proverb in the mouth of a fool.
> Like an archer who wounds everybody
> is one who hires a passing fool or drunkard.

> (Prov 26:9–10)

I hope the above comments will draw people to personal engagement with the texts. However, we will limit our study to Proverbs, Sirach (Ecclesiasticus), and the Wisdom of Solomon to indicate some varied perspectives, with select examples, on issues of justice and poverty in these books.

BOOK OF PROVERBS

The book itself, attributed to Solomon, is generally thought to be the oldest Wisdom collection and parts may actually date to the court of Solomon (cf. 10:1—22:16), though it contains other collections, often in the form of random sayings, and its final redaction is postexilic.

Proverbs continues the two-way theology of Deuteronomy 30:19 by contrasting the way of the just and the way of the wicked: "The memory of the righteous is a blessing, / but the name of the wicked will rot" (10:7). See also verses 9, 11, 16, 20, 21, 24, 25, and the following:

> The hope of the righteous ends in gladness,
> but the expectation of the wicked comes to nothing.

---

1. William Wimsatt, *The Verbal Icon: Studies in the Meaning of Poetry* (Lexington: University of Kentucky Press, 1988), 91.

> The way of the LORD is a stronghold for the upright,
>> but destruction for evildoers.
> The righteous will never be removed,
>> but the wicked will not remain in the land.
>
> (Prov 10:28–30)

The collection criticizes practices and attitudes that would speak to issues of injustice in our world today: perversion of a system of justice and bribery (13:23; 17:8, 23; 18:5; 19:5; 24:23, 28); false weights and measures (11:1; 16:11; 20:10, 23); and greed (15:27; 19:22; 23:6–7).

Yet, the wicked are not simply identified with the rich, and in fact, poverty is often an evil brought about by humans (usually by sloth): "A little sleep, a little slumber, / a little folding of the hands to rest, / and poverty will come upon you like a robber, / and want, like an armed warrior" (6:10–11; 24:33–34 see also; 10:4, 15; 20:13; 21:17; 23:21) and it is a great misfortune to be poor (10:15; 13:8; 14:20; 19:4; 19:7; 19:22; 22:7; 28:3; 30:8–9).

Yet, the poor are victimized by the powerful (10:15; 13:23; 18:23; 22:7; 28:15; 30:13–14), and God "pleads the cause" of the poor and wants justice for them (14:31; 17:5; 19:17; 21:13; 22:2; 22:9; 22:22–23; 28:27; 29:14; 31:9). Riches can be evil and poverty and care of the poor can foster righteousness (16:19; 19:1; 19:22; 22:16; 28:6; 28:11; 29:7; 31:9, 20). Yet, while recommending care for the poor, Proverbs, like all the wisdom traditions, reflects primarily the values of the nonpoor and lacks the kind of passionate attacks on injustice found in the prophetic tradition (cf. Hoppe, *No Poor*, 105–8). David Pleins has captured the ambiguous reflections on the poor found in Proverbs:

> For the wise, "poverty is a reality to be avoided, but rarely protested against….Unlike the prophetic social critique the proverbial texts draw only the vaguest connections between the poverty of the poor and the wealth of the rich….How different are the prophetic texts, which consistently and extensively contend that much gain is made by those who take from the poor! For the wise, poverty, like wealth was

accepted as one of the givens of existence with which the student must learn to cope." ("Poverty," 67–78)

DEVELOPMENTS AFTER THE EXILE

A general description of the meanings of justice in the period from the exile to the time of Jesus is helpful not only in noting the transformations of the notions of justice within Judaism itself, but also in providing a context for New Testament statements on justice. During this period, the Hebrew terms for and the Greek translations of *justice* retain the same wide connotations that we find in the early period. Justice is associated with mercy (2 Esd 8:36; Tob 3:2; Sir 44:10); goodness of heart (Tob 14:11; Wis 1:1); love of neighbor (*Jub.* 7:20; 20:2); compassion for the poor and weak (*As. Mos.* 11:17); truth (Tob 1:3; 3:2; 4:6; Wis 5:6; 1 Macc 7:18; 4 *Ezra* 7:114); and harmony in family and social relations (*Jub.* 7:20; 31:12; 7:26). Along with these, justice is closely identified with a number of individual qualities—integrity, courage, constancy, self-control, steadfastness amid poverty and illness, intelligence, and knowledge.

While maintaining continuity with the meanings of justice in the Old Testament, justice in this period undergoes three major transformations: (1) emphasis on the justice of the individual and a sectarian stress between the just and the unjust; (2) the establishing of justice as a characteristic of the end-time, or the influence of eschatology on justice; and (3) the shift in language whereby *tsedaqah* means "almsgiving" or "care for the poor." While strident prophetic protests against the rich and heartfelt cries on behalf of the poor fade from the scene, the Wisdom literature continues to warn of the danger of wealth and expresses the need to come to the aid of the poor—perhaps the most pertinent message for our age.

THE JUST INDIVIDUAL

The legacy of Ezekiel's stress on individual responsibility (Ezek 18) leads to a stress on justice of the individual. Psalms, which were originally cultic laments, become codified in a book and become the prayers of individuals. In certain of these psalms (for example, Ps 18, 25, 26, 31, 35, 51), justice is keeping the statutes of the Lord, and freedom from guilt. The Lord is at one and the same time the only just one and the one who rewards a person "according to my righteousness" (Ps 18:24). During the intertestamental period, reflection on the call to be just before the Lord, coupled with a growing awareness of the transcendence of God, leads to a theology where God alone is just (Sir 18:2; 1QH 1:4) and that man alone is devoid of justice (Dan 9:18; Sir 5:8). The justice of the individual is a striving for innocence and purity in the face of Hellenization and religious syncretism. This individualization of justice is vividly portrayed in the departure address of Tobit to his son, Tobias (Tob 4:1–21). Tobit tells his son:

> Revere the Lord our God all your days, my son, and refuse to sin or transgress his commandments. Live uprightly all the days of your life, and do not walk in the ways of wrongdoing. (4:5)

Tobit goes on to counsel his son to give alms and share his goods with the poor, but the social motive is absent: "For charity delivers from death and keeps you from entering the Darkness" (Tob 4:10). The son is also urged to avoid immorality, to marry a woman from the Jewish people, to avoid pride, to honor the dead, and to persevere in prayer. What in the earlier period were manifestations of justice incumbent on the whole community, become for Tobias a personal rule of life.

In this context, the rise of later Pharisaic notions of justice can be understood. The Pharisees originated in the movement of the pious or "separated ones" who were conscious of the evils of Hellenization and sought to preserve the sanctity of God by careful observance of his revelation, the Torah. The *Psalms of Solomon* give examples of early Pharisaic piety. God is a "righteous judge" who is no respecter of persons (2:19), and at the same time he is "merciful and good" (10:7). The Lord is the vindicator of the just, since he will punish sinners, and those who fear the Lord will rise to life eternal (3:4). The just person remembers the Lord at all times (3:3), and "his will is always before the

Lord." True justice will be established with the advent of the Davidic Messiah who will be "a just king" (17:32), and who "will direct every man in the works of righteousness by fear of God" (18:8). Care should be exercised in describing Pharisaic piety as "works of righteousness." In observing the Torah, the Pharisees did not hope to merit or gain salvation, but attempted to recognize that the sovereignty of God applied to every area of human life and that the Torah made the distant God present to daily life. Still, during this period, the individualization of justice takes shape.

Allied to the individualization of justice is the rise of the motif of suffering as a sign of justice. In the Old Testament, the command was to remain faithful to the covenant God amid suffering, and see God's saving power as the vindication of his justice. In the intertestamental period, suffering itself becomes a sign of justice or righteousness. This emphasis culminates in the picture of the "suffering just one" in the *Wisdom of Solomon* (2:1–20; 5:1–8)—which greatly influenced the depiction of Jesus in the New Testament. Here the foolish "lie in wait for the righteous man, / because he is inconvenient to us and opposes our actions; / he reproaches us for sins against the law" (2:12). The just one is a reproof to their thoughts "because his manner of life is unlike that of others, / and his ways are strange" (2:15). The unjust plan to test the just one with torture and put him to death (2:18–20). However, the death of the just one will be a vindication of God's justice since "the righteous man who had died will condemn the ungodly who are living" (4:16). At the final judgment, the vindication of this suffering just one will take place (5:1), and those who persecuted him will say:

> We thought that his life was madness
> and that his end was without honor.
> Why has he been numbered among the sons of God?
> And why is his lot among the saints?
> So it was we who strayed from the way of truth,
> and the light of righteousness did not shine on us.
>
> (5:4–5, NAB)

In this diptych (chapters 2 and 5) from the *Wisdom of Solomon*, suffering itself becomes a stage in the manifestation of God's judgment on sinners and a prelude to the hope of vindication. This conjunction of justice and suffering provides the background for the Pauline idea of the cross as a stumbling block (1 Cor 1:23) as well as a manifestation of the saving justice of God (Rom 4:25).

THE BOOK OF SIRACH: JUSTICE REFASHIONED

Shifts in both the meaning of justice and in concern for the poor can best be seen by some engagement with the Book of Sirach. Though not listed as canonical by the Jewish and most Protestant traditions, this work had immense influence on the emerging Christian moral teaching. Origen and Augustine referred frequently to Sirach; Gregory the Great, Bishop of Rome in the second half of the sixth century, quoted Sirach so profusely that after his death, his immediate disciple, Paterius, a notary of the Roman Church decided to arrange Gregory's writings on Sirach into an almost continuous commentary, and the work had great influence on medieval monasticism. Many of Jesus ben Sira's aphorisms found their way into the Talmud. Also called Ecclesiasticus (lit. "the church book"), it was written around 180 BC in Jerusalem by an instructor of wealthy youth, and translated into Greek around 132 BC by the author's grandson, most likely in Egypt. Ben Sira was a wisdom teacher in Jerusalem, and his work is an anthology of advice mainly to young students on how to live and how to achieve success in their lives (see Harrington, *Jesus Ben Sira*, 1–13). This literature, from a time when Jerusalem was under Hellenistic rule, most likely originated among the growing number of city dwellers engaged in commerce and in governmental bureaucracy. In today's world, ben Sira might be teaching in a business school.

Though reflecting a Hellenistic context, the author knows of the threefold division of Jewish writings in the Torah, the Prophets, and other writings. The work contains a lengthy praise of the Jewish ancestors (chapters 44—50), whose "bodies are buried in peace, but their name lives on generation after generation" and "the assembly declares their wisdom" (44:14–15). This long encomium concludes with an elaborate description of the temple liturgy and vestments of the high priest Simenon II (219–196 BC), and a benediction (50:22–24).

Advice on wealth and possessions are scattered throughout the work. Throughout the Bible possessions and the goods of the earth are a blessing from God (see, for example, Mic 4:4), while poverty brings sorrow and suffering and, in itself, is not praised. Sirach offers a nuanced view of wealth and poverty. On the one hand, "Good things and bad, life and death, / poverty and wealth, come from the Lord" (Sir 11:14). Wealth is a blessing but relative to deeper values:

> Wealth and wages make life sweet,
>> but better than either is finding a treasure.
> Children and the building of a city establish one's name,
>> but better than either is one who finds wisdom.
> Cattle and orchards make one prosperous;
>> but a blameless wife is accounted better than either.
> Wine and music gladden the heart,
>> but the love of friends is better than either.
>
> (40:18–20)

At the same time wealth can be a danger:

> Do not depend on dishonest wealth,
>> for it will not benefit you on the day of calamity.
>
> (5:8)

Wealth is ultimately fleeting:

> One becomes rich through diligence and self-denial,
>> and the reward allotted to him is this:
> when he says, 'I have found rest,
>> and now I shall feast on my goods!'
> he does not know how long it will be
>> until he leaves them to others and dies.
>
> (11:18–19; cf. Luke 12:16–21)

And:

> One who loves gold will not be justified;
>> one who pursues money will be led astray by it.

Many have come to ruin because of gold,
and their destruction has met them face to face.

(31:5–6)

Still, in Sirach, the lot of the poor is miserable:

A rich person does wrong, and even adds insults;
a poor person suffers wrong, and must add apologies.
A rich person will exploit you if you can be of use to him,
but if you are in need he will abandon you.
If you own something, he will live with you;
he will drain your resources without a qualm.

(13:3–5)

And also:

What peace is there between a hyena and a dog?
And what peace between the rich and the poor?
Wild asses in the wilderness are the prey of lions;
likewise the poor are feeding grounds for the rich.

(13:18–19)

However, DiLella and Skehan note that "Ben Sira derived his teaching on social justice from the biblical tradition" and that "the principal ethical concerns that Ben Sira speaks of are social justice and almsgiving" with Sirach 4:8–10 illustrative of the former:

Give a hearing to the poor,
and return their greeting politely.
Rescue the oppressed from the oppressor;
and do not be hesitant in giving a verdict.
Be a father to orphans,
and be like a husband to their mother;
you will then be like a son of the Most High,
and he will love you more than does your mother.

(4:8–10)

This advice crystallizes much of the biblical tradition on the concern for marginalized and suffering people, for example, Exodus 22:22; Deuteronomy 24:17–22; Leviticus 19:9–10; 23:22; Amos 5:10–15; Isaiah 1:17; and Proverbs 14:3; 28:27 (DiLella and Skehan, *Wisdom*, 89).

Sirach is also illustrative of one of the more interesting transformations of the older biblical notions of *tsedaqah* (justice that translated not by the usual Greek *dikaiosynē* ["justice"] but by the Greek *eleēmosynē* ["almsgiving"] from the Greek root *eleēmōn*, meaning "having compassion or concern for a suffering person").

As water extinguishes a blazing fire,
   so almsgiving atones for sin.

(3:30)

One's almsgiving is like a signet ring with the Lord,
   and he will keep a person's kindness like the apple of his eye.

(17:22)

Nevertheless, be patient with someone in humble circum-
    stances,
   and do not keep him waiting for your alms.
Help the poor for the commandment's sake,
   and in their need do not send them away empty-handed.

(29:8–9)

Justice in the sense of almsgiving is also found in Tobit 1:3; 12:8–9; and 14:11, and when the Greek text of Sirach employs *eleēmosynē* in such sayings as "almsgiving atones for sins" (3:30) and "do not be fainthearted in your prayer, nor neglect to give alms" (7:10, RSV), the Hebrew original has *tsedaqah* in these places. The change in meaning of the term can be seen from a comparison of Proverbs 10:2 with Tobit 12:9:

Righteousness (*tsedaqah*) delivers from death.

(Prov 10:2)

Almsgiving (*eleēmosynē*) delivers from death.

(Tob 12:9)

Jacob Lauterbach describes the significance of this development when he says that in later Judaism charity and concern for neighbor are conceived as justice and not simply as an excess of love.[2]

The roots of this view lie in the Old Testament identification of doing justice with concern for the poor, the widow, the orphan, and the sojourner (Heb. *ger*). The development lives on in both Christianity and Judaism. In Judaism, it produced a large system of care for the poor in the communities in Judaea and in the diaspora. In the New Testament, it is mirrored in Paul's concern for the poor and in the Letter of James where true faith demands acts of charity (Jas 2:16–17). Furthermore, in the early Church, the command to give alms and share the goods of the earth is seen as a manifestation of justice rather than an act of unselfish charity, crystallized in St. Augustine's statement: "Justice is assisting the needy" (*Justitia est in subveniendo miseris*).

This development represents a very important facet of biblical thought that was obscured by later distinctions between justice and charity. Concern for the poor and a desire to lessen the inequality between rich and poor either individually or collectively, in a biblical perspective, should not proceed simply from a love for or compassion with the sufferings of others, but is rooted in claims of justice; that is, how one can be faithful to the Lord who has given the goods of the earth as common possession of all and be faithful to others in the human community who have equal claim to these goods? Both in terms of its linguistic background (*tsedaqah/eleēmosynē*), and of its use in significant texts, almsgiving as practiced in various ways in Church life today should not be seen as an optional activity but as a sign of true faith.

---

2. Jacob Lauterbach, "The Ethics of the Halakah," in *Rabbinic Essays* (Cincinnati: Hebrew Union College, 1951), 292.

HOPE FOR THE MARGINALIZED

Though not stressed adequately in this study, eschatology is important in all the Old Testament traditions. Fundamentally, it describes "a form of radical orientation to the future, which may involve a sort of social and/or cosmic arrangement fundamentally different from that which currently exists" (David L. Peterson, "Eschatology," *ABD*, 2:575). This general orientation assumes different expectations, for example, the hope for a renewed or restored covenant (Jer 31 and Ezek 11); expectation of a royal Messiah (2 Sam 7; Isa 9:2–7; 11:1–9); prophetic images of hope (Isa 35) and restoration (Jer 23:5–6); as well as warnings often of the "day of Yahweh" (Amos 5:18–20; Isa 2:11–17; Zech 14:2–7), when the enemies of Israel will be defeated and the infidelity of the people will be manifest and punished. Such expectation of the future is to shape religious belief and ethical action in the present. In the preexilic literature, these hopes are to unfold at the end of human history and inaugurate a new age.

A very important development in the postexilic period is the motif that the true justice of God will be manifest only at the end-time. This motif is anticipated in the Old Testament, especially in the messianic oracles of Isaiah 9:2–7 and 11:1–9, and in the Isaiah Apocalypse (24:1—27:13), where themes like the eschatological judgment, the messianic banquet, and the cosmic upheavals will prepare the command: "Open the gates / that the righteous nation which keeps faith / may enter in" (Isa 26:2), and in the prophecies of Deutero-Isaiah that look to a time when the conversion of the nations will be due to the justice of God (45:23–25); salvation will be granted (60:18); and the people will be just and possess the land forever (60:21). Such prophetic sayings provide the matrix for the view that justice is no longer something that Yahweh will establish in the sphere of history, but will be reserved to the end-time when human history will end and a new age will emerge.

These hopes for justice will unfold in a new form of eschatological hope, described generally as apocalyptic thought. While complex in origin and development, it generally describes revelations of the future (Gk. *apokalyptein*, meaning "uncover" or "disclose") communicated to a seer or prophet, defined by John Collins as "a genre of revelatory literature with a narrative framework, in which a revelation is mediated by an otherworldly being to a human recipient, disclosing a transcendent reality which is both temporal, insofar as it envisages eschatological salvation, and spatial insofar as it involves another supernatural world." (*Apocalyptic Imagination*, 40). Certain characteristics appear frequently:

> Apocalyptic literature portrays a deterministic view of history. The present evil is willed—for example, phrases like "this must happen"—but God has determined a timetable for the conquest of evil. Those who are the perpetrators of evil will be punished; in fact, it has been determined in advance that they will be punished.
>
> The final victory of God will be preceded by a period of suffering often designated as the "messianic woes" (1 Thess 1:4), or the "birth pangs" of the Messiah. Coincident in much apocalyptic literature, especially in Christian apocalyptic, is the arrival of "false messiahs" or false prophets.
>
> Apocalyptic literature is heavily dualistic on many levels: cosmological dualism, where struggles on earth reflect struggles in the heavenly sphere; ethical dualism, where people are divided into good and evil.

This literature and worldview thrives among people suffering persecution or alienation from their culture and fosters trust in a God who will reverse the injustice they suffer and create a new age of peace and justice. The literature functions also as a "hidden transcript" of resistance to the values and practices of the dominating and oppressive culture (Portier-Young, *Apocalypse*).

Among the canonical Scriptures, the Book of Daniel provides the archetype of apocalyptic literature. Though composed of different traditions, it takes shape during the forced Hellenization of the Jews under Antiochus IV Epiphanes (167–164 BC). The traditional stories of chapters 1—6 set in the context of the victory of Daniel and his companions over Babylonian kings give hope to an oppressed people, while the final chapters 7—12 offer visions of the vindication of the suffering people and the hope of future glory.

Concerns for social justice in Daniel are more implicit than explicit. Throughout, a refrain is the attacks of ruthless and powerful rulers upon the holy ones of the Most High (Dan 7:21, 25; 8:24), which will end in the destruction of the hostile kingdoms. The ultimate vindication of God's justice (fidelity to his promises) occurs with the arrival of "Michael, the great prince, the protector of your people" (12:1), which will inaugurate "a time of anguish, such as has never occurred since nations first came into existence" that will be followed by the double resurrection:

> "But at that time your people shall be delivered, everyone who is found written in the book. Many of those who sleep in the dust of the earth shall awake, some to everlasting life, and some to shame and everlasting contempt. Those who are wise shall shine like the brightness of the sky, and those who lead many to righteousness, like the stars forever and ever." (Dan 12:1–3)

Resurrection as vindication of God's justice emerges as an essential element of biblical thought and provides the matrix for the proclamation of the resurrection of Jesus as the ultimate victory of God's justice.

Justice as the vindication of the suffering poor and the punishment of the rich is a major theme in noncanonical second temple Jewish literature, especially in *1 Enoch*, which is a collection of visionary literature attributed to Enoch, a descendent of Adam mentioned in Genesis 5:24, as one who "walked with God; then he was no more, because God took him." The "Epistle of Enoch" comprises chapters 92—105 in the form of admonitions and encouragement to his descendants (George Nickelsburg, "Enoch, First Book of," *ABD*, 2:508–15). A major theme here is the oppression of and violence on the poor by the rich who await God's punishment.[3] Some examples would be:

> Woe to you, rich, for you have trusted in your riches; and from your riches you will depart, for you have not remembered the Most High in the days of your riches. You have

---

3. See especially George E. Nickelsburg, "Riches, the Rich, and God's Judgment in *1 Enoch* 92–105 and the Gospel According to Luke," *New Testament Studies* 25 (1979): 324–44.

committed blasphemy and lawlessness, and you have been prepared for the day of bloodshed and the day of darkness and the day of great judgment. Thus I say to you and make known to you: he who created you will overturn you, and for your fall there will be no compassion, and your Creator will rejoice over your destruction. (*1 Enoch* 94:8–10)

The unjust are characterized by a series of actions that destroy the social fabric of the community. They are lying witnesses (95:6); they trust in riches (94:8); they acquire gold and silver unjustly (97:8); they persecute just people (95:7); and they spread evil by making false weights and measures. The world as described by *1 Enoch* is a world where injustice is rampant and the just suffer, and the harsh judgment on the wealthy provides the background for similar indictments in the New Testament, for example, Luke 6:24–26, the "woes on the rich," James 1:9–11, and Revelation 18. Coupled with this indictment of the unjust, *1 Enoch* contains a series of exhortations for the readers. The just are told to "take courage" for sinners will perish (97:1); a bright light will enlighten them and "the voice of rest you will hear from heaven" (93:6). The just will be companions of the hosts of heaven (104:6).

The final judgment is simultaneously revelation and vindication. It uncovers the sins of the unjust and vindicates the just. Eschatology does not function simply as speculation on the end-time. It provides a double answer: (1) to the problem of theodicy—how a just and loving God can permit the unjust to prosper; and (2) to the problem of salvation history—what the history of God's saving acts means to a people who experience oppression and loss of political power. Therefore, in eschatological thought, not only are the faithful "justified" at the end-time, but God himself is shown to be just and faithful. The meaning of history is seen not simply from the course of events but from the perspective of the goal or end of history. The "God who acts" of the Old Testament is here the Lord of hope. This type of eschatology is important for understanding Paul's teaching in the New Testament on the contrast between this age and the age to come, and his statements that the end-time, that is, the judgment on the powers of the age, has come in Jesus Christ.

CONCLUDING REFLECTIONS ON THE OLD TESTAMENT

Our brief tour through the Old Testament has been selective with a twofold purpose: to encourage study of the texts themselves, along with many other texts and themes that were omitted, and to broaden that study with additional resources.

The Bible proclaims what it means to be just and do justice; it is less interested in what justice is in the abstract. It gives concrete instances of justice and injustice in the lives of people. The task of translation is to make alive in our present age the vision of justice that formed the lives of the biblical writers. Interpretation of the Bible is always determined by the social context of the interpreter. Luther wrestled with the late medieval problem of a just and often angry God and sinful creation, and translated the God of justice into a God of love. The task of our age may well be the reverse—to translate the love of God into the doing of justice.

The God of the Old Testament is a God who loves justice and righteousness. What God loves, God brings to pass. As a just God, he is faithful to his covenant by revealing to people how they may turn to him and return to him when they fail. His justice is manifest both in the saving deeds whereby he frees people from slavery and oppression, and in his indicting of sinfulness. In God, justice and mercy are not in opposition, but, as Heschel states: "God is compassion without compromise; justice, though not inclemency" (*The Prophets*, 1:16).

Biblical justice is fidelity to the demands of a relationship. To be just is to be faithful to the covenant God, as he reveals himself in history, in the law, and in the prophets. Covenant faithfulness means that justice is shown to the neighbor as a sign of the saving justice received from God. Peace and harmony are the fruits of justice as well as its signs.

Characteristic of Israel's faith is the revelation of God as protector of the helpless, the poor, and the oppressed in the community. In order to become a faithful and just people, Israel is summoned to true knowledge and true worship of God that is not simply the recognition that another person has equal rights to the goods of God's creation, but is active engagement in securing these goods for them. The mirror of

136

this concern is the almost relentless suspicion of abusive power and wealth, shown not only in the Torah and prophetic texts but enduring through the wisdom tradition. As we will discuss later in the Gospel of Luke, these two strains merge seamlessly.

No Christian theology or practice of social justice can unfold without deep engagement with the Old Testament, with the texts themselves, with study and reflection on them, and with an awareness of the ways that Jewish people have lived and interpreted these texts. Often, even when avoiding the more blatant forms of anti-Jewish readings of the Bible, Christians slip into latent Marcionism, named for the second-century bishop and heretic who wanted Christianity free of Judaism. Marcion rejected the Old Testament as revelation of an inferior God, and had a canon limited to ten Pauline letters and parts of the Gospel of Luke. One still hears views that the God of the Old Testament is a God of justice (in a distorted sense) in contrast to the New Testament God of love and mercy, or that violence characterized the Hebrew Bible, while peace is the legacy of Christianity—both of which are a travesty.

In the development of biblical faith, the quest for justice presents gift and demand, and the full realization of the quest is future hope. The heir to biblical faith lives between the times with a mission both to confront the evils of injustice and to offer to the world visions and practices of justice.

RESOURCE BIBLIOGRAPHY

Anderson, Gary A. *Sin: A History*. New Haven/London: Yale University Press, 2009. An original, scholarly study that argues that sin is understood as debt, so that almsgiving especially in the Wisdom literature becomes central to biblical understandings of the right relation to God.

Bergant, Dianne. *Israel's Wisdom Literature: A Liberation–Critical Reading*. Minneapolis: Fortress Press, 1997.

Ceresko, Anthony. *Introduction to Old Testament Wisdom: A Spirituality for Liberation*. Maryknoll, NY: Orbis Books, 1999.

Collins, John J. *The Apocalyptic Imagination: An Introduction to the Jewish Matrix of Christianity*. New York: Crossroad, 1984.

Crenshaw, James L. *Old Testament Wisdom: An Introduction*. Revised and enlarged. Louisville, KY: Westminster John Knox Press, 1998. Crenshaw notes "the sages' attitude toward wealth and poverty is elusive partly because of their assumption that one controls one's own destiny" (84).

Dell, Katherine J. *The Book of Proverbs in Social and Theological Context*. Cambridge: Cambridge University Press, 2006.

DiLella, Alexander, and Patrick Skehan. *The Wisdom of Ben Sira*. AB 39. New York: Doubleday, 1989.

Harrington, Daniel J. *Jesus Ben Sira of Jerusalem: A Guide to Living Wisely*. Collegeville, MN: Liturgical Press, 2005. An excellent overview of the nature, content, and setting of this most influential book with awareness of its importance for spiritual growth.

Heschel, Abraham. *The Prophets*. 2 vols. New York: Harper and Row, 1962. Reissued in 2001 as a one-volume edition by Perennial Classics (HarperCollins).

Hoppe, Leslie J. *There Shall be No Poor Among You: Poverty in the Bible*. Nashville, TN: Abingdon Press, 2004. A treatment of the poor in Old and New Testament literature. Ideal for classroom use.

Malchow, Bruce. "Social Justice in the Wisdom Literature." *Biblical Theological Bulletin* 12 (1982): 120–24.

Nickelsburg, George W. "Enoch, First Book of," *ABD*, 2:508–16.

Perdue, Leo G. *Wisdom Literature: A Theological History*. Louisville, KY: Westminster John Knox Press, 2007.

Pleins, J. D. "Poverty in the Social World of the Wise." *Journal for the Study of the Old Testament* 37 (1987): 61–78.

Portier-Young, Anathea E. *Apocalypse against Empire: Theologies of Resistance in Early Judaism*. Grand Rapids, MI: Eerdmans, 2011. A major scholarly study of second temple Jewish apocalyptic works, which shows that this literature does not function only to give oppressed people a hope of future vindication, but is itself a form of resistance.

Schmidt, T. Ewald. "Hostility to Wealth in Philo of Alexandria." *Journal for the Study of the New Testament* 19 (1983): 85–97. I have added this for the sake of historical completeness since Philo represents an important voice in diaspora Judaism of the first century AD.

Scott, James C. *Domination and the Arts of Resistance: Hidden Transcripts.* New Haven: Yale University Press, 1990. Widely used by those studying literature of marginal or oppressed people to show how their writings provide an alternate view of reality to that of the dominant groups.

Whybray, R. N. *Wealth and Poverty in the Book of Proverbs.* JSOT Sup 99. Sheffield: JSOT Press, 1990. A thorough study of the terminology, literary, and social setting of sayings with a careful summary of the teachings on wealth and poverty.

CHAPTER 7

JESUS

Prophet of God's Reign

When reading the New Testament through the prism of social justice, some initial comments are important. First, the twenty-seven books of the New Testament cover a very short period compared to the literature of Israel, yet they are extremely diverse, ranging from quasi-biographical portraits (Gospels), a narrative of the initial spread of those "who belonged to the Way," (Acts 9:2), through various letters to specific groups, and concluding with a long homily (Letter to the Hebrews) and vivid apocalyptic visions (the Book of Revelation). Second, they reflect the initial stages in the lives of people, both people from a completely Jewish background, and Jews living in the diaspora and mainly in the major cities of the Greco-Roman world, who accepted the crucified Jesus of Nazareth as the hoped-for Messiah. These comprised those from Antioch, Ephesus, Corinth, Alexandria, and Rome, along with Greek-speaking non-Jews, who had been attracted by Jewish theology and morality (God fearers), and pagans, who had little contact with Judaism. Third, the witness of these books comes from people who had little power over the external circumstances of their lives. While the biblical prophets could confront kings and rulers with a set of shared fundamental values, the early Christians were a barely noticed minority. Fourth, while contemporary research has enriched our knowledge of the impact of the Greco-Roman culture on emerging Christianity, the Jewish Scriptures are the prime and almost exclusive *literary* matrix. Beyond a scattered quote or two, there is no citation of Hellenistic literature, while works such as Isaiah and Psalms are constantly evoked. Finally, no longer valid are formerly voiced pejorative

140

contrasts between the Jewish Scripture and Tradition and the New Testament material (for example, religion of law vs. religion of love; God of judgment vs. God of mercy).

Our discussion of the New Testament is necessarily selective. After some reflections on aspects of the life and teaching of Jesus (drawing primarily on Markan texts), we will examine in some detail the Gospels of Matthew and Luke (with comments on Acts) and try to highlight the major themes of Paul's writings, with some concluding comments on the Johannine writings.

It has become axiomatic to say that Jesus was not a social reformer; nonetheless, his teachings and actions had strong social implications during his lifetime and continue to shape the consciences of his followers today. A key to his life is his proclamation of the imminence of God's reign or kingdom through direct proclamation or in parable. He also enacts the kingdom through acts of power (healings and exorcisms), and by his association with and offer of God's love to the marginalized of his day, especially tax collectors and sinners.

Reconstruction of the life and teaching of the Jesus of history has been a dominant part of New Testament studies since the middle of the nineteenth century with the first "quest for the historical Jesus," "the new quest," and now "the third quest" and complete agreement on most issues is rare. Based on the emerging consensus in specific areas and in debt to the massive research of John Dominic Crossan, John P. Meier, and James Dunn, as well as insightful shorter studies (for example, by Daniel Harrington and Gerhard Lohfink), we will examine elements of his kingdom proclamation and praxis and highlight factors that led to his execution.

PROCLAMATION AND PRACTICE OF THE KINGDOM

In the books of the Hebrew canon, the expression "kingdom of God" appears rarely, but pervasive is the image of God as "king," for example, "Your throne, O God, stands forever; / your royal scepter is a scepter for justice. / You love justice and hate wrongdoing" (Ps 45:7–8, NABRE; see Pss 5:2; 47:6–7; 95–100). In the New Testament, however, there is wide agreement that the fundamental mission of Jesus was as prophet of the "kingdom of God," but with diverse interpretations of its meaning. An initial problem is the androcentric and authoritarian tone of "kingdom" (Gk. *basileia*). Nonetheless, in respect to the original use of the term and also as an aid for the use of biblical dictionaries and concordances, we will speak of "kingdom."

Yet "kingdom of God," itself, is multivalent and there is no one-to-one correspondence with "kingdom of God" and any concept or expression of it. It is a "tensive symbol," which "can have a set of meanings that can neither be exhausted nor adequately expressed by any one referent, in contrast to a 'steno symbol,' which has a single referent" (for example, mathematical symbols; Perrin, *Jesus and the Language*, 196). As such, it evokes a host of associations rooted in both the Old and New Testament understandings and is summarized by three terms: *reign(ing)*, the power of God active in creation and history; *realm*, it is not simply a spiritual power but seeks a "home" or situation where this power is exercised and recognized so much so that people can "enter" it; and *rule*, guidelines for a way of life according to its proclamation and presence. John Dominic Crossan has described it well:

> But what we are actually talking about is power or rule, a state much more than a place, or, another, state means way of life or mode of being, not nation or empire. The basic question is this: how does human power exercise its rule, and how, in contrast, does divine power exercise its rule? The kingdom of God is people under divine rule, and that, as ideal, transcends and judges all human rule. (*Historical Jesus*, 266)

Jesus inaugurates his public ministry by proclaiming that the kingdom of God is at hand and summons people to reform and renewal (*metanoia*, that is, a change of heart or a new way of looking at things; Mark 1:16–17), and that the kingdom is "among you" or "in your midst" (Luke 17:21)—not "within you," which is an inaccurate translation that suggests that the kingdom is only an interior spiritual reality. Jesus' mighty works of healing, confrontation with demons, and power over nature are the signs of this power of God now at work in his life and teaching. The kingdom is "of God" (about and from God), both as gift and challenge, and despite common parlance, nowhere does the New Testament speak of humans "building the kingdom of God." Jesus speaks often of the kingdom in parables drawn from the ordinary lives of his hearers. Human experience is the path toward the transcendent.

Future expectation is also strong. Disciples are to pray that the kingdom will come, in the same vein that they pray God's will be done on earth as in heaven (Matt 6:10). Other sayings of Jesus reflect Jewish apocalyptic thought with its emphasis on the end of the world, when the exalted Son of Man will reign as king to judge evildoers and restore justice to the elect (the parable of the sheep and the goats, Matt 25:31–46). Eschatological fulfillment of the reign of God, in Pauline terms, is that at the end-time the risen Jesus will hand over his kingdom to "his God and Father" (1 Cor 15:24).

Jesus proclaims the reign of God as a radical challenge crystallized in a series of sayings on "entering." Rather than scandalize a child or commit other sins, one should be willing to enter the kingdom of God blind (Mark 9:47). Those who wish to enter the kingdom should be powerless like a little child, and riches provide an overwhelming obstacle to entering the kingdom. Disciples who seek the prestige of sitting at the right hand of Jesus in the kingdom are rather urged to become servants and slaves (Mark 10:32–45; Matt 20:21–25).

The reign and power of God is not otherworldly, but embodied in history. Its arrival brings special hope to the poor, the suffering, and the marginalized. When Jesus calls the poor blessed because "the kingdom of God is yours" (Luke 6:20), he declares that God's reign is on their behalf. The rich young man seeking eternal life is urged to give his wealth to the poor, and Jesus reflects on his reluctance, "how hard it is for the rich to enter the kingdom of God" (Mark 10:23).

THE "WHEN" OF GOD'S REIGN

A host of problems accompany this proclamation. There are three principal groups of sayings of Jesus: the first stresses the presence of the kingdom, the second its future coming, and the third describes its demands on people who wish to accept or enter it. There is a seemingly endless debate on which sayings are closest to the *ipsissima vox* of

Jesus (his actual statements). Advocates of the presence of the kingdom interpret Jesus primarily as a prophet of reform (John Dominic Crossan), while those who stress the future coming of the sayings view Jesus as an apocalyptic preacher (Albert Schweitzer). Current exegesis leans toward some version of the thesis of Joachim Jeremias that regards God's reign as present and unfolding in the ministry of Jesus, while its fullest realization is in the future.[1]

SOCIAL JUSTICE AND THE KINGDOM OF GOD IN PARABLE

The prophets of Israel spoke on behalf of God and on behalf of those who had no voice to whom they offered visions of hope; they challenged powerful leaders and castigated distortions of religious traditions. The prophets conveyed their messages in the vivid language of metaphor and parable. Jesus stands in this tradition, and characteristic of the Gospels, "began to teach them many things in parables" (Mark 4:2), so that the parables have been and remain a rich resource for discipleship and ethical reflection. The formal characteristics of parables have themselves ethical implications. Jesus used realistic images from daily life that caught his hearers' attention by their vividness and narrative color. Yet his parables have a surprising twist; the realism is shattered and the hearers know that something more is at stake than a homey illustration to drive home a point. The parables raise questions, unsettle the complacent, and challenge the hearers to reflection and inquiry. Parables are open-ended; they are invitations waiting for a response. The parable does not really exist until it is freely appropriated. The response of the reader or hearer in a real sense creates the meaning of the parable. Parable is a form of religious discourse that appeals not only to the imagination or to the joyous perception of paradox or surprise, but to the most basic of human qualities, freedom. Jesus chose a form of discourse that put his life and message at the risk of free human response (see J. R. Donahue, "Use of Parables in Ethics," in *DSE*, 575–78).

---

1. For a full discussion of the position of Jeremias and others who hold an "already" and "not yet" view of the kingdom proclamation see, Norman Perrin, *The Kingdom of God in the Teaching of Jesus* (London: SCM Press, 1963), 79–90.

The symbolic phrase "kingdom of God" finds expression in images taken from and oriented to the mystery of growth and human engagement in it. Initially, we will look at select "seed parables" (Mark 4:1–9, 26–32) where their poetic images are able to evoke a network of meanings: the mystery of growth, its hidden quality, the rhythmic and unhurried pace of nature, the need to respect the times and seasons, the urgency of the harvest, as well as eschatological sifting and judgment. These images point to the ways in which God's power and presence intersect with human history. Yet the ordinary process of growth is surpassed and new meanings emerge.

In Mark 4:11, when asked about the meaning of the parables, Jesus says that to you has been given the "mystery of the kingdom." The "seed parables" of Mark 4 draw hearers into this mystery. The first parable (Mark 4:3–9), though called the parable of the sower, really deals with the contrast between three failed sowings and one extravagant yield. Its hearers are caught up in the rhythm of planting and failed growth, but their expectations are shattered by the final yield. A sevenfold harvest is bountiful; thirty-, sixty-, and a hundredfold are unheard of. By highlighting the difference between the time of sowing and that of harvest as well as the discrepancy between the three failures and the great harvest, Jesus assures his disciples that what God has begun in his ministry, despite apparent failure, contains hope for the future. This calls attention to the gift-like nature, the graciousness, and the surprise of the advent of the bountiful harvest—all suggestive of the advent of the kingdom, which shatters the way in which we feel that life normally operates and the patterns it follows. In effect, this parable becomes one about how the proclamation of the kingdom will affect people.

At the time of Jesus, farming was a fragile operation with frequent droughts and crop failures. Coupled with this was a system of high taxation by both civil and religious authorities so that people were often on the brink of famine. The images used by Jesus point to a God who brings forth life and wants people to share in the bounty of creation, and are an implicit criticism of those who would dominate it or control its bounty.

The allegory of the seeds (Mark 4:13–20) that follows the sayings about the mystery of the kingdom in Mark is actually the earliest inter-

pretation of the four sowings. Mark has applied the failure of the sowings to the lives of those who would follow Jesus. Discipleship permeates chapter 4 and is highlighted by the repeated demands for
"hearing" (4:3, 9, 23, 24, 33). In biblical thought, *hearing* (*akouō*) is
intimately related to *obedience* (*hypakouō*), and the demands of God are
expressed in the daily prayer that begins, "Hear, O Israel" (Deut 6:4–9;
see also 11:13–21; Num 15:37–41; Mark 12:29). The three failed sowings in the allegory of Mark become examples of not hearing the Word
of God and warnings for the pitfalls of discipleship: destruction by
Satan's power (v. 15; cf. 8:31–32); initial enthusiasm, quashed by subsequent scandal (vv. 16–17)—which summarizes the action of the disciples in Mark; worldly cares, the lure of wealth, and desires for other
things that "strangle the word" (vv. 18–19; see 10:23–25, the rich
young man). The fruitful harvest (v. 20) is a virtual summary of the
process of conversion: hearing the Word, accepting it, and bearing
fruit. This is one of the earliest instances where wealth and power
become obstacles to responding to Jesus' proclamation that "the kingdom is at hand, repent and believe in the good news" (Mark
1:14–15)—obstacles much alive in our contemporary world.[2]

In the final two kingdom parables of Mark 4, the Markan Jesus
takes images from his early years in rural Galilee to portray the mystery
of God's reign, that is, God's power being made manifest in his ministry.
In the first parable, often called the parable of the seed growing secretly
(Mark 4:26–29), a rather unconcerned farmer just scatters the seed,
resumes a restful life, and the seed sprouts and grows; how, he doesn't
know. This action of the sower seems a bit strange since in an earlier
parable (Mark 4:1–9), Jesus speaks of the perils of agriculture. Yet here
the seed grows "on its own," and the farmer returns only to harvest.

What was Jesus trying to say in the parable? Perhaps many
things. To those of his followers who expected the kingdom to blossom
forth immediately, he may caution that God's times are not human
times. To others who wanted to hurry the arrival of the kingdom by
violent or extraordinary means, the parable says that God's reign has a

---

2. See John R. Donahue, "The Lure of Wealth: Does Mark Have a Social Gospel?" in *Unity and
Diversity in the Gospels and Paul: Essays in Honor of Frank J. Matera*, ed. Christopher W. Skinner
and Kelly R. Iverson, Society of Biblical Literature Early Christianity and Its Literature 7 (Atlanta:
Society of Biblical Literature, 2012), 71–93.

power of its own. To both groups the stress is on being ready for the harvest. A time will come to act, and we must stand ready.

In the parable of the mustard seed (4:30–32), the contrast between insignificant beginnings (the small mustard seed) and the luxuriant shrub that shelters all the birds of the air (Mark 4:32) provides an image of the contrast between Jesus with his small band of disciples and the hoped-for eschatological community (cf. Ezek 17:22–24; Dan 4:10–12). There is even an element of humor in this parable. The mustard bush, as Crossan has stressed, is a pungent shrub with dangerous takeover properties; it grows out of control and attracts birds into unwanted places (*Historical Jesus*, 278–79).

In various Old Testament texts, a tree becomes a symbol of kingdoms or empires (Judg 9:7–15; Dan 4:10–12, 20–27), and nesting birds stand for the subjects of imperial rule (Ezek 31). Yet the kingdom that Jesus proclaims turns this image on its head. Where the birds (that is, the nations) will gather is not a mighty tree but "the greatest of all shrubs" that will harbor all the birds of the air, symbolizing the diverse and inclusive nature of the kingdom proclaimed by Jesus and a subtle hint that God's kingdom is not to be like the mighty trees (that is, empires) of old, which are established through power and violence.

These parables suggest ways for reflecting on the kingdom today. God's reigning or kingdom is precisely that: it is God's doing, not human effort. God's reign is a power that affects life in strange and wonderful ways, but we, like the farmer of Mark 4:26–30, often "know not how." Despite repeated failures, the power of God's reign can produce results all out of proportion to those failures. Like the mustard seed that becomes a huge plant, the kingdom evokes hope that startling results may follow insignificant beginnings, and like the mustard bush, God's way of reigning and the realm he seeks can be disturbing. Any engagement in the quest for social justice will involve persecution, failure, and often meager results, and can be made fruitless by riches and the lure of wealth, but can be sustained by hope of a harvest often still in the unseen future.

JESUS AND THE MARGINALIZED

EATING WITH TAX COLLECTORS AND SINNERS

A shocking element of Jesus' ministry was his acceptance of and familiarity with "tax collectors and sinners," epitomized in Mark 2:15–17:

> While he was at table in his house, many tax collectors and sinners sat with Jesus and his disciples; for there were many who followed him. Some scribes who were Pharisees saw that he was eating with sinners and tax collectors and said to his disciples, "Why does he eat with tax collectors and sinners?" Jesus heard this and said to them (that), "Those who are well do not need a physician, but the sick do. I did not come to call the righteous [just] but sinners."

This association is at the bedrock of stories of Jesus and appears in every block of tradition especially in Luke (see chapter 9). Matthew recounts a tradition about Jesus that surely must have caused embarrassment among some followers of Jesus. After stating that the kingdom of God suffers violence and castigating the crowds for rejecting the preaching of John because they viewed his wild and ascetic lifestyle as demonic possession, Jesus says that they did not accept him because he was just the opposite: "The Son of Man came eating and drinking and they say, 'Look, [he is] a glutton and a drunkard, a friend of tax collectors and sinners!'" (Matt 11:19). In this early text, before Jesus was called "Messiah" or "Lord," he is the "human one" known for his association with rejected groups. This is all the more startling since some Jewish groups yearned that a Davidic king would arise who "wisely, righteously [he] shall thrust out sinners from (the) inheritance; he shall destroy the arrogance of the sinner as a potter's jar" (*Psalms of Solomon* 17:21).

In the cultural milieu of Jesus, the concept of "eating with" was totally in contrast to our informal and hurried society. Two aspects are crucial: hospitality shown in sharing food was a paramount social value (1 Kgs 17:12–24; Luke 11:5–7), and rarely, if ever, did shared meals cross religious, social, and economic boundaries. Observant

Pharisees gathered and shared meals in religious fraternities (*habura*) out of concern for proper observance of food laws. The Essenes had elaborate rules of attendance and seating arrangements for shared meals. The Greco-Roman world celebrated stylized *symposia* meals (lit. "drinking together") with stated rituals of precedence and acceptance.

The practice of Jesus shatters these conventions. Tax and toll collectors, though not the corrupt "publicans" of earlier portrayals, but rather local toll collectors of indirect taxes, were scorned not only as agents of a repressive tax system, but were often accused of enhancing personal profit from their tasks. Sinners could embrace a wide variety of people and are often equated with sexual immorality: "Amen, I say to you, tax collectors and prostitutes are entering the kingdom of God before you" (Matt 21:31; see also Luke 7:36–50). With these people Jesus practiced what Dominic Crossan has called "open commensality," welcoming such people for meals, but with the deeper implication of personal acceptance and trust (*Jesus: A Revolutionary Biography*, 66–70). Jesus also instructs his followers not to invite the powerful and prestigious to banquets but the marginalized of the land: "the poor, the crippled, the lame, and the blind" (Luke 14:13). In contrast even to the preaching of John the Baptist, who said that conversion would lead to acceptance by God, Jesus first practices communion as a symbol of the acceptance offered. By accepting and eating with such groups, Jesus shatters those conventions of exclusion that dominate human societies. Any actions on behalf of social justice today must find ways to confront those structures of exclusion that are enshrined in law and custom, both in civil society and, sadly, equally in our churches.

"LET THE LITTLE ONES COME TO ME"

A solid element of the Jesus tradition is those narratives dealing with Jesus and the acceptance of children and proposing them as a model for followers (Mark 9:33–37, 42; 10:13–16; cf. also Matt 18:1–6; 19:13–15; Luke 9:46–48; 18:15–17). Mark places the first of these incidents after the second time the disciples misunderstand Jesus' prediction that he will suffer and die and they bicker over positions of power (9:33–37). After countering their aspirations with an exhortation to be "last of all and servant of all," Jesus takes a child in his arms, brings it before the disciples, and says "Whoever receives one child such as this in my name, receives me" (v. 37).

In the following section (Mark 9:38–41), the disciples forbid someone who is not part of their group from casting out demons in the name of Jesus, but Jesus counters, "Do not prevent him. There is no one who performs a mighty deed in my name who can at the same time speak ill of me. For whoever is not against us is for us" (v. 39–40). A second allusion to children occurs where Jesus then utters some of the harshest denunciations in the Gospels: "If any of you put a stumbling block before one of these little ones who believe in me, it would be better for you if a great millstone were hung around your neck and you were thrown into the sea" (Mark 9:42).[3] The little ones in the Gospel are both children and those of little faith, and the harsh judgments—drowning with a large millstone thrown around their neck, or self-mutilation—are the punishments for those who trap or trip up these little ones by placing obstacles to their faith.

In the third "children incident" (Mark 10:13–16), sandwiched between Jesus' defense of marriage and his warnings about the danger of wealth, people are bringing children to Jesus so that he might bless them, but with practiced obtuseness, the disciples "rebuke them" (*epetimēsan*, the same term used when Jesus rebukes demons). Jesus becomes "indignant" and relates the kingdom of God to welcoming children: "Let the children come to me; do not prevent them, for the kingdom of God belongs to such as these. Amen, I say to you, whoever does not accept the kingdom of God like a child will not enter it" (Mark 10:14–16).

These "children stories" lead us to a greater understanding of Jesus' kingdom proclamation and its relation to social justice. Often these stories are used to urge people to have childlike innocence in accepting official teaching with the correlation that religious leaders can treat people like children. In the Jewish world of the first century,

---

3. The "Catholic" translation of this verse creates completely wrong interpretations: "Whoever causes one of these little ones who believe [in me] *to sin*" (NABRE). There is no Greek word for *sin* and the onus of the condemnation is on those who cause little ones to stumble or trip since *skandalizein* in Greek comes from the noun *skandalon*, "a trap or device for catching someone or tripping someone up." The condemnation is directed at those who harm the little ones, not some "sin" these little ones will commit.

children are not symbols of innocence, but until they can learn and observe Torah (celebrated today with a bar or bat mitzvah), children are not really capable of moral actions crystallized in the saying that the *yetzer hara* (the evil inclination) is twelve years older than the *yetzer hatov* (the good inclination). Children are not symbols of innocence but of powerlessness and vulnerability. In many portions of the Greco-Roman world, where the words of Jesus took root, infanticide or exposing children to be picked up by slavers was common practice. When Jesus exhorts his disciples to be like children, he is urging them to renounce dominating power; when he accepts and embraces children, he says that God's realm is like this, accepting and defending the powerless and vulnerable.

Sadly, this book took shape at the beginning of the second decade of the 2000s, when the sex abuse of children by clergy and the concealment of it and inaction to address it by Church leaders permeate the news. Actually, there has not only been a "sex abuse scandal," but also a "power abuse scandal," and here the dissonance from the kingdom proclamation is striking. Sick or distorted people within the Church, sadly most often priests, used the power of their position to trap children, and leaders used positions of power to conceal the abuse or to avoid effectively confronting it. Also, the latter never really listened to the voices of victims in the early days of the scandal and were even hostile to people who lodged complaints. They were not attuned to the values that Jesus embodied when he both accepted and defended vulnerable children in his ministry. The kingdom proclamation of Jesus must always stand over and against all attempts to dilute it by existing Church structures or practice.

KINGDOM IN CONFLICT

In the Old Testament, one of the roles of God as king is as a "divine warrior" who fights on behalf of a beleaguered people and confronts evil power. An early paean of triumph for the exodus is "Yahweh is a warrior, / Yahweh is his name. / Pharaoh's chariots and army he cast into the sea" (Exod 15:3–4), and the psalms are replete with images of God as a warrior. Since much of this imagery is rooted in ancient Near Eastern conflicts of deities, in the Bible God is also engaged in a cosmic struggle and vanquishes primordial forces of evil: "It was you who crushed the heads of Leviathan / and gave him as food to the creatures of the desert" (Ps 74:14; cf. also Pss 2; 18; 24; 46; 48; 76; 89; 97; 132; 144). In the Gospels, this takes the form of Jesus' conflicts with two forces opposed to the kingdom: demonic power and human opposition.

The first mighty work of Jesus after the proclamation of the good news of the kingdom is cosmic conflict: a violent confrontation with a man possessed by an unclean spirit. When Jesus drives out the spirit, who recognizes him as a holy one of God, the people are amazed at his new teaching with authority (or "power," *exousia*, Mark 1:21–28). The subsequent exorcisms then represent a clash of kingdoms, as Jesus himself says, "But if it is by the finger of God that I cast out demons, then the kingdom of God has upon you" (Luke 11:20).

The clash between kingdoms is dramatic in Mark 3:20–35. The narrative begins with opposition from the family of Jesus who think that he is "out of his mind," apparently because of his frantic activity and wonder-working. This is quickly followed by the more serious charge by Jerusalem scribes that Jesus is possessed by Beelzebul and "by the ruler of demons he drives out demons." Jesus turns the charge back on his accusers by proposing some parables (riddles): "How can Satan drive out Satan? If a kingdom is divided against itself, that kingdom cannot stand. And if a house is divided against itself, that house will not be able to stand. And if Satan has risen up against himself and is divided, he cannot stand; that is the end of him" (vv. 23–26). Matthew, who is more direct in recounting this controversy, adds a "clincher" argument, "And if I drive out demons by Beelzebul, by whom do your own people drive them out?" (12:27). Jesus was not the only exorcist among first-century Jewish teachers. The substance of this narrative is that the kingdom proclaimed and enacted by Jesus is stronger than the rule and realm of evil manifested by Satan (lit. "the opponent").

Today as people struggle for social justice, the forces of injustice seem to assume a cosmic dimension and certainly have a global dimension. The economic crisis beginning in 2008 with lasting effects, constituted an assault on the most vulnerable in the world, and though ultimately orchestrated by ambitious and greedy men, it seems to be a power that ordinary people cannot control. Other manifestations of evil such as child slavery and trafficking for sexual abuse, the brutal treatment of women, the arms trade, and the exploitation of natural resources are manifestations of the *mysterium iniquitatis* ("the mystery of evil"). Action on behalf of justice motivated by the kingdom proclamation of Jesus necessarily involves conflict in its wake: false accusation, rejection by loved ones, and even loss of life, as it ultimately did for Jesus. Yet it is nurtured by the hope that the house of the strong man can be plundered by Jesus, the stronger one (Mark 3:29), and ultimately by those who live his message.

A second level of opposition to the kingdom proclamation of Jesus comes from within Jesus' own followers, and one incident found in all three Synoptic Gospels is paradigmatic. The middle section of Mark (8:27—10:52) recounts Jesus' journey to Jerusalem and is punctuated by three predictions of his suffering and death and three misunderstandings by the disciples. We noted above the bickering over power in Mark 9:33–37. This rhythm of prediction and denial culminates in the final more elaborate prediction of suffering and death that is ignored by James and John, who rather ask "Grant that in your glory [Matt 20:21, "in your kingdom"] we may sit one at your right and the other at your left," which makes the other ten disciples "indignant" (Mark 10:37, 41).

Jesus' response provides a digest of the meaning of power in God's kingdom. When the disciples are angry at the request of James and John to share in the power of Jesus, his response is pregnant with meaning. He states:

> You know that among the Gentiles those whom they recognize as their rulers lord it over them, and their great ones are tyrants over them. But it is not so among you; but whoever wishes to become great among you must be your servant, and whoever wishes to be first among you must be slave of all. For the Son of Man came not to be served but to serve, and to give his life a ransom for many. (Mark 10:42–45)

Virtually every word of Jesus is a diagnosis of the misuse of power: "recognized" rulers is a poor translation of the Greek, *hoi dokountes*; better would be "supposed" rulers, as used by Paul in Galatians in a derogatory sense (2:6), as their power is illusory; "among the Gentiles" suggests the history of Roman violence in Palestine; "great ones" (*megaloi*) echoes the "leading men" (*megistanes*) attending Herod's debauched banquet (Mark 6:20); the Greek original for their actions, "lord it over them," and "make their authority felt" both convey oppressive use of power. Jesus' response completely delegitimizes any similar use of such power by his disciples, where, rather, precedence will be the ironic status of servant and slave, and where he himself as a model of such service will give his life, so that people may be free or as a ransom for many. Desire for power and prestige and lording it over others are the driving forces of injustice in both civil society and in the Church.

DEATH OF A PROPHET

As prophet of God's reign, Jesus came to a violent end at an early age through one of the most horrible modes of execution in antiquity: crucifixion, used by the Romans primarily as a warning against any actual or perceived threat to their rule. He died between two *zelotai*, not simply thieves, but most likely "revolutionary bandits." The inscription on the cross, "Jesus of Nazareth, King of the Jews," is an ironic mockery of his kingdom proclamation and of his nonviolent life and action. While the events surrounding his death are complex, a century of historical research questions elements of the Gospel portrayals, principally that Jesus was executed because he claimed to be God and broke Jewish law. The most obvious counter to this view is that the Romans ordered and carried out his execution, and that stories of Jewish involvement, which nurtured the centuries-long charge of deicide against the Jews, emerged decades after his death.

Jon Sobrino has noted that we must distinguish two questions: (1) Why was Jesus killed?—a historical question, and (2) Why did Jesus die?—a theological question (*Jesus the Liberator*, 195). Let us consider some suggestions about the situations leading to the death of Jesus. Jesus was clearly associated with the mission and message of

John the Baptist, a preacher of reform, who castigated both Jerusalem leaders and the client king, Herod Antipas, who had him executed. Jesus was executed in Jerusalem, though he preached mainly in Galilee. In the Gospel of John, the ministry of Jesus involves at least three visits to Jerusalem and is clearly longer than one year. The Johannine chronology is gaining more acceptance, and crucial to this chronology, is that Jesus' action against the temple occurred earlier in his ministry rather than a week before his execution.

There are clear conflicts in the Gospels, but mainly these are with scribal and priestly groups associated with the Jerusalem temple; disputes with the Pharisees were often over points of law debated by different Jewish groups and the Pharisees play virtually no role in the passion narratives. Though the temple remained the center of the cycle of festivals, the center of sacrificial rites, and a pilgrimage site, the high priests were often hated and scorned. The position was hereditary and, when under Roman governance, owed its existence to careful cooperation with the Romans. The Jerusalem aristocracy (priests and scribes) constituted a wealthy class that often exploited the poor, and "devoured the houses of widows" (Mark 12:38–44). Even the poor among the local priests were victimized by the Jerusalem hierarchy. Josephus, himself from a priestly family who lauds the institution of the high priest, recounts that the high priests sent their servants to Galilee to collect tithes from the threshing floor, "with the result that the poorer priests starved to death" (Feldman, *Jewish Antiquities*, 20, §180).

The remark of Jesus that the children of a king would not pay taxes (Matt 17:24–26) would have sent shudders through the Jerusalem leadership, and his declarations of direct forgiveness of sin by God could have been seen as an attack on the sacrificial cult. His action in the temple recounted in all four Gospels, whether it was a criticism of the commercialism practices, or a prediction of its destruction (similar to the temple sermon of Jer 7) along with a following by large crowds, even in Jerusalem, would have fomented opposition by the Jerusalem leadership.

These elements coupled with the Roman prefect's (Pontius Pilate) constant fear of Jewish resistance movements lie at the decision to do away with Jesus. Jesus was not a political revolutionary in the modern sense, but he proposed an alternate vision of the realm and presence of

God that represented a threat to the existing society, its sociopolitical organization, and its religious justification.

Those today who look to the kingdom proclamation of Jesus and to his concern for the poor and marginalized, and who challenge the existing structures of power can expect persecution and opposition, and continue to pay with their lives as the examples mount: Sr. Dorothy Stang, who was helping indigenous farmers in Brazil to preserve and live off land, spoke out against criminal gangs working on behalf of ranchers who were after their land. On February 25, 2005, two killers hired by the ranchers approached her home and asked if she had any weapons. She claimed that the only weapon would be her Bible and proceeded to read a passage from the Beatitudes, "Blessed are the poor in spirit...," as they shot her multiple times. Other examples would be the lay and religious women, and the Jesuits murdered in El Salvador (1989); the recently beatified Fr. Jerzy Popieluszko, tortured and killed by the Polish secret police in 1984; along with senseless killings of priests, religious, and aid workers in parts of Africa because of their solidarity with or defense of marginal or suffering people. In the early Church, people were martyred because they would not deny their faith; today people are martyred because they are living their faith openly and courageously. Martyrs for the faith are now martyrs for justice.[4]

The ringing manifesto of Jesus as he begins his ministry, "the decisive moment (*kairos*) has arrived; God's reign (*basileia*) is at hand; change your way of thinking and place your trust in the Good News" (Mark 1:14–15, *au. trans.*) echoes throughout our world and, like the disturbing mustard bush, continues to gather people under its shadow.

RESOURCE BIBLIOGRAPHY

GENERAL STUDIES IN NEW TESTAMENT ETHICS

Brawley, Richard L. *Character Ethics and the New Testament: Moral Dimensions of Scripture*. Louisville, KY: Westminster John Knox Press, 2007: Sixteen essays by leaders in the field on: the Gospels,

---

4. Karl Rahner, "Dimensions of Martyrdom: A Plea for the Broadening of a Classical Concept," *Concilium* 163 (1983): 9.

ethics and Paul, forgiveness and reconciliation, and political issues and peacemaking.

Burridge, Richard A. *Imitating Jesus: An Inclusive Approach to New Testament Ethics.* Grand Rapids, MI: Eerdmans, 2007. An important work suggesting that the Gospels invite us to imitate and be transformed by the diverse words and deeds of Jesus, while other New Testament writings indicate various ways this occurred.

Harrington, Daniel, SJ, and James Keenan, SJ. *Jesus and Virtue Ethics: Building Bridges between New Testament Studies and Moral Theology.* Lanham, MD/Chicago, IL: Sheed and Ward, 2002. An important study by a New Testament scholar and moral theologian.

Hays, Richard B. *The Moral Vision of the New Testament: Community, Cross, New Creation: A Contemporary Introduction to New Testament Ethics.* San Francisco: HarperSanFrancisco, 1996. Attention to questions of methods for study of New Testament ethics, and organizing themes (community, and so on), with helpful application to important contemporary issues, for example, nonviolence, divorce and remarriage, and homosexuality.

Matera, Frank J. *The New Testament Ethics: The Legacies of Jesus and Paul.* Louisville, KY: Westminster John Knox Press, 1996. An excellent descriptive study that covers each book of the New Testament with a final synthetic chapter.

Schrage, Wolfgang. *The Ethics of the New Testament.* Philadelphia: Fortress Press, 1988. A comprehensive study that synthesizes the best New Testament scholarship. The section on Jesus (13–106) presents accurate exegesis of important texts, especially on the kingdom and the love command.

Verhey, Allen. *Remembering Jesus: Christian Community, Scripture and the Moral Life.* Grand Rapids, MI: Eerdmans, 2002. Verhey has been writing on the relation of Jesus to the moral life for two decades. Especially helpful is chapter 4, "Remembering Jesus in the World of Adam Smith."

LIFE AND TEACHING OF JESUS

Major Works

Crossan, J. Dominic. *The Historical Jesus: The Life of a Mediterranean Jewish Peasant.* San Francisco: HarperSanFrancisco, 1991. A massive (507 pages) reconstruction of the life of Jesus, with stress on the social implications of Jesus' teaching and actions. A more popular presentation is: *Jesus: A Revolutionary Biography*. San Francisco, HarperSanFrancisco, 1994.

Dunn, James D. G. *Jesus Remembered*. Grand Rapids, MI: Eerdmans, 2007. Dunn has been a decades-long leader in Jesus research, and this massive work is the fruit of his historical and theological research. See especially chapter 12: "The Kingdom of God."

Dunn, James D. G., and Scot McKnight. *The Historical Jesus in Recent Research*. Winona Lake, IN: Eisenbrauns, 2005. Extracts and comments on thirty-five important essays on the historical Jesus research, with preference for representatives of "the third quest."

Meier, John P. *A Marginal Jew: Rethinking the Historical Jesus*. Garden City: Doubleday, 1991—. Encyclopedic study of Jesus, four volumes thus far: vol. 1: *The Roots of the Problem and the Person*; vol. 2: *Mentor, Message and Miracles* (kingdom proclamation is treated here); vol. 3: *Companions and Competitors*; vol. 4: *Law and Love*. For an early statement of his views see "Jesus." *NJBC*, 1320–22.

Sanders, E. P. *Jesus and Judaism*. Philadelphia: Fortress Press, 1985. Sanders is especially sensitive to the Jewish background and context of Jesus' teaching, see especially 123–245. See also *The Historical Figure of Jesus*. New York: Penguin, 1993.

Schweitzer, Albert. *The Quest of the Historical Jesus: A Critical Study of Its Progress from Reimarus to Wrede*. Baltimore: Johns Hopkins University Press, 1998.

Wright, N. T. *Christian Origins and the Question of God*. Minneapolis: Fortress Press, 1992. Vol. 1: *The New Testament and the People of God*; vol. 2: *Jesus and the Victory of God* (extensive discussion of kingdom); vol. 3: *The Resurrection of the Son of God*. This work combines solid historical research with original theological insight. Wright has multiple shorter studies of Jesus, recommended are: *The Contemporary Quest for Jesus*. Minneapolis: Fortress Press, 2002, excerpted from *Jesus and the Victory of God* and *The Original Jesus: The Life and Vision of a Revolutionary*. Grand Rapids, MI: Eerdmans, 1996.

General Works

Blount, Brian K. *Go Preach! Mark's Kingdom Message and the Black Church Today.* Maryknoll, NY: Orbis Books, 1998. An original work that applies insights from Mark's Gospel to issues of social transformation in the black Church.

Borg, Marcus J. *Uncovering the Life, Teachings, and Relevance of a Religious Revolutionary.* New York: HarperCollins, 2006. Borg has been writing on Jesus for two decades and here presents him as a Jewish mystic whose healings and exorcisms manifest God's concern for the marginalized.

Bussmann, Claus. *Who Do You Say?: Jesus Christ in Latin American Liberation Theology.* Maryknoll, NY: Orbis Books, 1985. An excellent survey of the important contributions of liberation theologians to an interpretation of Jesus.

Charlesworth, James H. *The Historical Jesus: An Essential Guide.* Nashville, TN: Abingdon Press, 2008. A concise and very informative coverage of major issues.

Chilton, Bruce, and J. H. McDonald. *Jesus and the Ethics of the Kingdom.* Grand Rapids, MI: Eerdmans, 1987. An excellent synthetic treatment that unites kingdom and ethics.

Donahue, John R. *The Gospel in Parable: Metaphor, Narrative and Theology in the Synoptic Gospels.* Philadelphia: Fortress Press, 1988. Primarily treats the parables in the context of each Gospel.

Feldman, Louis B., trans. *Josephus: Jewish Antiquities*, Bk. 20. Loeb Classical Library 456. Cambridge: Harvard University Press, 1965. An essential work for understanding the background and context of the life of Jesus.

Fiorenza, Elisabeth Schüssler. *Jesus: Miriam's Child, Sophia's Prophet: Critical Issues in Feminist Christology.* New York: Continuum, 1994. A very important approach by a leading feminist theologian.

Fredriksen, Paula. *Jesus of Nazareth: King of the Jews: A Jewish Life and the Emergence of Christianity.* New York: Knopf, 1999. In opposition to some trends in Jesus research, Fredriksen stresses the Jewishness of Jesus and makes interesting suggestions on the reasons for his death.

Herzog, William R, II. *Jesus, Justice and the Reign of God: A Ministry of Liberation*. Louisville, KY: Westminster John Knox Press, 1999. An interpretation of Jesus from a liberationist perspective.

Horsley, Richard. *Jesus and the Powers: Conflict, Covenant, and the Hope of the Poor*. Minneapolis: Fortress Press, 2011. For Horsley, Jesus presents a socioeconomic vision that gives hope to the poor in contrast to the structures of power both of Rome and the priestly aristocracy.

————. *Jesus and the Spiral of Violence: Popular Resistance in Roman Palestine*. San Francisco: Harper and Row, 1987. Horsley locates Jesus' teaching among broad-based social unrest in the early first century. See especially chapters 6 and 7 on "Jesus and Nonviolent Social Revolution," and "The Kingdom of God and the Renewal of Israel."

Lohfink, Gerhard. *Jesus of Nazareth: What He Wanted, Who He Was*. Collegeville, MN: Liturgical Press, 2012. Based on solid scholarship, eminently readable, with stress on the proclamation of God's reign in the context of the hopes of Israel.

Lohfink, Norbert. "The Kingdom of God and the Economy in the Bible." *Communio* 13 (1986): 216–31. A short but very original examination of kingdom and its background, with continued reflection on how the kingdom evokes a "contrast society."

Mott, S. C. *Jesus and Social Ethics*. Grove Booklets on Ethics 55. Malden, MA: Institute for Christian Renewal, 1984. A strong criticism by an evangelical scholar of the view that, since Jesus founded no political system, his life and teaching cannot be invoked for systemic social justice concerns today.

Myers, Ched. *Binding the Strong Man: A Political Reading of Mark's Story of Jesus*. Maryknoll, NY: Orbis Books, 1988. A very influential study that argues that Mark's community engaged in passive resistance to both Roman power and to the violent strategy of the zealots.

Nolan, Albert. *Jesus Before Christianity*. Twenty-fifth anniversary edition. Maryknoll, NY: Orbis Books, 2001. A popular and influential study of Jesus with relevance to issues of justice and liberation.

Perrin, Norman. *Jesus and the Language of the Kingdom*. Philadelphia: Fortress Press, 1976. A fine study on kingdom in ancient Jewish literature and the teaching of Jesus.

Ringe, Sharon H. *Jesus, Liberation and the Biblical Jubilee.* Philadelphia: Fortress Press, 1985. An excellent study of the jubilee in biblical thought and how its images influence our understanding of Jesus' proclamation.

Sanders, E. P. *Jesus and Judaism.* Philadelphia: Fortress Press, 1985. A landmark study that locates Jesus within the life and practice of his contemporaries.

Sobrino, Jon. *Jesus the Liberator: A Historical-Theological View.* Maryknoll, NY: Orbis Books, 1993. An important and convincing study by a major liberation theologian who argues that Jesus lived and died in the service of God's kingdom.

Sölle, Dorothee, and Luise Schottroff. *Jesus of Nazareth.* Louisville, KY: Westminster John Knox Press, 2002. A powerful presentation by two leading German feminists.

Song, C. S. *Jesus and the Reign of God.* Minneapolis: Fortress Press, 1993. An important study by an Asian liberation theologian.

Theissen, Gerd, and A. Merz. *The Historical Jesus: A Comprehensive Guide.* Minneapolis: Fortress Press, 1998.

Thurston, Bonnie B. *Maverick Mark: The Untamed First Gospel.* Collegeville, MN: Liturgical Press, 2013. Readable and challenging essays on Mark, especially chapter 3, "Mark and Economic Justice," and chapter 4, "Brother Jesus: Asceticism and Its Implications for Mark."

Witherington, Ben, III. *The Jesus Quest: The Third Search for the Jew of Nazareth.* Downers Grove, IL: Intervarsity Press, 1995. The most comprehensive survey of recent "Jesus" books.

CHAPTER 8

THE GOSPEL OF MATTHEW AND THE LETTER OF JAMES

These two New Testament books, though very different, reflect a similar background. Matthew, the most "Jewish" of the Gospels in its language and content, is written in both conflict and dialogue with Jewish movements at the end of the first century for a community composed of a great number of recent converts from Judaism. Similarly, the Letter of James is directed at a Christian-Jewish community with a theology heavily influenced by the Hebrew Bible. They both stress that belief and discipleship should be translated into action on behalf of powerless and poor people.

THE GOSPEL OF MATTHEW

Alone among the Gospels, Matthew refers frequently to *dikaiosynē* (Heb. *tsedaqah*—"justice/righteousness"), 3:15; 5:6, 10, 20; 6:33; 21:32, 6:1 (mistranslated as "piety" in NRSV) and *krisis* (Heb. *mishpat*—"judgment/justice"), 12:18, 20; 23:23. Again the translation problem looms large. As noted earlier, "righteousness," however rightly understood by biblical scholars, involves unfortunate overtones of a stress on personal piety and propriety. Furthermore, Matthew is heir to the individualization of "justice," and most likely in conflict with a brand of Pharisaic Judaism that stressed fidelity to the law. Most commentators argue that by "righteousness," Matthew means living according to a norm or law, but for his community, it is the law as proclaimed and enacted by Jesus. Yet, such observance of the law as interpreted by Jesus (Matt 5:20), presupposes the gift of being in right relation to God

162

that is expressed in actions toward others. At the final great gathering of the nations, the Greek term used for those who ministered to suffering people is *dikaioi*, "just."[1]

Matthew uses "kingdom of heaven" thirty-two times and "kingdom of God" four times (12:28; 19:24; 21:31, 43), with virtually little difference in meaning. Margaret Hannan has summarized well the usages of *kingdom*:

> Not only is the content of the message of John the Baptist (3.2), Jesus (4.17), and the disciples (10.7) the proclamation of the imminent coming of the Kingdom of the Heavens, but as well, Matthew, in line with the traditional Jewish interpretation of the term, gives it a metaphorical and spatial characteristic by imaging it as a place to which people can gain entrance, refuse to enter, or place obstacles in the way of others entering (5.20; 7.13; 7.21; 18.3; 18.9; 19.23; 21.31; 23.13).
>
> God's Kingdom is also inherited (19.29; 25.34) or sought for (6.33). It is imaged as belonging to the poor, those persecuted for righteousness' sake and children (5.3, 10; 19.14). Scribes can be trained for it (13.52), and people can make themselves eunuchs for the sake of it (19.12). In parables, the Kingdom is compared to a vast variety of well-known household and agricultural objects, and human activities (13.24, 33, 44, 45, 47; 18.23, 20.1; 22.2; 25.1). Finally, Jesus, on the eve of his passion and death, looks forward in hope to once again sharing table fellowship with his disciples in the Kingdom of the Father (26.29 cf. 8.11). Not only is the content of the message of John the Baptist (3.2), Jesus (4.17), and the disciples (10.7) the proclamation of the imminent coming of the Kingdom of the Heavens, but as well, Matthew, in line with the traditional Jewish interpretation of the term, gives it a metaphorical and spatial characteristic by imaging it as a place to which people can gain entrance, refuse to enter, or place obstacles in the way

---

1. In treating Matthew, when alluding to the above texts, I will prefer *justice* to *righteousness* that is used by current translations, and translate *krisis* as "judgment."

of others entering (5.20; 7.13; 7.21; 18.3; 18.9; 19.23; 21.31; 23.13).

If Matthew formulates Jesus' message, as proclaiming the gospel of the Kingdom of heaven (4.23; 9.35; 24.14; cf. 13.19), it is because Matthew roots the community's subsequent proclamation of the Kingdom in what Jesus himself had taught (cf. 28.20). (*Nature and Demands*, ix–x)

Davies and Allison indicate how the juncture of kingdom and justice in Matthew 6:33, "Seek first God's Kingdom and his righteousness [justice]" epitomize the whole Gospel:

Probably the thought is that the kingdom, which has already begun to manifest itself in Jesus and the church, can be entered not only in the future but in the here and now, and since entering the kingdom is synonymous with salvation, one should make it one's overriding concern. On this reading, striving for the kingdom means in practice the same thing as striving for righteousness, for this last does not mean God's eschatological vindication of the saints or divine justice, but the conduct God requires to enter the kingdom. So to seek the kingdom is to seek righteousness, which is its precondition, and to seek righteousness is to seek the kingdom, to which it leads. (*Commentary*, 1, 102)

Echoes of covenant theology sound throughout Matthew, primarily as often noted in parallels between the story of Moses and Jesus. Like the Sinai covenant revealed to Moses, the Sermon on the Mount begins with fundamental pronouncements (Decalogue and Beatitudes), and continues with specific directives (the antitheses, 5:17–48). The characteristic gifts of the covenant renewal in Hosea 2:21—right, justice, love, mercy, and fidelity—reverberate throughout Matthew, and Jesus criticizes the scribes and Pharisees for neglecting the "weightier things of the law: judgment and mercy and fidelity" (Matt 23:23). The promise of Emmanuel, "God with us" that brackets the beginning and end of the Gospel (1:23; 28:20) recalls the covenant promise to Abraham ("I will establish my covenant as an everlasting covenant between me and you and your descendants after you for the generations to come, to be your God…" Gen 17:7). Jesus' final meal with his disciples seals a covenant by his blood (Matt 26:26–29), and continues the promise to Jeremiah of a new covenant ("So you will be my people, and I will be your God," Jer 30:22).

With these overviews in mind, we will now discuss Matthew's contribution to the quest for social justice by a dialogue with select passages: John the Baptist as the herald of justice; the Beatitudes (Matt 5:3–12); the mission of Jesus as the servant who will bring justice to the nations (12:15–21); the difficult parables of the laborers in the vineyard, and the sheep and the goats; the final grand scenario of the last judgment (25:31–46).

JOHN THE BAPTIST AS HERALD

The Synoptic Gospels all begin the public ministry of Jesus preceded by John the Baptist crying out in the wilderness: "prepare the way of the Lord" and inviting people to a baptism of repentance (Matt 3:1–6; Mark 1:2–6; Luke 3:1–6). However, Matthew and Luke draw on the sayings source ("Q") to add, immediately prior to the arrival and baptism of Jesus, John's attack on those ("brood of vipers") who invoke religious privilege ("we have Abraham as our ancestor") in place of true conversion (Matt 3:7–10; Luke 3:7–14). In recounting the baptism, only Matthew begins with the demur of John, "I need to be baptized by you, and do you come to me?" (3:14), which is followed by the first words of Jesus spoken in the Gospel: "Let it be so now; for it is proper for us in this way to fulfill all righteousness [justice]" (3:15), which anticipates a subsequent attack by Jesus in Jerusalem in the last week of his life on temple officials, "For John came to you in the way of righteousness [justice] and you did not believe him, but the tax collectors and the prostitutes believed him; and even after you saw it, you did not change your minds and believe him" (21:32)—which echoes Jesus' praise of John in Matthew 11:7–14, as "Elijah." The "way of justice" also evokes the choice of Abraham and the charge to his descendants: "to keep the way of the LORD by doing righteousness and justice" (Gen 18:19).

When Jesus fulfills all righteousness (justice) "he is fulfilling Scripture" which is embodied in "the saving activity of God" (Davies and

Allison, *Commentary*, 1:326–27), made manifest not only in the proclamation of the kingdom but "by justice which is concerned for the rights of the oppressed…those in most need of God's mercy or justice," "the poor and the dispossessed, and those starved of justice—lepers, blind men, women, the deaf, the dumb, the ritually unclean and those normally excluded from Temple worship" (Hannan, *Nature*, 231).

THE BEATITUDES

The Beatitudes inaugurate the Sermon on the Mount, the first of five great speeches of Jesus in Matthew. They are the Sermon on the Mount (chapters 5—7); the Sermon on Mission (chapter 10); the Sermon on Parables (chapter 13); the Sermon on the Church (chapter 18), and the Sermon on the End-Time (chapters 24—25). The Sermon on the Mount begins after a scenic summary by Matthew (4:23–25) of the healing work of Jesus and is immediately followed by a healing miracle (8:5–13), which signifies that the sermon is a collection of powerful and healing words, which follow from the experience of the healing power of the presence of Jesus where gift precedes demand and that the experience of grace and love is a precondition for discipleship. As the first of the blessings of Jesus, the Beatitudes form a great arch to the final blessings of Jesus, the last words of the final sermon of Jesus, the parable of the sheep and the goats (Matt 25:31–46). Here, there are two classes as in the Beatitudes, that is, people who are passive and suffer, and those who actively help people, who are called "the just" and are brothers and sisters of Jesus.

Their traditional title "Beatitudes" and the translation "blessed" are a bit confusing. In Greek, each verse begins with the term *makarios*, meaning "happy, joyful," usually in the sense of a privileged recipient of divine favor (Lat. *beatus*); related to but different from *eulogetos/omenos*, which means "blessed" (Lat. *benedictus*), which is most often used in praise of God (Luke 1:68; Rom 1:25; 9:5) or of a person "blessed" by God (Luke 1:28, 42; Matt 25:34). In the Old Testament, people are called "happy" because of a state that de facto exists: "Happy is the nation whose God is the LORD, the people whom he has chosen as his heritage" (Ps 33:12, cf. Ps 144:15), with an indirect exhortation to adopt a certain attitude (Pss 1:1; 32:1–2). Throughout these compact verses, we hear echoes of groups and attitudes of the Old Testament: the poor, mourners, the merciful, seekers after justice, and peacemakers. By calling the named groups "happy" or "blessed," Matthew reflects the initial psalm of the five books of psalms ("Happy are those who do not follow the council of the wicked," Ps 1:1). The Beatitudes are read with a certain irony that marginal and suffering people possess true happiness as a gift from God and convey an exhortation to adopt their attitudes. The Beatitudes are eschatological in promising ultimate happiness with God, but it is a joy that is inaugurated by the ministry of Jesus.

The Beatitudes (Matt 5:1–12) are based on sayings of Jesus in the Q source (that is, material that Matthew and Luke have in common but not found in Mark), and found parallel in Luke 6:20–26. Matthew gives them a particular stamp by careful poetic arrangement and through the addition of added sayings of Jesus. The initial four (vv. 3–6) all begin with letter *P* in Greek, and in each case, the people are passive. The second group of four (vv. 7–10) describe actions or active dispositions, and the fourth Beatitude in each group mentions "justice" (*dikaiosynē*); either thirsting for it, or being persecuted because of it, which anticipates a major motif of the whole sermon (see 5:20; 6:1; 6:33). The ninth (v. 11), directed not at the crowds but the disciples, indicates the cost of discipleship for those who pursue justice.

While discussion of each Beatitude is beyond the scope of this work, some brief observations may stimulate personal engagement and evoke reflection and criticism.

Happy are the poor in spirit, for God's reign is for your sake (5:3, au. trans.). As we have seen, the Old Testament, while showing God's concern for the poor, does not praise poverty itself. In taking over the Beatitudes from Q, and in contrast to Luke 6:20: "Blessed are you who are poor," Matthew stresses interior dispositions and attitudes rather than simply a sociological state. Yet the meaning of "poor in spirit" is ambiguous with various suggested meanings: (1) "lacking in spirit," cf. IQM 14:7; (2) voluntarily poor; and (3) humble, cf. Isaiah 66:2. Behind Matthew's praise of both the poor and the meek (v. 5) lies Isaiah 66:2, where the Lord speaks assuringly "to him who is poor and contrite of spirit." In that verse, Isaiah himself interprets the meaning of the poor who appeared earlier in his prophecy at 61:1. "The originally bare term stressed the humiliation of poverty. Matthew's addition emphasizes relying on God within the spirit, as opposed to depending on visible means of support such as wealth and the power it brings" (Gundry, *Matthew*, 67). Today poverty of spirit is used to suggest total openness to God, but the Matthean meaning suggests that one does not rely on wealth or power. In "A Meditation on the Two Standards" in his *Spiritual Exercises*, St. Ignatius speaks of the "standard of Satan," as "riches, honor, and pride." Matthew's Beatitudes embody the counter-standard of Christ. The opposite of the poor in spirit are the greedy. In our world today, if any solution to material poverty can be found, it must grow from those who are "poor in spirit," who do not place their hopes in wealth and power. When Matthew and Luke state that "the kingdom of God is yours," it should be understood not simply as a promise of future glory, but rather that the kingdom is "for you," that the practice and values of the kingdom as embodied and proclaimed by Jesus are for the sake of suffering people.

Happy are those who cry out in lament, for God is their comfort (5:4, *au. trans.*). This Beatitude is a paraphrase of Isaiah 61:1 (also paraphrased in Luke) to inaugurate Jesus' ministry:

> The spirit of the Lord GOD is upon me,
>   because the LORD has anointed me;
> he has sent me to bring good news to the oppressed,
>   to bind up the brokenhearted.

The chapter in this book on the psalms stressed the importance of lament in Old Testament theology as a form of protest against injustice (Pss 9—10; 12). The mourners in Matthew 5:4 are "those who grieve over the power of the wicked who oppress the just people" (BDAG, 795), and express a sense that the world is out of joint (Isa 33:9, "the land mourns and languishes," also Jer 4:23–28). Those who mourn and lament the suffering and injustice are the truth tellers in our society. The all too frequent memorial services after mass shootings at schools and colleges are a lament not only for the loss of innocent life but a judgment on the insanity of the U.S. gun culture.

The paradoxical joy of the mourners, communicated by a "divine passive" should be understood as "comforted by God" but also comforted by community support and protest. The term *comfort* (Gk. *paraklēthēsontai*) recalls the beginning of the "book of consolation," "Comfort, O, comfort my people, says your God" (Isa 40:1) and foreshadows the Johannine gift of the *paraklētos* (John 14:26, the comforter or advocate).

Happy are those whose strength is not violent, for they will truly own the land (5:5, au. trans.). Virtually every translation describes this group as "the meek" (*praeis*) where English nuances of the term create problems. Often it suggests a divinely sanctioned religion of weaklings (Nietzsche), and seems foreign, but is ultimately challenging to U.S. society today, consumed by a desire to be "number one," and that celebrates violence in all its forms. The original Greek, while translated as "gentle or kind," also suggests "not being overly impressed by a sense of one's own self-importance" (BDAG, 861). Moses is described as "by far the meekest man on the face of the earth" (Num 12:3 [NAB]), and Jesus to whom others should bring their burdens is "meek and humble of heart" (Matt 11:29 [NAB]) and as king he enters Jerusalem "meek" (Matt 21:5 [NAB]) riding on a donkey (not a war horse). Neither Moses, who led the people out of exile and through the wilderness, nor Jesus, who confronted the power of demons and stood up against false accusations, could be "weaklings."

This Beatitude echoes Psalm 37, which is a long acrostic (each section beginning with a letter of the Hebrew alphabet) and combines elements of a lament with teaching on wisdom. It grapples with the age-old and enduring enigma of the power of the evildoers, for example, "The wicked plot against the righteous [just], / and grind their teeth at them" (v. 12), and "The wicked draw the sword and bend their bows / to bring down the poor and needy, / to kill those who walk uprightly" (v. 14). The speaker in the psalm, attributed to David, counsels against resentment and anger, with the hope that the wicked will be destroyed and then multiple times offers hope: "those who wait for the LORD shall inherit the land" (v. 9); "But the meek [or poor] will possess the land, / will delight in great prosperity" (v. 11); "For those blessed by the LORD will possess the land" (v. 22); and near the conclusion of the psalm: "The righteous [just] will possess the land, / and live in it forever" (v. 29). The people who are given hope in the

Beatitudes are those in the psalm oppressed by the wicked. But they will inherit the land that no longer refers to the land of Israel but to the earth itself and to the lands where the Gospel will be spread not by violence but by biblical "meekness."

Happy are those starved and thirsting for justice, for they will receive food and drink (v. 6, *au. trans.*). Each of the quatrains ends with a "justice" Beatitude, and this simultaneously provides a culmination of the first four Beatitudes and a transition to the final, more active ones. "Hunger and thirst" are the two things that the people of the exodus suffer most when wandering in the wilderness (cf. Exod 16:3; 17:3; Ps 107:4–5) and are also used metaphorically of desire for God (Pss 42:2–3; 63:2; 107:4–9; 143:6). Here the blessed ones are not those who achieve justice but those who long for it. In this Beatitude converge the sufferings of the first three: the poor in spirit, the mourners, and the meek, who hunger for justice, and a right relationship with God and among humans. The "satisfaction" or answer to the hunger and thirst comes from God. This is not to encourage passivity, but to support faith in God who ultimately "makes right" the world with the cooperation of humans. Humanity is transformed by its hopes and hungers and those working for social justice are attuned to these.

Happy are all who bring saving help (the merciful) to others for they will also receive this in return (v. 7, *au. trans.*). "Mercy" (Gk. *eleos*), most often translates the Hebrew *chesed* ("steadfast love") and is closely related to compassion. It is one of the prime covenant qualities in Hosea 2:19–20 and appears as one of the prime attributes of God (Exod 20:6; 34:6: "a God merciful and gracious, / slow to anger, / and abounding in steadfast love and faithfulness"). To be "merciful" is to imitate God.

Matthew adds a distinctive understanding of mercy. When Jesus is criticized for eating with tax collectors and sinners, and when he defends his disciples against the charge of violating the Sabbath, he quotes Hosea 6:6, "I desire mercy and not sacrifice" (Matt 9:13; 12:7). Luke captures this meaning of mercy by stating that the Samaritan was the one who showed "mercy" to the half-dead man by the side of the road (10:37). Mercy is not simply a negative concept, that is, forgiving wrongdoing or forsaking punishment, but connotes sympathetic and faithful love translated into transforming action most often on behalf of the poor and vulnerable.

Happy are those whose hearts are centered on God, for their eyes will be open to the presence of God (v. 8, *au. trans.*). The traditional translation "clean or pure of heart," while often limited to sexual or ritual purity, rather reflects Ps 24:3–4:

> Who shall ascend the hill of the LORD?
>   And who shall stand in his holy place?
> Those who have clean hands and pure hearts,
>   who do not lift up their souls to what is false,
>   and do not swear deceitfully.

Happy in Matthew are those people of integrity who "do not life up their souls to what is false," and are not seduced by the idols of power and greed; they will "see God." One sense of seeing is certainly eschatological. Judaism and early Christianity hope that God, who in this world was invisible even to Moses, can be seen face-to-face in the eschaton. Catholic tradition describes this as the "beatific vision." However, there is another interpretation dating back to Martin Luther. At the end of Matthew, in the parabolic narrative of the sheep and the goats (25:31–46), which describes the enthronement of Jesus as Son of Man, the just are welcomed to his Father's kingdom because when Jesus was hungry, thirsty, a stranger, naked, or in prison, they cared for him. Three times they ask, "when was it that *we saw* you hungry and fed you?" and so on, and Jesus responds: "Truly just as you did it to one of the least of my brothers or sisters, you did it to me." The difference between the just and the unjust is that the former *saw* Jesus in the marginal and suffering and thus will see him in the glory of the Father's kingdom, while the unjust did not see Jesus in these people. The clean of heart are pronounced happy because they will be able to see Jesus hidden within suffering humanity and so among the just.

Happy are the peacemakers [or peace builders], for they will be called sons and daughters of God (v. 9, *au. trans.*). "Peacemaker" appears only here in the New Testament, but see Colossians 1:20 and James 3:18: "A harvest of justice is sown in peace for those who cultivate peace" (*au. trans.*). Peace (*shalōm*) is a foundational biblical concept. It suggests not simply absence of conflict but security as well as wholeness. In the Old Testament, the hoped for king will be "a prince of peace"

(Isa 9:6–7); a hymn to God's glory concludes "may the LORD bless his people with peace" (Ps 29:11), and a psalmist looks to God's salvation when "steadfast love and faithfulness will meet; / righteousness and peace will kiss each other" (Ps 85:10). The close connection between peace and justice found here and later in James is most vivid in Isaiah 32:16–17:

> Then justice will dwell in the wilderness,
>   and righteousness abide in the fruitful field.
> The effect of righteousness will be peace,
>   and the result of righteousness, quietness and trust forever.

The frequent greeting of "grace and peace" in the Pauline letters (for example, Rom 1:7; 1 Cor 1:3) is a symbol of the benefits of the messianic age, and in John, peace is the legacy of the departing Jesus (John 20:26). In *Pirke Abot* ("Sayings of the Fathers"), the oldest tractate in the *Mishnah*, in a saying attributed to Gamaliel we read: "On three things does the world stand: On justice, truth, and peace" (1:18).

The reward of peacemakers is that they will be "children of God," a term used of people chosen especially by God and by baptized Christians (Gal 3:26). Regrettably, the imaginary visitor from Mars, reading our Scriptures and hearing about our history, would be hardpressed to think that Jesus preached and lived peace and called his followers to be peacemakers. Christian history has more consistently lauded "war makers," for example, Crusaders, and the language of our hymns is replete with martial language. The connection between violence, war, and injustice is almost too obvious to mention. Every pope in the last sixty years has warned against the arms race and spelled out the horrible consequences of unjust aggression and violence. The Beatitude itself does not praise "pacifism" but "peacemaking." The preferred terminology today is "peacebuilding," which came into widespread use after 1992, when Boutros Boutros-Ghali, then United Nations Secretary-General, announced his "Agenda for Peace" that suggested a wide range of activities not so much to stop violence but to analyze its causes and move toward prevention. A wide array of public and private institutions has heard the call to be "peacemakers/ builders" even if they have no connection with the teaching of Jesus.

But the teaching of Jesus presents even more radical demands. The final antitheses that follow the Beatitudes counsel nonretaliation in face of evil (Matt 5:38–42) and state that those who love their enemies will be perfect and named sons and daughters of God (5:43–48). While Christian pacifism has always been chosen by a prophetic minority, the challenge of this section of the Sermon on the Mount is necessary for survival, as Ulrich Luz has noted: "It is not so important for the church that a minority of its members who are pacifists are dependent on the responsible politics of the churches, but that they themselves and Christian politicians for the sake of the Gospel are dependent for the sake of the gospel on Christian pacifists. Today's practice of the text must express this in a credible way" (*Matthew 1—7*, 282).

Happy are they who are persecuted because they work for justice, for you have entered the realm of God (v. 10, au. trans.). This Beatitude concludes the second set of four and is related to the blessing of the poor by the repetition of "theirs is the kingdom of heaven." It is also related to verse 6, the last Beatitude in the first set of four. While in verse 6, the "thirsting and hungering" is praised, here the active pursuit of justice is explicit. Justice or righteousness has the nuance of both personally "being right" with God and of "making right" the human condition.

Both this Beatitude addressed to the crowds and the very next Beatitude stress this and link the disciples with persecuted prophets (5:11). Following Jesus reflects persecution that the Matthean community experienced: they are to pray for persecutors (5:44); the missionaries will be persecuted from town to town (10:23); persecution on account of the Word causes the seed with little root to endure only a short time (13:21). In addition, both John the Baptist and Jesus suffer violent deaths, and Jesus is betrayed by a trusted follower (26:14–25) and his closest disciples run away during his suffering (26:56). Simon Peter, who first confessed him as Messiah, denies knowing him (26:74). Christians can expect to be betrayed by loved ones and to suffer external persecution (10:34–36; 24:9–10).

The Beatitudes present a series of dispositions and attitudes that make of Christianity a contrast society. They state a massive paradox, that those seemingly on the outside are the true heirs of the kingdom, and act as a shock to the values of the world. In the Gospel, Jesus embodies and enables the Beatitudes. Jesus is the "lowly one" (Matt

11:29; 21:5) and the merciful compassionate one, who brings saving help to others (Matt 9:13, 36; 12:7; 14:14; 15:32; 20:34; cf. 23:23), and in the passion especially, Jesus is the suffering just one (Matt 27:4, 19, 24). While stressing interior dispositions and extraordinary demands, they are not directed to a select few but to all who would be followers of Jesus, and to all who would seek the justice of the kingdom.

JESUS AS THE SERVANT WHO BRINGS JUSTICE TO THE NATIONS (MATT 12:15–21)

A well-known theological device of Matthew is the use of "fulfill-ment quotations" from the Old Testament that emphasize the continu-ity between the biblical tradition and events in the life of Jesus. Most appear in the infancy narratives (1:23; 2:5, 15, 17, 23) and at impor-tant moments in the life of Jesus (4:14; 8:17; 12:17; 13:14, 35; 21:4; 26:56; 27:9). From birth to death, the life of Jesus is a retelling of Old Testament narratives. Especially influential is the figure of the Suffering Servant from Isaiah (42:1–4; 49:1–6; 50:4–9; and 52:13—53:12). These Servant Songs (or poems) describe the Servant as the one God chose to "bring…justice to the nations" (42:1) and "to lead back the people of Israel" to God (49:5). But the Servant will also be "a light" so that other nations will recognize God's "saving power" (49:6). Unlike others in the Jewish Scriptures who are called the Lord's servant (for example, Abraham, Jacob, and Moses), the Servant in Isaiah suffers physical pain and humiliation (50:6; 52:14; 53:3–5, 7) in the work the Lord called him to do. The last of these songs, however, recognizes that the suffering of the Servant will help accomplish the work he was called to do. In other words, his own suffering will ultimately take away the sins and guilt of others (53:4, 5, 10, 11), and the Lord will reward the Servant for sacrificing his life for others (53:12).[2]

But only Matthew cites in 12:18–21 the full text of Isaiah 42:1–4 (though somewhat freely):

---

2. Joseph Blenkinsopp, *Opening the Sealed Book: Interpretation of the Book of Isaiah in Late Antiquity* (Grand Rapids, MI: Eerdmans, 2006), 251–52. See especially chapter 5, "Interpretations of Isaiah in Early Christianity with Special Reference to Matthew's Gospel."

When Jesus became aware of this, he departed. Many crowds followed him, and he cured all of them, and he ordered them not to make him known. This was to fulfill what had been spoken through the prophet Isaiah:
"Here is my servant, whom I have chosen,
  my beloved, with whom my soul is well pleased.
I will put my Spirit upon him,
  and he will proclaim justice to the Gentiles.
He will not wrangle or cry aloud,
  nor will anyone hear his voice in the streets.
He will not break a bruised reed
  or quench a smoldering wick
until he brings justice to victory.
  And in his name the Gentiles will hope."

(12:15–21)

This citation has been called "the hermeneutical key" for Matthew's entire Gospel (Keener, *Matthew*, 360), and many scholars link it to the earlier citation of Isaiah 53:4, in Matthew 8:16–17, where he "cured all the sick, to fulfill what had been said by Isaiah the prophet: 'He took away our infirmities and bore our diseases.'" An initial problem, as always, is the meaning of "justice" proclaimed by the spirit-inspired Servant as a description of his mission to the Gentiles. Usually the Greek translates the Hebrew *mishpat* by the word *krisis*, which, we have seen, suggests enacting a just decision. Contemporary authors then translate the term here as either "judgment" with a negative overtone of final judgment on the ungodly, or "justice" as salvific action of God, especially since in the Old Testament it appears in concert with other terms such as *justice* (*tsedaqah*), *mercy*, and *compassion* (Hos 2:21–23) and in contexts of delivering and defending suffering people (Isa 1:17, 21; Jer 22:3; Mic 6:8; Hos 6:6). Equally important is that, in the above text, the action of the Servant will be gentle and healing, rather than harsh and destructive. In another text central to Matthew's theology, the Pharisees will be indicted for neglecting "the weightier matters of the law: judgment and mercy and faith" (23:23). When the Servant brings justice to victory, the Gentiles (*ethnē*) will hope in his name, which foreshadows the mission of the disciples to make disciples of all nations (*ethnē*).

The larger context of this citation of Isaiah 42:1–4 is important. Between the discourse on mission (ch. 10) and before the parable discourse (ch. 13), Matthew 11 begins with Jesus' response to the question of John's disciples as to whether he is the one "who is to come." Jesus' response is a prelude to the following chapters, "Go and tell John what you hear and see: the blind regain their sight, the lame walk, the lepers are cleansed, the deaf hear, the dead are raised, and the poor have the good news proclaimed to them. And blessed is the one who takes no offense at me" (11:4–6). Service of the marginalized and opposition to Jesus are the key themes of Matthew 11 and 12. After praise of John and criticism of the crowds for rejecting John as possessed by a demon and of himself as a "glutton and a drunkard, a friend of tax collectors and sinners" (11:19), the chapters modulate between warnings against unbelieving cities, a call to the weary and burdened to find rest in Jesus, and further disputes about the healing activity of Jesus.

The mission of the Servant in 12:18–21 is thus a mission of justice in its fullest sense, concern for those who are suffering, but now the mission extends beyond the people of Israel as Jesus proclaims and will bring justice to the nations, which echoes Isaiah 51:4–6 where the justice of God will go out to the whole world. The Servant who will not break the bruised reed recalls the values of the Beatitudes and of 11:28–29 ("gentle and humble of heart"). The work of the Servant, understood here as saving help and liberating people from various infirmities, foreshadows the grand scenario of the final judgment in Matthew 25:31–46. We will consider this text in more detail, but for now, emphasize that those people who are called "just" (*dikaioi*) are precisely those who respond to people suffering from different forms of injustice. The mission of the Servant to "bring justice to victory" creates an arch that spans the activity of Jesus in Matthew, and culminates in the last words of the final discourse of Jesus in Matthew (25:31–46). Matthew's Jesus heralded as "God with us" is beloved Son and Servant who manifests God's justice to his followers and commissions his followers to proclaim this same message to all the nations (28:16–20).

THE PARABLE OF THE VINEYARD WORKERS (MATT 20:1–16)

Two attitudes vie for center stage in American life. One is a great sense of fairness and concern for equal rights (especially for individuals), for example, "equal pay for equal work"—"equal opportunity for all." The other is a concern for the underdog: a joy when the last become first; the small college upsetting a national power on an autumn afternoon; rooting against the Yankees in the "fall classic"; rags-to-riches success stories. Today's Gospel seems to challenge fairness at the expense of concern for the "last."

Though called the parable of the vineyard workers, the central character is the landowner who appears at the axial moments in the story and determines its shape. In a scene, not unlike the stirring images from *On the Waterfront*, day laborers are lined up waiting for work, most likely as the harvest season draws to a close. The landowner offers them the usual daily wage (a denarius), and happily they go off to work. Then a strange sequence unfolds. He goes out again at nine, noon, and three in the afternoon and hires more for a wage simply called "just." More surprisingly, he goes out near the end of the work day, finds straggling would-be workers and hires them with no stipulated salary. At this point, the parable is about a surprisingly generous landowner. Jesus' hearers might think of a bountiful God always ready to share his goodness.

The mood shifts dramatically when payment time comes. Not the owner but his foreman is told to distribute the wages, somewhat illogically, "beginning with the last and ending with the first" (the twelve-hour workers). This is an instance of the power of the parables to orient by disorienting. When the realism of the parable breaks down, the deeper meaning of the parable emerges. Those who had barely worked up a sweat receive a denarius, and we can almost hear the rest of the workers chatting approvingly in the hope of receiving more. Yet each received the same daily wage.

Their anticipated joy turned immediately to grumbling: "these last ones worked only one hour, and *you have made them equal to us* who have borne the day's burden and the scorching heat" (20:12;

177

emphasis mine). The generous and good landowner now seems to be both legalistic and arbitrary, saying that he did them "no injustice," and that he can do with his resources what he wants.

Does this parable summon us simply to stand in awe with Isaiah over the mysterious ways of God? The surprise of the parable is provocative today. Essential to its interpretation is that the order of strict justice is maintained; the grumbling workers received what they agreed upon. Justice provides the background against which goodness can appear as true goodness. The grumblers' complaint is not simply economic; they resent that others are treated equally. They are defining their personal worth in contrast to others; they are not so much angered by what happened to them, but instead are envious of the good fortune of others. They are so enclosed in their understanding of justice that it alone becomes the norm by which they relate to others, and want to order the world by their norms that limit the landowner's freedom and exclude startling generosity.

The final words of the owner unmask their deeper problem: "are you envious because I am good?" (20:15, lit. "is your eye evil because I am generous?"). In Matthew, "the eye is the lamp of the body" (6:22) that should be plucked out if it causes one to sin (5:29). The attitude of the grumbling servants distorts their view of the world. As ever with envy, an act of goodness and generosity to others blinds people to their own and others' good fortune.

The parable summons us to believe that God's justice played out in this world is not limited by human conceptions of strict mathematical judgment, where reward is in proportion to effort or merit. Mercy and goodness challenge us as they did the workers in the parable to move beyond justice, even though they do not exist at the expense of justice. The parable teaches that "equal treatment" is different from "treatment as equals" (the complaint of the grumbling workers). Much progress in social justice today has been made by attempts to assist different groups to achieve equality, even when it involves actions that transcend a narrow definition of justice, for example, affirmative action and compensatory justice (see Donahue, *Gospel in Parable*, 79–86).

But God's ways are not human ways. Categories of worth and value by which humans separate themselves from others are reversed in God's eyes. When divine freedom is limited by human conceptions of God's goodness, men and women may never be able to experience undeserved goodness. Not to rejoice in the benefits given others is to cut ourselves off from those benefits we have received. Our eyes too become evil.

THE PARABLE OF THE SHEEP AND THE GOATS (MATT 25:31–46)

Matthew's grand pageant of the last judgment has become the "gospel within the Gospel," for people dedicated to works of charity and justice for the multitudes today suffering hunger, thirst, horrible illness, and imprisonment. Most surprising in this parable is that Jesus is identified with such people and was unknown even to those who ministered to him. A "universalistic interpretation" has become commonplace and supported by a large number of scholars: anyone (Christian or non-Christian) who does such works of mercy to another person is doing them to Christ and will be rewarded by Christ.

Many recent commentators, however, are not at ease with the universalistic interpretation and prefer a "discipleship interpretation." This narrative concludes a long discourse *to disciples* telling them how they are to live during Jesus' absence (24:22—25:31), involving fidelity, watchfulness, and the proper use of God's gifts. When Jesus departs after the resurrection, he commissions his disciples as missionaries to the ends of the earth, baptizing in the name of the Father, Son, and Spirit and spreading his teaching, but always with the consciousness that he would be "with them" until the end of the age (Matt 28:16–20). The parable of the sheep and the goats takes place at the end of the age where we learn that Jesus was always "with them" among the least of his brothers and sisters. These least are called "brothers," a term that Matthew reserves for disciples of Jesus. In this reading of the parable, the Gentile nations will be judged on how they received Christian disciples, the least of Jesus' brothers and sisters who carry the presence of the absent Jesus.

Over the years, I have vacillated between these two interpretations but have come to favor the discipleship interpretation. The least of Jesus' brothers and sisters are disciples, who bear the same kinds of apostolic suffering that Paul speaks of: hunger, thirst, living as a stranger, nakedness, sickness, and imprisonment (1 Cor 4:8–13; 2 Cor 11:23–29). Paul sees these as signs that "power is made perfect in weakness…so that the power of Christ may dwell in me" (2 Cor 12:9). Apostolic sufferings hide the power and presence of Christ.

Matthew is not simply concerned about the reward and punishment of Gentiles (nations). Those Gentiles who ministered to Christ hidden in the missionaries are called "just" (*dikaioi*). The horizon of this narrative is apocalyptic. In apocalyptic thought, scenes of judgment disclose the transcendent values that should have been operative prior to the end of history. Creation narratives tell us what the world *should be* like; whereas visions of the end-time tell us what the world *should have been* like. Apocalyptic is a view of history and human life from God's side. The parable reveals that justice is constituted by acts of loving-kindness and mercy to those in need; the world will be made "right" or "just," when the way the least are treated becomes the norm of action. The sufferings of the followers of Jesus and the way they are treated reveals what justice should be, and those who practice such justice need not themselves be followers. What is done positively *for* Jesus' followers is not to be limited *to* them.

The sufferings born by the least of the brothers and sisters of the Son of Man summon the Church to be an authentic and faithful witness of the gospel. The Church cannot preach acts of loving-kindness to the hungry, the thirsty, the imprisoned, and the naked unless it, too, is a Church in mission that bears these same sufferings. No Gospel is harsher than Matthew regarding an ethic of words without deeds (7:15–23). Much Church leadership today suffers from a massive credibility gap, and the values that it proposes *to* the nations must be those that the Church itself witnesses *in the midst of* the nations (Donahue, *Gospel in Parable*, 109–25).

In recent decades, a river of words on injustice, dangers of wealth, care for immigrants, concern for the homeless, and a wide variety of human rights issues have flowed forth from powerful statements of Pope John Paul II, continued by Pope Benedict XVI and by local bishops' conferences, and Pope Francis is clearly committed to serving the poor and living a modest lifestyle. Still, "social justice" is often for external consumption rather than internal assimilation. Concern for social justice is a marginal qualification among most episcopal appointees, and one sad fallout of the recent scandals within the Church is the reduction of staff and offices dedicated to social justice issues. In spite of this, the understaffed agencies of bishops' conferences, priests, religious, and laypeople in all walks of life, often at the cost of their own lives, continue to seek "first the kingdom of God and God's justice" (Matt 6:33).

THE JEWISH-CHRISTIAN LETTER OF JAMES

Until recently, the Letter of James was the neglected child of biblical criticism, perhaps due to Martin Luther's description of it as "a right strawy epistle," since its emphasis that "faith of itself, if it does not have works, is dead" (2:17) seemed opposed to his fundamental vision of justification by faith alone. Contemporary scholars, however, call it one of "the most tantalizing of the New Testament writings" (Hartin, *Spirituality of Perfection*, 1). It is very Jewish in character and is written for "the twelve tribes in the dispersion," yet it is characterized by Hellenistic language and style. Though mentioning Jesus explicitly only in 1:1 and 2:1 and omitting any reference to the cross and resurrection, once negative comparisons with Paul are abandoned, its own richness can unfold (Johnson, *Letter*, 114). Though in form it is a "wisdom collection" of sayings often joined by catchwords or grouped thematically, it also contains prophetic denunciations reminiscent of Amos eight centuries earlier. There are almost as many diverse outlines of the letter as commentaries. Contemporary concern for issues of social justice and especially the option for the poor have given this letter new vitality today.

The letter echoes many of the sayings of Jesus, especially as found in the Gospel of Matthew. Matthean Beatitudes are echoed in statements such as "Did not God choose those who are poor in the world to be rich in faith and heirs of the kingdom that he promised to those who love him?" (2:5, cf. Matt 5:3); "For the judgment is merciless to one who has not shown mercy; mercy triumphs over judgment" (2:13, cf. Matt 5:7); and "the fruit of righteousness is sown in peace for those who cultivate peace" (3:18, cf. Matt 5:9). Just as Matthew stresses that belief should be expressed not in words alone (7:15–23), James offers a demanding and pragmatic spirituality: "be doers of the word and not hearers only, deluding yourselves" (1:22), which is followed by the definition of true religion as "to care for orphans and widows in their affliction and to keep oneself unstained by the world" (1:27).

In vivid language, James continues the Jewish heritage of concern for the poor and marginalized:

> My brothers, show no partiality as you adhere to the faith in our glorious Lord Jesus Christ.
>
> For if a man with gold rings on his fingers and in fine clothes comes into your assembly, and a poor person in shabby clothes also comes in, and you pay attention to the one wearing the fine clothes and say, "Sit here, please," while you say to the poor one, "Stand there," or "Sit at my feet," have you not made distinctions among yourselves and become judges with evil designs?
>
> Listen, my beloved brothers. Did not God choose those who are poor in the world to be rich in faith and heirs of the kingdom that he promised to those who love him?
>
> But you dishonored the poor person. Are not the rich oppressing you? And do they themselves not haul you off to court? Is it not they who blaspheme the noble name that was invoked over you? (2:1–6)

These verses are part of a larger section that rejects partiality or favoritism, initially on the basis of social and economic discrimination. The situation is conduct in an "assembly" (synagōgē), a generic term in the Jewish diaspora for places of worship and other gatherings. In light of verse 6, this assembly seems to have a judicial function, and the warning against favoritism reflects concerns in Leviticus 19 for the poor and marginalized, but especially Leviticus 19:15, "You shall not act dishonestly in rendering judgment. Show neither partiality to the weak nor deference to the mighty, but judge your fellow men justly," which is clear from the subsequent citation by James of the "royal law" of Scripture, "You shall love your neighbor as yourself" (Jas 2:8, cf. Lev 19:18). Other Old Testament texts strongly criticize judicial partiality especially toward the rich and powerful (Sir 7:6: "Seek not to become a judge / if you have not strength to root out crime, / Or you will show favor to the ruler / and mar your integrity" [cf. also Exod 23:2–6]).

Rabbinic writers continue strongly this strain of thought, often in language similar to James. A saying of R. Ishmael (second-generation Tannaite) is given:

> If before a judge two men appear for judgment, one rich and another poor, the judge should say to the rich man, "Either dress him in the same manner as he is dressed, or clothe him as you are clothed."[3]

This saying is also found in the Babylonian Talmud (*Shebu'oth* 31a), where a description of the clothing of the two men is given:

> How do we know that, if two come to court, one clothed in rags and the other in fine raiment worth a hundred manehs, they should say to him: "Either dress like him, or dress him like you"? (followed by a reference to Exod 23:7)

James likewise describes the difference between the rich and the poor in vivid images (2:1–13). Echoing the rich man of Luke 16:19, the symbols of wealth and power are named: gold rings on his finger, fine clothes, a warm welcome, and a reserved seat, while the poor man (*ptōchos*, lit. "beggar") walks in with shabby clothes (*rhypara*, lit. "filthy") and is told to sit on the floor. The evil here is not simply the risk of judicial partiality but the dishonor shown to the poor (v. 6), and similar to the situation we will see when looking at the abuse of the Lord's Supper in 1 Corinthians 11:17–22, where the action of the more prosperous community members humiliates the "have nots." James's response equates such conduct as blaspheming "the excellent name that was invoked over you" (that is, their baptism), and then recalls Jesus' own "preferential option for the poor" who were chosen to be rich in faith and contrasting them with the rich who oppress his "beloved brothers" through judicial actions (2:6–8, cf. 1 Cor 6:1–11). Having portrayed the situation of the poor man in shabby clothes,

---

3. *Deuteronomy Rabbah Shofetim* V, 6 on Deut 16:19.

James follows this section with an exhortation to clothe and feed the needy brother or sister, and ask what good is faith if one does not give others the necessities of the body (Jas 2:14–16). Judicial corruption in the small communities whom James addresses is repeated today as poor and marginal people do not receive equal justice, and one of the chief sources of injustice occurs when people of great wealth or self-serving ideology can pervert the systems of justice.

Near the end of the letter, James, after various exhortations about the wisdom from above that should guide the community and warnings about divisions within the community addresses "you rich" in the community:

> Come now, you rich people, weep and wail for the miseries that are coming to you. Your riches have rotted, and your clothes are moth-eaten. Your gold and silver have rusted, and their rust will be evidence against you, and it will eat your flesh like fire. You have laid up treasure for the last days. Listen! The wages of the laborers who mowed your fields, which you kept back by fraud, cry out, and the cries of the harvesters have reached the ears of the Lord of hosts. You have lived on the earth in luxury and in pleasure; you have fattened your hearts on a day of slaughter. You have condemned and murdered the righteous one, who does not resist you. (5:1–6)

This invective is resonant of attacks on the rich not only in the Old Testament prophets, but also in noncanonical Second Temple literature:

> Woe to you, rich, for you have trusted in your riches; and from your riches you will depart, for you have not remembered the Most High in the days of your riches. You have committed blasphemy and lawlessness, and you have been prepared for the day of bloodshed and the day of darkness and the day of great judgment. (1 Enoch 94:8–9)

> Woe to you sinners, for your riches make you appear to be righteous…woe to you, who devour the finest of wheat, and

drink wine, quaffing it from the pitcher, and tread down the lowly with your might…woe to you, mighty, who with might oppress the just; for the day of your destruction is coming. (*1 Enoch* 96:4–6, 8)

Though James may appear to echo sectarian resentment, his attack is consonant with a major theme of the letter—the opposition between the wisdom of God and human wisdom (3:13–15). In language similar to the Johannine suspicion of the "world" as a collection of forces aligned against God, James warns his brothers and sisters: "Do you not know that to be a lover of the world means enmity with God?" (4:4). This love is manifest in "bitter jealousy and selfish ambition in your hearts" (3:16) and coveting the possessions of others (4:2). The invective against the rich fits the immediate context of 4:11—5:6, called by Johnson (*Letter*) "examples of arrogance" (*alozeneia*, which in 1 John 2:16, is "pride in riches"). The evils of the rich are primarily depriving laborers of the just wages and of living in luxury, but they killed "the righteous one," who in this context is not Jesus but the suffering just one of Wisdom 2 and 5. Unjust wealth results in the "arrogance of power," which makes one "a lover of the world."

MANDATES FOR CHRISTIANS

Though not affirming a direct literary connection between the Gospel of Matthew and the Letter of James, both remain important resources for the theology and practice of justice today, mainly since both actualize elements of the heritage of the *Tanakh*—those Scriptures that gave identity to the people of Israel and continue to form consciences today. Jesus' final words in Matthew are to teach them (the nations) "to observe all that I have commanded you" (28:20), and James exhorts his communities: "Be doers of the word and not hearers only" (1:22)—both mandates for Christians of the twenty-first century.

RESOURCE BIBLIOGRAPHY

GOSPEL OF MATTHEW: REFERENCE COMMENTARIES

Davies, W. D., and Dale C. Allison. *A Critical and Exegetical Commentary on the Gospel According to Saint Matthew.* ICC. 3 vols. Edinburgh: T & T Clark, 1988–97. A superb resource for all aspects of Matthew.

Gundry, Robert H. *Matthew: A Commentary on His Literary and Theological Art.* Grand Rapids, MI: Eerdmans, 1982. Careful attention to and commentary on the texts.

Keener, Craig S. *The Gospel of Matthew: A Socio-Rhetorical Commentary.* Grand Rapids, MI: Eerdmans, 2009. A careful exposition with a massive list of secondary sources.

Luz, Ulrich. *Matthew 1—7: A Commentary.* Hermeneia. Minneapolis: Fortress Press, 2007; *Matthew 8—20: A Commentary.* Minneapolis: Fortress Press, 2001; *Matthew 21—28: A Commentary.* Minneapolis: Fortress Press, 2005. A thorough discussion of all aspects of the text in context with comments on the history and influence of particular passages and themes.

Nolland, John. *The Gospel of Matthew: A Commentary on the Greek Text.* Grand Rapids, MI: Eerdmans, 2005. A thorough study of the Gospel of Matthew.

FURTHER COMMENTARIES ON MATTHEW

Allison, Dale C., ed. *Matthew: A Shorter Commentary.* London: T & T Clark International, 2004. An abbreviated version of Davies and Allison (above).

Harrington, Daniel. *Matthew.* Sacra Pagina. Collegeville, MN: Liturgical Press, 1991. An excellent commentary ideal for the religious professional.

Meier, John P. *Matthew.* New Testament Message 3. Wilmington, DE: Glazier, 1980. A popular commentary on Matthew; insightful and readable.

Schweizer, Eduard. *The Good News According to Matthew.* Atlanta: John Knox, 1975. An excellent commentary with theological sensitivity.

Senior, Donald. *The Gospel of Matthew.* Interpreting Biblical Texts Series. Nashville: Abingdon, 1997.

Smith, Robert H. *Matthew*. Augsburg Commentary on the New Testament. Minneapolis: Augsburg, 1989. A readable and thorough popular commentary.

Witherup, Ronald D. *Matthew: God With Us: Spiritual Commentaries*. Hyde Park, NY: New City Press, 2000. One of the best commentaries available for priests and parishioners.

SELECTED WORKS ON MATTHEW

Aune, David E., ed. *The Gospel of Matthew in Current Study: Studies in Memory of William G. Thompson, S.J.* Grand Rapids, MI: Eerdmans, 2001. A fine collection of essays by major Matthean scholars.

Brown, Raymond E., and John Meier. *Antioch and Rome: New Testament Cradles of Catholic Christianity*. New York: Paulist, 1983. Situates Matthew in first-century Antioch.

Carter, Warren. *Matthew and Empire: Initial Explorations*. Harrisburg, PA: Trinity Press International, 2001. This work combines knowledge of the practices and ideology of the Roman Empire with a study of Matthew. It concludes "Matthew as a work of resistance to the Rome's empire *trains contemporary readers to be suspicious of the structures and actions of all ruling powers whether national, ethnic, political, economic, social, cultural or religious*" (173, emphasis in original).

Crosby, Michael. *House of Disciple: Church, Economics, and Justice in Matthew*. Maryknoll, NY: Orbis Books, 1988. An early study that addresses Matthew as a resource for reflection on social justice.

Donahue, John R., SJ. *The Gospel in Parable*. Minneapolis: Fortress Press, 1988.

Hamm, Dennis. *Building Our House on Rock: The Sermon on the Mount as Jesus' Vision for Our Lives: As Told by Matthew and Luke*. Frederick, MD: The Word Among Us Press, 2011.

Hannan, Margaret A. *The Nature and Demands of the Sovereign Rule of God in the Gospel of Matthew*. London/New York: T & T Clark, 2006.

Kealy, Sean P. *Matthew's Gospel and the History of Biblical Interpretation*. 2 vols. Lewiston, NY: Mellen Biblical Press, 1997. A comprehensive history of interpretation (*until 1996*) with helpful summaries of individual works.

Kingsbury, J. D. *Matthew as Story*. 2nd ed. Minneapolis: Fortress Press, 1988. A good literary reading of the Gospel.

————. *Matthew: Proclamation Commentaries*. Philadelphia: Fortress Press, 1977. An excellent presentation of Matthew's theology.

Levine, Amy Jill, ed. *A Feminist Companion to Matthew*. Sheffield: Sheffield Academic Press, 2001. Part of a series that covers virtually every book of the Bible with fine articles by leading scholars.

Love, Stuart. *Jesus and Marginal Women: The Gospel of Matthew in Social Scientific Perspective*. Eugene, OR: Cascade Books, 2009. Using social scientific methods and focusing on specific stories of women, Love offers a picture of social interactions and tensions in Matthew's community.

Luz, Ulrich. *Matthew in History: Interpretations, Influence, and Effects*. Minneapolis: Fortress Press, 1994. An excellent study of the impact of Matthew.

————. *The Theology of the Gospel of Matthew*. Cambridge: Cambridge University Press, 1995. One of the best short presentations of Matthew's theology.

Meier, John P. *The Vision of Matthew: Christ, Church and Morality in the First Gospel*. New York: Paulist, 1979. An excellent series of essays in commentary style.

Powell, Mark Alan. *God With Us: A Pastoral Theology of Matthew's Gospel*. Minneapolis: Fortress Press, 1995. This work approaches material not from the perspective of traditional "theological" categories, but from pastoral ones, for example, Mission, Stewardship, Social Justice.

Przybylski, Benno. *Righteousness in Matthew and His World of Thought*. SNTSMS 41. New York/Cambridge: Cambridge University Press, 1980. An academic study of the terminology and use of *righteousness* with stress on observance of norms.

Saldarini, Anthony. *Matthew's Christian-Jewish Community*. Chicago: University of Chicago Press, 1994. A scholarly and readable study, which provides a wealth of information on Matthew and Judaism.

Senior, D. *What Are They Saying About Matthew?* New York/Ramsey: Paulist Press, Rev. ed. 1996. An excellent survey of the recent state of scholarship on Matthew. Highly recommended for teachers.

Thompson, W. G. *Matthew's Story: Good News for Uncertain Times.* Mahwah, NJ: Paulist Press, 1989. A reading of Matthew for contemporary spirituality, with a special stress on the use of Matthew for prayer.

SELECTED WORKS ON THE BEATITUDES

Crosby, Michael H., OFM. *Spirituality of the Beatitudes: Matthew's Vision for a Church in an Unjust World.* Rev. ed. Maryknoll, NY: Orbis Books, 2005. This work deals explicitly with how the Beatitudes bear on issues of social justice.

Forest, James. *The Ladder of the Beatitudes.* Maryknoll: Orbis Books, 1999.

Green, H. Benedict. *Matthew: Poet of the Beatitudes.* Sheffield: Academic Press, 2001.

Hamm, Dennis. *The Beatitudes in Context: What Luke and Matthew Meant.* Collegeville, MN: Liturgical Press, 1990.

————. *Building Our House on Rock: The Sermon on The Mount as Jesus' Vision for Our Lives As Told By Matthew and Luke.* Frederick, MD: Word Among Us Press, 2011. An exposition of sermons based on solid exegesis with application to the contemporary world.

Stortz, Martha Ellen. *Blessed to Follow: The Beatitudes as a Compass for Discipleship.* Minneapolis: Augsburg Fortress Press, 2008. A creative journey through the Beatitudes.

THE LETTER OF JAMES: COMMENTARIES

Dibelius, Martin. *A Commentary on the Epistle of James.* Revised by Heinrich Greeven. Hermeneia. Philadelphia: Fortress Press, 1976.

Hartin, Patrick. *James.* Sacra Pagina. Collegeville, MN: Liturgical Press, 2003. A scholarly work with fine insight into a difficult letter.

Johnson, Luke T. *The Letter of James.* AB 37A. New York: Doubleday, 1995. Johnson locates James in its historical setting while explaining difficult passages.

Laws, Sophie. *A Commentary on the Epistle of James.* London: Adam & Charles Black, 1980. Very influential on subsequent work on James.

Wall, Robert. *Community of the Wise: The Letter of James*. The New Testament in Context. Valley Forge, PA: Trinity Press International. 1997.

SELECTED WORKS ON JAMES

Hartin, Patrick J. *A Spirituality of Perfection: Faith in Action in the Letter of James*. Collegeville, MN: Liturgical Press, 1999. A fine discussion of the setting and theology of James with insight on "perfection," and direction on the contribution of James to contemporary spirituality.

Johnson, Luke T. *Brother of Jesus, Friend of God*. Grand Rapids, MI: Eerdmans, 2004. Collected essays that identify James as the blood brother of Jesus and the letter written in Jerusalem before AD 69.

Maynard-Reid, Pedrito U. *Poverty and Wealth in James*. Maryknoll, NY: Orbis Books, 1987. One of few works addressed specifically to these issues.

Tamez, Elsa. *The Scandalous Message of James*. New York: Crossroad, 1990. A fresh and powerful reading "from the perspective of the oppressed."

CHAPTER 9

LUKE–ACTS

Guideposts for a Pilgrim Church

The two-volume work attributed to Luke comprises roughly one-fourth of the New Testament and has exerted immense influence on Christian life, art, and spirituality. The Christian imagination would be impoverished without *The Annunciation* of Fra Angelico; *The Nativity* by Giotto; *The Adoration of the Shepherds* by Caravaggio; Rembrandt's *The Return of the Prodigal*; and, early in the last century, the stunning *Annunciation* by the African American artist Henry Ossawa Tanner. For Christian and non-Christian alike, the parables of the Good Samaritan and the Prodigal Son have been icons of care and reconciliation within a family. Wonderful personalities rise up from Luke's pages: Mary, an unmarried teenage woman told that she would be a mother, hurrying to visit her older relative Elizabeth, who proclaims a canticle that has resounded in prayer and music through the centuries; a newborn child, who is laid in an animal's feeding trough and grows to be a prophet and brings good news to the poor and liberty to captives, while continuing the legacy of those other prophets who warned of the danger of wealth and the abuse of power.

The Gospel of Luke was crafted not only for Greek-speaking communities in the last decades of the first century but is especially relevant to the Church of the twenty-first century. The Second Vatican Council called the Church "the people of God" and spoke frequently of the "pilgrim church," a Church on a journey. The Gospel begins with a journey of Joseph and Mary of Nazareth to Bethlehem, and the distinctive themes center on a journey of Jesus to Jerusalem (Luke 9:31, *exodos*, translated as "departure"). Acts chronicles the spread of the gospel in an

191

ever-expanding journey of the early Church from Jerusalem to Rome, a foreshadowing of the universal mission of the Church. Luke's Jesus proclaims and lives a message that should shape the journeys of Christians today.

Only multiple volumes can capture the varied ways this Gospel speaks to us today, so we will limit our study to a schematic listing of major themes that bear on larger issues of social justice, and then focus on four ways in which Luke breaks down barriers within the human family: (1) the barrier of social location; (2) the barrier of religious hatred and division; (3) the barrier of rich and poor; and (4) the barrier of gender.

MAJOR THEMES OF LUKE

Jesus is more clearly a prophet in Luke than in any other Gospel; as such, he is a spirit-inspired person who speaks on behalf of God (*pro-phēmi*) and on behalf of those who have no one to speak for them (see 7:16, 39; 9:19). Before his birth, he is heralded "a light for the revelation of the Gentiles" or "nations" (*ethnōn*, 2:32; cf. Isa 42:6). His inaugural sermon is an overture to the major prophetic themes. Luke initiates the public ministry of Jesus as in Matthew and Mark with Jesus being led by the Spirit into the wilderness where he is tested by Satan, but only Luke notes that "full of the Spirit," he enters the wilderness, and "filled with the Spirit," he returns to Galilee to preach in the synagogue (4:16–30). Then linking his ministry with Israel's prophetic heritage, Jesus identifies himself as one anointed by the Spirit (4:18), followed by a mixed quotation of Isaiah 61:1 and 58:6 on the mission of the prophet, "to bring good news to the poor / ...to proclaim release to the captives, / and recovery of sight to the blind, / to let the oppressed go free [Isa 58:6], / to proclaim the year of the Lord's favor." In the Gospel, Jesus will fulfill this mission with good news to the poor (6:20, "blessed are the poor"; 7:22, "the poor have good news brought to them") by healing the blind (7:21–22; 18:35), release from sin, (same Greek term *aphesis*, often used for "forgiveness"), and liberating those oppressed by demons (Johnson, *Prophetic Jesus*, 79).

The narrative then continues where Jesus, having invoked Isaiah, and in response to the anger of the people at Nazareth that he has not done "things that we have heard you did at Capernaum" now cites Elijah and Elisha, who did mighty works to outsiders (non-Israelites). This anticipates the story of the Samaritan who embodies God's mercy (10:37) and another who gives praise to God (17:18), which precipitates the prophetic rejection that awaits Jesus since no prophet will be "killed away from Jerusalem" (13:33), and finally after his death the followers on the way to Emmaus see him as a prophet (24:19).

Luke–Acts is very much the Gospel of the Holy Spirit, with seventeen references in the Gospel, and fifty-seven in Acts, in contrast to six in Mark and seventeen in Matthew. Important moments in salvation history are characterized by the intervention of the Spirit (Luke 1:15; 1:35; 3:22; 4:1; 4:18). The Spirit is present at turning points in the life of Jesus: the Holy Spirit descends upon him at his baptism (3:22); "filled with the Holy Spirit he is led by the Spirit into the desert" (4:1); he returns to Galilee "by the power of the Spirit," and preaches his inaugural sermon at Nazareth (4:14–30); he promises the gift of the Spirit to his followers (12:12). Where Matthew speaks of the good things the heavenly Father gives to those who ask, Luke speaks of the Holy Spirit as the gift *par excellence* (11:13).

The presence of the Spirit is especially characteristic of Acts, which has been called "The Acts of the Holy Spirit." As in the life of Jesus, important movements in the spread of the Gospel arise from the presence of the Holy Spirit. Acts describes that first day of Pentecost as the fulfillment of the promise of Jesus that they will "receive power when the Holy Spirit comes upon you," so that they will become witnesses "in Jerusalem, and in all Judaea, and Samaria and to the ends of the earth" (Acts 1:8). In Acts, the Holy Spirit is the empowering and creative gift of God and moves the community outward in mission, breaking through geographical, religious, and social barriers.

The Spirit forms a Church that is inclusive. Gathered at Pentecost are not only the Twelve, but women who were most likely those who followed Jesus in Galilee (8:2–3), were present at his death (22:49), and received first the resurrection proclamation (24:8, Acts 1:12–14). Mary, who was not mentioned by name after Luke 1—2, is present, and all receive the gift of the Spirit, which provides an overture to the expanding mission of the Church as it moves centrifugally outward from Jerusalem. Filled with the Spirit, the disciples begin to witness the power of God, when, speaking their own language, they are understood by peoples representing the geographical boundaries of the known world (Acts 2:1–12). The coming of the Holy Spirit reverses the confusion of tongues at the tower of Babel in Genesis 11. When humans raise themselves up to God to "make a name for themselves," they are dispersed and confused in language. When God's Spirit comes down upon them, divisions are broken down. In Acts 10, after Peter is commanded in a vision to break through ritual food laws, the gift of the Holy Spirit is poured out on the Gentiles, and they are baptized into the community (10:45–48). Under the influence of the Spirit, the Church is exocentric, moving into new lands and breaking through old barriers—certainly a mandate for the contemporary Church.

BREAKING THE BARRIERS OF SOCIAL LOCATION

In chapter 7, we noted that "friend to tax collectors and sinners" was not only an early title of Jesus but it characterized his ministry. Luke adopts completely this tradition and enhances it. Only in Luke, tax collectors and sinners come to John to be baptized and seek his advice, "Teacher, what should we do?" And we hear John's answer, "Collect no more than the amount prescribed for you" (3:12–13), and later in the Gospel "all the people who heard this [Jesus' praise of John in 7:25–28], including the tax-collectors, acknowledged the justice of God, because they had been baptized with John's baptism" (7:29). Significant parables of Jesus are in response to his acceptance of tax collectors and sinners (15:1–32), and a tax collector is a model of prayer (18:8). Jesus summons Zacchaeus, a chief tax collector who is rich to abandon his perch in a tree, and is welcomed by Zacchaeus in his home while bystanders grumble: "he has gone to be the guest of one who is a sinner" (19:7). Hearing of Zacchaeus's conversion to give half his possessions to the poor and to make restitution for fraud, Jesus then says, "Today salvation has come to this house, because he too is a son of Abraham. For the Son of Man came to seek out and to save the lost" (19:9–10).[1] José Comblin

---

1. Alan Mitchell has argued that the actions of Zacchaeus giving possessions to the poor and restitution to those he defrauded, were done before his conversion. See "Zacchaeus Revisited: Luke 19:8 as a Defense," *Biblica* 71 (1990): 153–76.

has captured the foundation of Jesus' practice and its contrast to much contemporary Church activity: "the message of Jesus is the forgiveness of sins," while too often, "priests did not regard their mission as forgiving sin but preventing it" (*Called for Freedom*, 192).

SHOCKING THE BANQUET GUESTS

More than in any other Gospel, Luke portrays Jesus at meals, not only with tax collectors and sinners, as mentioned, but with a wide variety of groups, which are a setting for important teaching: Martha and Mary (10:38–42); a Pharisee (11:37–52); a Pharisee and other "guests of honor" (14:1–24); a Passover meal with disciples (22:14–38); and a postresurrection meal with travelers on the way to Emmaus (24:28–30). By this setting, Luke evokes the ancient literary convention of the symposium, where teachers instruct their followers. Important among these instructions is the banquet etiquette of Luke 14.

When invited by a Pharisee, Jesus warns the guests not to be ostentatious by seeking a privileged place lest they be humiliated by the host who sends them to a lower place, reminiscent of the advice of Sirach 32, but then Jesus offers shocking advice: "do not invite your friends or your brothers or your relatives or rich neighbors, in case they may invite you in return, and you would be repaid. But when you give a banquet, invite the poor, the crippled, the lame, and the blind" (14:12–13).

Jesus then underscores this advice by telling the parable of the great dinner. While based on the Q source, found also in Matthew 22:1–13 (the wedding feast), Luke retells it in keeping with his theological concerns (14:15–24). The original narrative is very similar: A host holds an important feast and invites important guests who refuse to attend. In Matthew, the host reacts by first slaughtering them and ordering the banquet hall filled with people gathered from the main road; in Luke, the angry host invites substitute guests and, when they do not fill the hall, has yet another invitation. Our focus is on the substitute guests who are the same people mentioned as part of the banquet etiquette.

An eschatological meal was part of the hope of Israel when all the nations gather and death will be "swallowed up" (Isa 25:6–8), and this hope appears in Luke (14:13 and 22:30) and other parts of the New

Testament (Matt 8:11–12; 1 Cor 11:26; Rev 19:7–9). The community at Qumran awaited a final holy war between good and evil that was to usher in an eschatological banquet (1QSa 2.11–22, the *Rule of the Community*). Among those not eligible to participate, neither in the full life of the community nor in the final meal, were "the lame, the blind, the crippled" (1QM 7:4–6, the *War Scroll*) or "the paralyzed, the lame, the blind or the deaf" (1QSa 2:6–10), people socially and religiously marginalized. Jesus shatters such boundaries in the banquet discourse of Luke 14, and the parable of the great dinner offers an image of the kind of meals the community itself will celebrate not only as it awaits the end-time, but also in their daily lives.

THE BARRIER OF RELIGIOUS HATRED AND DIVISION

One of the saddest aspects of recent history has been the rise of hatred and violence with ethnic and religious roots. It has brought suffering and tragedy almost equal to the devastation of the Second World War, and is the source of injustice in many other areas: education, employment, living conditions, health care, and political participation—to mention but a few. The Gospel of Luke contains three paradigmatic narratives that challenge Christians to view people who are "other" or "different" through a different lens.

The Samaritans (Luke 9:51–56)

"Samaria" is the name of the ancient capital of the Northern Kingdom (Israel), roughly forty-two miles north of Jerusalem and twenty-five miles east of the Mediterranean Sea, and also of the territory between Galilee and Judea. Tension between this region, which became part of Israel, and Judah (Judaea in New Testament times) is rooted in the division of the kingdom after the death of Solomon (922 BC). This tension, which broke out often into warfare and violence, was especially strong during the New Testament period, with Josephus, a first-century Jewish historian and the New Testament itself providing the principal evidence.

During the time of the Roman prefect Coponius (AD 6–9), when the Jews were celebrating the festival of unleavened bread, some

Samaritans scattered human bones in the temple, so polluting the temple that the sacrifices could not be offered (*Jewish Antiquities*, 18.2.2 §29–30). After a clash between Galileans and Samaritans, the Galileans elicit the help of Eleazar, the son of Dineus, a robber, and with his assistance plunder the villages of the Samaritans.

This hatred between Jew and Samaritan is reflected in the Gospels. In the Gospel of John, the Samaritan woman at the well says to Jesus, "how is that you a Jew, ask a drink of me, a woman of Samaria," and the Johannine editor notes, "Jews do not share things in common with Samaritans" (John 4:9). Later the opponents of Jesus in John say, "Are we not right in saying that you are a Samaritan and have a demon?" (8:48). Jew and Samaritan looked on each other as "the hated other," each of which was a threat to their respective religious and national identities.

As is well known, Luke organizes his Gospel around a great journey narrative where Jesus travels from Galilee in the North through Samaria to Jerusalem in the South (9:51—19:46). The journey is announced in a solemn manner that echoes the beginning of the Gospel: "And when it came to pass (cf. Luke 1:5, 8, 23), when the days were fulfilled for his taking up, he set his face toward Jerusalem" (9:51, *au. trans.*). The impending "taking up" of Jesus suggests both his crucifixion and ascension, so that the whole ensuing text contains a narrative theology of the meaning of these events. At the outset of the journey, Jesus dispatches his disciples to a "village of the Samaritans," but "the people would not receive him, because his face was set toward Jerusalem" (9:53), which typifies the mutual hostility between Jew and Samaritan. James and John ask Jesus if he wants them to call fire down from heaven and destroy them, but Jesus rebukes them (Gk. *epetimēsen*, 9:55), the same term used when he rebukes demons.

The desire of James and John reflects the Elijah narrative of 2 Kings 1:1–17. Elijah requests that fire come down to kill the messengers of Ahaziah, king of Samaria, who rejected the God of Israel by turning to Baal-zebub, the god of Ekron. Jesus' rebuke of the disciples' request to destroy the Samaritans who reject Jesus helps to show the kind of prophet Jesus will be and points to the arrival of a new era when God will act in a new way. The theme of reversal is also paramount since early in Luke 10 Jesus pronounces harsh judgments of destruction on the cities of Chorazain, Bethsaida, and Capernaum (vv. 13–15), "while here he apparently refuses to condemn the 'foreigners' or 'outcasts.'"[2]

The Samartian Who Stopped and Saved a Life (Luke 10:29–37)

The major Samaritan story of the Gospel is the ever-familiar and ever-challenging parable of the Good Samaritan (Luke 10:25–37). A lawyer tests Jesus about the requirements for eternal life. Jesus turns the question back on him and he, rightly, articulates the two great commands of the Jewish law, total love of God and love of neighbor as one's self (Lev 19:18; Deut 6:5). Not surprisingly, the lawyer has a follow-up question, and asks, "Who is my neighbor?" which elicits the parable. It does not answer the lawyer's question, but tells him what it is to be neighbor and subtly who is neighbor.

The story describes a man beaten, robbed, and left half dead on the road to Jericho. All identifying characteristics are gone; we don't know whether he is rich or poor, Jew or Samaritan. Three travelers were coming down the road. The first, a priest, arrived "by chance," saw him and walked past, as did the second, a Levite. The third traveler was a Samaritan. Given the intense hatred between Jews and Samaritans at the time of Jesus, Jesus' hearers may have expected the Samaritan to finish the man off. Yet the rhythm of "seeing" and "passing by" is broken by the explosive Greek verb *esplanchnisthē*, "moved with compassion." Only then does the Samaritan enter the world of the injured man with saving help. Luke combines "seeing" and "compassion" when Jesus sees and has compassion on the widow at Nain (7:13), and when the father welcomes home the returning prodigal son (15:20). Compassion is that divine quality that, when present in human beings, enables them to feel deeply the suffering of others, and move from the world of observer to the world of helper.

Like all parables, this story has multiple meanings. Most shocking in the parable is not that someone stopped. It would be a story of compassion if a Jewish layperson stopped. The parable forces us as readers to put together "good" and "Samaritan." The outsider provides the

---

2. G. K. Beale and D. A. Carson, eds. *Commentary on the New Testament Use of the Old Testament* (Grand Rapids, MI: Baker Academic, 2007), 315.

model of love of neighbor; the apostate fulfills the law. We might also put ourselves battered in the ditch and ask if we are ready to be helped by those whom we would class as outsiders. The parable forces us to ask who today teaches us and enacts for us the meaning of love of God and neighbor. The lawyer grudgingly answers, "the one who treated him with mercy." Mercy that was twice heralded by Mary as God's gift flowing from her "yes" to his call (Luke 1:50, 54) and is repeated in Zechariah's thankful blessing of God's love, is not simply forsaking punishment, but rather is active entry into the world of helpless and suffering people (1:78). In holding up a mirror to the life of the lawyer and to our lives, Jesus says then, "Go and do likewise" (10:37).

This parable challenges a major source of conflict and hatred. In her evocative study of the way in which the Bible has undergirded violence and hatred, Regina Schwartz argues that "through the dissemination of the Bible in Western culture, its narratives have become the foundation of ethnic, religious, and national identity as defined negatively over against others."[3] This parable challenges such identification. The paradigmatic "other," the hated Samaritan, appears as the neighbor who saves the person in the ditch. The admission by the lawyer that the Samaritan does mercy is also a veiled allusion to Hosea 6:6: "I desire mercy and not sacrifice," which is doubly ironic since the Samaritans did not recognize the authority of the prophets, but only of the Torah of Moses, and yet the outsider fulfills the deepest meaning of the Jewish Scriptures. The "other" teaches us what it means to love God and neighbor.

A Samaritan Leper Praises God (Luke 17:11–19)

Just as the parable of the Good Samaritan occurs during the initial stages of Jesus' journey to Jerusalem, the healing of the ten lepers occurs at the beginning of the third and final phase of this journey (17:11a; see 9:51; 13:22). Though showing traces of the traditional form of miracle story (for example, the request for healing; healing by powerful word; the demonstrative sign, that is, showing oneself to the priest; the simple mention of healing), the Lukan focus is clearly on the second part of the narrative, the actions of the Samaritan in verses 15–18.

---

3. Regina Schwartz, *The Curse of Cain: The Violent Legacy of Monotheism* (Chicago: University of Chicago Press, 1997), x (from the preface).

Here, for the first time, it is mentioned that one of those healed was a Samaritan, even though the reader has been alerted by the introductory verse that Jesus is on the border of Samaria. Suspense builds in verses 15–16, especially in the Greek word order: one of those who has been healed returns; he is "glorifying God [*doxazōn*] in a loud voice;" (*au. trans.*), and in a gesture of worship, he falls with face bowed at the feet of Jesus; only then is it stated: "And he was a Samaritan." As in the parable of the Good Samaritan, where the Samaritan is the third to pass by, the suspense builds to highlight the presence of the Samaritan. The major thrust of the narrative then unfolds in the pronouncements of Jesus in verses 17–18: "Were not ten made clean? But the other nine, where are they? Was none found to return and give glory [*doxan*] to God except this foreigner (*allogenēs*)." The postponement of the reference to "this foreigner" to the final words of Jesus is similar in structure to the word order of verses 15–16 so that the reference to the Samaritan again stands out. Jesus' final words of the story are a praise of the faith of the Samaritan.

Throughout Luke's Gospel, "glorifying God" is a fundamental response to the presence of God in the actions of Jesus (for example, angels and shepherds at birth, 2:14, 20; crowds at the entry to Jerusalem, 19:38; and the centurion at the cross, 23:47). In these significant places, those who give such glory are people on the margin of Jesus' society. Shepherds (along with tax collectors) are listed among those whose occupations no observant Jew should pursue. Samaritans, as we noted, were hated and suspect, and a leper who was a Samaritan was doubly scorned, both for his disease and for his religious and ethnic identity. A Gentile centurion is *allogenēs*, like the Samaritan leper, as well as a representative of an occupying power.

The actions of the Samaritan in the parable and of the Samaritan leper also comprise two religious attitudes that are fundamental to both Judaism and the teaching of Jesus. At the time of Jesus, Jewish teachers defined the two fundamental obligations as worship of God (*eusebeia* or *dikaiosynē*) and love of neighbor (*philanthropia*). Worship of God was shown especially through offering praise and glory to God. The Samaritan leper who twice gives glory to God embodies the first of these fundamental dispositions, while the Good Samaritan is a model of love of neighbor. Luke forcefully says that those who are called enemy and scorned as outsiders are fulfilling fundamental religious attitudes expected of both Jews and all followers of Jesus.

One lasting value of the Samaritan stories of the New Testament is that they continually challenge the tendency to dehumanize people by classifying them as enemies. They offer alternate images and a different way of thinking about people who are not only different, and with whom one may share a common history and heritage, but who have grown apart for religious, social, and ethnic reasons.

In an important study on the images of the enemy, sociologists Robert W. Rieber and Robert J. Kelly have analyzed those qualities that people attribute to enemies and that become the presupposition of violent action toward them. They write:

> From a religious point of view, the enemy becomes nothing less than evil incarnate, a "fake person," an impostor, a malefactor pretending to be human. In more general terms, the enemy may be characterized as racially, linguistically, ethnically, or physically different; but the difference is held to be both fundamental and noxious.[4]

In the still relevant novel *All Quiet on the Western Front*, Erich Maria Remarque captures the tragedy of not seeing the enemy as a fellow human.[5] Originally published in 1929, Remarque's book was burned by the Nazis in 1933 because it countered the heroic view of war proclaimed by the regime. The novel, and later the film, portrays a rabidly nationalistic teacher, Kantorek, in Germany, prior to the First World War, stirring up hatred of the French among his teenage charges and exhorting them to join in the combat. As the story unfolds, the horror of trench warfare overwhelms these boys never to be men. In a particularly haunting scene, one of the young Germans kills a French soldier who jumps into his trench. He then reflects:

---

4. Robert W. Rieber and Robert J. Kelly, "Shadow and Substance: Images of the Enemy," in *The Psychology of War and Peace: The Image of the Enemy*, ed. Robert W. Rieber (New York and London: Plenum, 1991), 15.

5. Erich Maria Remarque, *All Quiet on the Western Front* (Boston: Little, Brown and Company, 1966), 159–60. See also John R. Donahue, "Love of Enemies in an Age of Hatred," *Seattle Theology and Ministry Review* 4 (2004): 68–79.

Comrade, I did not want to kill you. If you jumped in here again, I would not do it, or you would be sensible too. But you were only an idea to me before, an abstraction that lived in my mind and called forth the appropriate response. It was the abstraction that I stabbed. But now for the first time I see that you are a man like me. I thought of your hand-grenades, of your bayonet, of your rifle; now I see your wife and your face and our fellowship. Forgive me comrade. We always see it too late. Why do they never tell us that you are poor devils like us, that your mothers are just as anxious as ours and that we have the same fear of dying and the same agony—Forgive me comrade; how could you be my enemy?[6]

The question facing the Christian churches today is whether they can plant the alternate vision offered by the New Testament into the minds and imaginations of people and thus confront the violence and hatred that cause such injustice. Can we see the enemy or "the other" as a fellow human being like ourselves before we pray, "Forgive me comrade; we always see it too late"?

THE GOOD NEWS OF PEACE:
AN ALTERNATE VISION

A horrid fact of history is that since the rise of historical criticism of the Bible in the nineteenth century, humanity has witnessed the most destructive wars in human history with hundreds of millions of innocent victims whose numbers mount every day. Yet one of the most familiar biblical phrases quoted in world literature is "on earth peace among those whom he favors."[7] Along with the Matthean Beatitudes and the sayings of Jesus on the rejection of violent responses to evil, the Gospel of Luke provides the best resource for the message of peace.

---

6. Ibid., 75.

7. The older King James Version of Luke 2:14 captures well the original Greek, "on earth, peace, good will toward men." The most inaccurate translation is in the *Order of the Mass*, imposed on the Catholic Church in 2011, "and on earth peace to people of good will," which is a mistranslation of both the Greek and Latin since it suggests that the gift of peace is limited to those of good will, while in the original languages peace is a result of the favor or good will of God.

Chapter 10 of the Acts of the Apostles has been described as the "Pentecost of the Gentiles," since it recounts the conversion and gift of the Spirit to Cornelius as the opening scene of the dramatic spread of the gospel to the Gentile world. Prior to the baptism of Cornelius, Luke recounts a speech of Peter that incorporates much of the missionary theology of the early community. Peter begins by describing God as the one "who does not show favoritism, but accepts those from every nation who fear him and do what is right" (10:34), and then goes on to give a kerygmatic summary of the life of Jesus (10:37–43), in a manner similar to other places in Acts (for example, 3:12–16; 5:30–32). However, here the summary is introduced by an even shorter epitome (10:36): "You know the word which he sent to Israel, preaching the good news of peace [*euangelizomenos eirēnēn*] through Jesus Christ." The subsequent narration of the life, death, and resurrection of Jesus are thus called the good news of peace. Though this peace is removal of hostility between the idolatrous Gentiles and the God of Jesus Christ, in the Gospel, Jesus is also the herald of a peace that breaks through human enmity and violence.

In biblical thought, peace (*shalōm*) is not simply the absence of conflict and the presence of concord or security, but also well-being, a full and whole life manifest in the blessings of God, fertility of the land, and joy in community. In his own language of peace, Luke reflects the different shades of meaning. In the infancy narratives, peace is virtually identified with that salvation that is to characterize the new age (1:79; 2:14); and it will characterize the new age inaugurated by the resurrection (24:36). The seemingly ritualized dismissals by Jesus of those healed: "Go in peace, your faith has saved you" (7:50; 8:48), combine the religious emphasis on the presence of God's saving power and the return of well-being with the normal biblical wish for a safe journey. Luke shows understandings of peace in less religious contexts such as security from theft (11:21), the averting of war (14:32; Acts 12:20), the respite from persecution (Acts 9:31), the reconciliation of clashing parties (Acts 7:26), and the resolution of conflicts within the Christian community (Acts 15:33). Luke's language of peace is located at those places that are structurally and dynamically important to the Gospel, where it is "in motion" and where barriers are broken down, be it the barrier between God and creation erected by sin or between peoples themselves. Structurally, Luke seems to say that peace is part of the Christian mission, which is involved in breaking down barriers.

Significant and even problematic statements on peace occur in Luke in a long discourse of Jesus on the demands of discipleship in preparation for the coming, in this case, the return of the Lord. The disciple is to forsake reliance on material wealth (12:1–21) and is not to be anxious or fearful, but to have trust in God (12:22–34). However, reliance on God is not to spawn passivity but rather a posture of active waiting, since the present is a time when much will be demanded (12:35–48). Jesus then speaks of his own purpose in coming: "I have a baptism with which to be baptized; and what stress I am under until it is completed! Do you think that I have come to give peace on earth? No, I tell you, but rather division" (12:50–51). The Matthean form of Luke 12:51 is perhaps more familiar, "I have come not to bring peace, but the sword" (Matt 10:34). At first glance, this saying harmonizes poorly with the mission command of Jesus in Luke 10:5, "Into whatever house you enter, first say, 'Peace to this household.'" Are we to assume that the disciples are to be bearers of the message of peace, while Jesus will bring the sword? Luke's alteration of the sword to division represents an attempt to obviate a violent interpretation of the saying, perhaps to disassociate Jesus and his followers from militant messianic movements like the later Zealots.

The most common line of interpretation is to take "sword" or "division" as alluding to the crisis brought on by the demands of the kingdom most vividly expressed by those sayings of Jesus which speak of division between family and loved ones (Luke 12:52–53; Matt 10:35–36; cf. Mark 10:29 and Luke 14:26: "If anyone comes to me and does not hate his own father and mother"). The saying immediately preceding (12:49–50) suggests that the kind of suffering Jesus will expect of his disciples is present in his own mission, since he has a baptism he must undergo. To this interpretation I would suggest another that builds on it. When Jesus says that he is not coming to bring peace, we hear echoes of Jeremiah's attack on pseudo-prophets who proclaim the hollow peace of a security built on injustice: "Everyone is greedy for unjust gain; / and from prophet to priest / every one deals falsely… / saying, 'peace, peace;' / when there is no peace" (Jer 6:13–14; see 8:11). Also the messianic expectations of Jesus' time were varied. The Messiah was to inaugurate a reign of peace, but this would involve the exclusion of the sinner from the holy community and the expulsion of the foreigner from the land, often by armed conflict in the name of the Lord. Jesus associates with the sinners, receives the centurion, praises the Samaritan, and rejects the way of violence. Paradoxically, his course of action brought violence, first to himself and then to his followers who suffer divisions within the family and often the kind of martyrdom he suffered (for example, Stephen in Acts 7:54). The Lukan Jesus is the true prophet who rejects false peace and that peace that can be achieved only through sectarian violence.

GOOD NEWS FOR THE POOR

No New Testament writing deals more extensively with the dangers of wealth, the proper use of possessions, and concern for the poor than Luke–Acts. As the Christian churches today become more aware of the immense gap between rich and poor, and massive manipulation of economic practices and structures to benefit a small minority of the super wealthy, the Gospel of Luke seems ever more topical and its message ever more urgent. Even a cursory survey of Lukan special material or of Luke's editing of the tradition shows the extent of the concern.

The infancy narratives show a special concern for the *anawim*—people without money and power. In her Magnificat, Mary praises a God who puts down the mighty from their thrones, fills the hungry with good things, and sends the rich away empty (1:52–53). The sacrifice offered at the presentation is that determined by law for poor people (2:24).

Luke adds to the Q tradition about John's preaching an exhortation that the one who has two coats or food should share with those who have none (3:10).

Luke begins the public ministry of Jesus not with the proclamation of the imminence of the kingdom (cf. Mark 1:15; Matt 4:17), but with Jesus citing Isaiah 61:1–2: "the good news to the poor" (Luke 4:17–19; cf. 7:22).

Only in Luke does Levi leave everything when he follows
  Jesus (5:28; cf. Mark 2:14; Matt 9:9).
In Luke it is simply "the poor" who are blessed, and Luke
  adds woes against the rich and powerful (6:20, 24–26).
Only Luke contains the parable of the rich fool (12:13–21) as
  well as the parable of the rich man and Lazarus
  (16:19–31).
Upon his conversion, Zacchaeus is willing to give half his
  goods to the poor (19:8).
Luke presents Jesus in the form of an Old Testament prophet
  who takes the side of the widow (7:11–17; 18:1–8), the
  stranger in the land (10:29–37; 17:16), and those on
  the margin of society (14:12–13, 21).
The early Christian community is one that shares its goods in
  common and where there is no needy person (Acts
  2:41–47; 4:32–37). Having things "in common" suggests also the Greco-Roman understanding of friendship.
In both the Gospel and Acts, almsgiving is stressed (Luke
  11:41; 12:33; 19:8; Acts 10:2, 4, 31; 24:17).
In Acts, Paul concludes his final address to the Ephesians
  with comments about the use of goods and the concern
  for the poor (20:32–35).

The recent awareness of the importance of these texts and of their
roots in the Old Testament has not solved all the connected issues. Basic
is the question, "Who are the poor?" Are they the economic poor, or is
poverty a metaphor for powerlessness and vulnerability? Why are the
poor called "blessed"? Is it because they are not blinded by wealth and
hence are open to God, or because they are to be the beneficiaries of the
kingdom as proclaimed by Jesus, which will reverse the structures of
poverty and oppression? Is the community addressed by Luke composed
mainly of the poor who are to be heartened by the message of Jesus, or
of relatively well-off people who are to be confronted by it? Does Luke
urge common possession, dispossession, or almsgiving as the most fundamental Christian posture toward wealth? (Luke Johnson presents
strong arguments that Luke–Acts recommends almsgiving as a sign of
Christian discipleship in *Prophetic Jesus* and *Sharing Possessions*).

Answering such questions is beyond the scope of the present reflection, but let us highlight some guidelines from Luke's Gospel, by focusing first on the parable of the rich fool, the directives on banquets, and the story of the rich man and Lazarus.

THE PARABLE OF THE RICH FOOL (LUKE 12:13–21)

This short parable is found only in Luke and appears in the context of a long sermon (12:1—13:9) by Jesus "to his disciples" (12:1, 22, 41) and to the multitude (12:1, 13, 54; 13:6). Much of the Q material found in Matthew's Sermon on the Mount and omitted from Luke's Sermon on the Plain is given here. This parable of the rich fool (12:13–21), which is sandwiched between groups of sayings to the disciples on trust and fearless confession (12:2–12, 22–31), is introduced by a question from the multitude. If the disciples are symbolic of those who have responded and followed Jesus, and the multitudes are those who are still being summoned to respond, then this parable has relevance for both groups. It will address both the conditions and consequences of discipleship.

Though this parable is introduced by a request from one of the multitude for Jesus to settle the question of a disputed inheritance (12:13), similar to the parable of the Good Samaritan, it does not really respond to this request but speaks of the deeper issue involved. The request is arrogant since the questioner asks Jesus to decide in his favor so Jesus responds somewhat harshly, "Who made me judge or divider over you?" and then underscores the real issue: "Beware of greed for a human life does not consist in the abundance of possessions" (12:14–15, *au. trans.*).

The phrasing of verse 15 is significant. "Covetousness" (*pleonexia*, lit. "the desire for more"), also translated as "avarice" or "greed," is one of the vices most scorned by Hellenistic moralists. They call it "the metropolis of all evil deeds" (Diodorus Siculus) or "the greatest source of evil" (Dio Chrysostom, examples taken from BDAG, 667). *Greed* appears in early Christian "vice lists" (Rom 1:29; *1 Clement* 35:5). In Colossians 3:5, it is equated with *idolatry*, which Romans 1:24–25 describes as serving "the creature rather than the Creator." Other places convey a similar judgment even when not using the technical terms *greed* or *avarice*. Desire of wealth chokes the growth of the seed in all interpretations of the parable of the sower (Luke 8:14; Mark 4:19; Matt 13:22), and deacons and bishops are warned against being "greedy for sordid gain" (*aischrokerdeis*, 1 Tim 3:8; Titus 1:7). Greed is a vice that turns its possessor away from both God and neighbor.

While the first half of the introductory verse is a warning, the second is a maxim: human life does not consist in an "abundance" of possessions (*en perisseuein*). The Greek literally means "in what is more than enough," with pejorative overtones, since moderation and having nothing in excess (*mēden agan*) was prized in the Hellenistic world. It is not the mere possession of material goods that will spell the downfall of the rich man, but his constant desire for more that leads to surplus possession, which today we might call "conspicuous consumption."

As often in Luke, the following parable illustrates the saying. The protagonist is rich (Gk. *plousios*). His land has brought forth "plenti-fully," and now the narrative switches to the soliloquy (12:17–19), which makes up the bulk of the parable. Instead of thanking God for the bountiful harvest, he decides to build ever larger barns in which to store the acquired grain and goods. The soliloquy is enhanced by a staged dialogue with "his soul." The text here is very subtle. While this is a dramatic parable (that is, with a human character rather than one about nature), there is no interaction with any other human being. The rich man can only be in dialogue with his own soul (his *psychē*, or self, 12:19). There is sad irony here; he does not share his joy with others but only with his soul that will soon be snatched away.

Despite his assurance of goods for many years and his careful plans to secure his future, his soliloquy is rudely interrupted: "God said to him, 'Fool! This night your soul is required of you; and the things you have prepared, whose will they be?'" This explosive intro-duction shocks the original hearers more than us. In no other parable does "God" enter so explicitly into the narrative and speak in a man-ner forbidden to human beings (see Matt 5:21–22). The word *fool* also recalls the wide Old Testament polemic against "folly" (for example, Pss 14:1; 53:1, "The fool says in his heart, 'There is no God'"; also Ps 49:10; Sir 11:19–20). The contrast between his complacency in his riches and the danger they pose is enhanced by the phrase: "This night your soul is required of you" (lit. "They are demanding your soul from you"). The word *demand* (Gk. *apaitousin*) is commonly used for collecting a loan. The rich man did not realize that the fruits of his harvest were "on loan" from God and not to be used for his own gratification. He forgets the most basic event of his religious heritage by not observing the law that gleanings from the harvest are to be left for the poor and the alien (Lev 19:9; 23:22), which Deuteronomy twice roots in the nature of God who freed the people from slavery:

> You shall not deprive a resident alien or an orphan of justice; you shall not take a widow's garment in pledge. Remember that you were a slave in Egypt and the LORD your God redeemed you from there; therefore I command you to do this.
>
> When you reap your harvest in your field and forget a sheaf in the field, you shall not go back to get it; it shall be left for the alien, the orphan, and the widow, so that the LORD your God may bless you in all your undertakings. When you beat your olive trees, do not strip what is left; it shall be for the alien, the orphan, and the widow.
>
> When you gather the grapes of your vineyard, do not glean what is left; it shall be for the alien, the orphan, and the widow. Remember that you were a slave in the land of Egypt; therefore I am commanding you to do this. (Deut 24:17–22)

The final question by God, "The things you have prepared, whose will they be?" (12:20) provides an *inclusio* with the dispute over an inheritance that evoked the parable (12:13). The covetousness of the rich person in the parable has so isolated him that he has not even provided for his heirs. Given the importance of family and heirs in first-century culture, his condition is pitiable. He is isolated amid his wealth, dies alone, and leaves only what will be a bitter dispute over the inheritance (cf. 12:13). The parable then has a "second application": such will happen to those who lay up treasure for themselves and are not "rich toward God" (12:21). The following verses, which urge trust in God and almsgiving, spell out what it means to be "rich toward God" (12:22–34), and the final verses of the chapter image the proper use of resources by giving alms, which foreshadows the practices of Acts.

In warning against greed, the Gospel and classical moral teaching seem shockingly close to our world today. In a major study that surveys the effect of greed on the social fabric, Ryan K. Balot describes greed as "an excessive desire to get more. Greed is a primarily materialistic type of desire, which is characteristically expressed by the attempt to satisfy bodily urges through the acquisition of money, material goods, and power."[8] After the collapse of the financial markets in 2008 and the ensuing deep recession, social analysts are somewhat belatedly linking greed to the contemporary practice of capitalism, and its mantra, "greed is good." The *London Guardian* (January 13, 2010) carried an article, "An American Cult of Greed," that warns of a greed that is causing massive global environmental damage, and book title after title now proclaim the impact of greed on the demise of major corporations and on millions of people out of work or underemployed, with hints that unbridled greed will bring the demise of capitalism.[9]

MAKING FRIENDS WITH MAMMON (LUKE 16:1–13)

The story of the unjust (or crafty) steward and the appended sayings contain the most enigmatic parable and puzzling advice of Jesus found in Luke (16:1–13). There have been more explanations of these texts than the "one hundred measures of olive oil" owed to the master.

We meet initially a steward (manager) of a wealthy person's land, roughly equivalent to a chief operating officer of a large corporation. Some kind of audit revealed that he had been squandering the resources of the estate, and he is called on the carpet to explain himself. Realizing that no defense is possible, and aware that he may be sent to the mines ("dig") or become a street beggar, he devises a plan.

---

8. Ryan K. Balot, *Greed and Injustice in Classical Athens* (Princeton, NJ: Princeton University Press, 2001), 1.

9. Some examples would be Jeff Madrick, *Age of Greed: The Triumph of Finance and the Decline of America, 1970 to the Present* (New York: Knopf, 2011); Gretchen Morgenson and Joshua Rosner, *Reckless Endangerment: How Outsized Ambition, Greed, and Corruption Led to Economic Armageddon* (New York: Henry Holt and Co., 2011); Roberto De Vogli, *Progress or Collapse: The Crises of Market Greed* (New York: Routledge, 2013).

By reducing the debts owed to his master, he hopes to curry favor with the debtors, so they may hire him later. He calls them in one by one for a "sit down." One owes the equivalent of 1,000 barrels of olive oil, which he immediately halves, and another roughly 1,100 bushels of wheat, which he reduces by 20 percent. Shockingly, the parable itself concludes with the simple statement: "the master commended that dishonest steward for acting prudently" (v. 8).

The most common explanation of the parable is a "Jesuitical" distinction that Jesus praises not the dishonesty of the manager, but his prudence, or shrewdness in a difficult time. Others stress the moral casuistry surrounding Jewish laws against lending money at interest. By letting the manager handle the loan terms, the owner can "stay out of the loop," while benefiting from exorbitant interest rates. When the manager juggles the books, he is simply reducing his own profit that would have been gained from the loans and restores to the manager the amount of the initial loan, perhaps with some profit included. Here, the manager is an example of a person who, when faced with a critical situation, (for example, the demands of Jesus' teaching) will sacrifice his or her own gain to respond (Fitzmyer, *Luke X—XXIV*, 1097–99). A third set of explanations focus on the parable as an instance of a common folk motif where a roguish but lovable inferior outwits a demanding master.

Such attempts prove the potential for multiple meanings for biblical texts. Too often overlooked is the similarity between the parables of the unjust steward and the preceding Prodigal Son. Both parables portray a person facing a life-threatening situation because the central character has "squandered" resources—the son, his father's; the manager, his master's. Each person so caught utters a soliloquy and evolves a plan to extricate himself, with a rather self-serving motivation. In each case, the hoped-for changed fortune will result in acceptance into a house, and in each case, the narrative flow of the parable is determined by unexpected actions by a figure of power (father, owner).

Most important, in both cases the plans of the schemers are not realized but transcended by the surprising action of first the father, and then the rich man. Both of the people caught in a dilemma think in terms of reestablishing a proper order of justice or obligation, and both receive unexpected acceptance and are rescued from danger by what they receive, not by what they accomplish. This parable might be called the parable of the foolish rich man, who acts illogically like the shepherd and the father of Luke 15 and thus evokes a world where God does not exact punishments but cancels debts even in the midst of human machinations.

The appended sayings (16:8b–13), whatever their original meanings, are now governed by Luke's understanding of the parable (16:1–8a). Free of a demanding and harsh God, the children of light can be as shrewd as the children of this world; they are not to flee engagement with "unrighteous mammon," but to remain faithful in its midst. Luke ends these sayings with the somewhat ambiguous phrase, "You cannot serve God and mammon" (16:13b; *au. trans.*). While Matthew (6:24) may preserve better the original context of this Q saying by appending to it a series of warnings against anxiety (6:25–33), Luke plays subtly on the etymology of *mammon*—that on which one relies or trusts. Although both the son and the steward seem to place their faith in possessions (that is, either obtaining or securing them), it is the free acceptance of the father/master that provides security. Christian disciples are summoned to be freed from slavery to wealth and from servile fear of God.

THE RICH MAN AND LAZARUS
AT HIS GATE (LUKE 16:19–31)

The parable of the crafty steward and the appended sayings that seem to offer a benign view of people with significant wealth are followed by one of the more frightening parables of Luke, the contrast in life and death between an obscenely rich man and a pitiful beggar. This parable is completely counter to the banquet teaching of Jesus. The narrative falls into three major parts: rich and poor in this life (16:19–21); the death of each protagonist and the reversal of fates in the afterlife (16:22–26); and a paraenetic dialogue between Abraham and the rich man over the fate of those still alive (16:27–31). The parable achieves its initial effect by a vivid contrast between the main characters. The man is rich (*plousios*); Lazarus is a destitute beggar (*ptōchos*). The rich man is clothed in purple and fine linen (that is, he lives like a king; cf. Prov 31:22; 1 Macc 8:14); Lazarus is covered with sores. The man feasts sumptuously every day (*euphrainomenos*, lit. "splendidly making merry every day"); Lazarus desires (the Greek text suggests a constant and unfulfilled longing) to be fed with scraps normally given to animals and has these as his only companions. Despite the vivid contrast, the audience would not necessarily see the rich man as evil and Lazarus as virtuous. Abundant possessions are a gift from God (Gen 24:35; Job 42:10–17; Eccl 3:10–13; 1 Tim 4:4–5), and the condition of Lazarus, like the pitiable state of Job, could be interpreted as a sign of divine disfavor.

The surprising reversal of fates is quick and immediate. The poor man dies and, without a funeral, is carried to Abraham's bosom; the rich man dies and has a decent burial (*etaphē*, v. 22)—which is important to the final section of the parable, since his remaining brothers presume he has received divine favor. The shock comes when we see him in Hades (16:23). The physical description underscores the reversal of fates: in contrast to sumptuous feasting, he is in great thirst; in contrast to his splendid garb, he is surrounded by flames. As Lazarus "desired" to eat the scraps from his table, he now begs Abraham to have Lazarus offer him a drop of water. The answer of Abraham in verse 25 simply puts in discourse what the narrative has portrayed: the fates are reversed; signs of power and favor in this life are no guarantee of joy in the afterlife. The time for decision and resolute action is past; now is the time only for realizing the consequences of one's action (cf. Matt 25:31–46). As a parable of the reversal of fates, it could end in verse 26, but the final verses, which show strong Lukan redaction, especially verses 30–31, are important for a deeper understanding of the text.

The story has different emphases. If it ended at verse 26, then it could be simply a continuation of the Old Testament polemic against the misuse of material possessions. The rich man is condemned not because he is rich but because he never even looked on Lazarus at his gate; the first time he sees him is from Hades, emphasized by the somewhat solemn phrase, "He lifted up his eyes, and saw" (v. 23). Here the text is bitterly ironic. In life, there was a chasm between himself and Lazarus because of his wealth and power; in death, this chasm still exists (16:26). As we will note below, one of the prime dangers of wealth is that it causes "blindness."

This danger provides the backdrop for the dialogue between the rich man and Lazarus. Too late, the rich man realizes that, in neglecting Lazarus, he was neglecting the Torah. He asks that Lazarus again be sent to warn the brothers. The reply of Abraham is also ironic. The brothers have Moses and the prophets, with their prescriptions on care for the poor, the orphan, the widow, and the stranger. They would be as blind to Lazarus as was their brother now in torment. The second request of the rich man (16:27) implies that he too understands this, and he says that they will repent "if someone goes to them from the dead" (16:30).

The response of Abraham (v. 31) that the brothers will not be convinced "even if someone should rise from the dead" provides a solemn conclusion to the narrative and shows considerable signs of Lukan redaction. Whereas the rich man wants someone to "go to them" from the dead, the answer of Abraham uses the technical Christian language of resurrection (Gr. *anastē*). The reference to "Moses and the prophets" occurs here and in Luke's narrative of the appearance of the risen Jesus, where he teaches his followers how his suffering and death were predicted in "Moses and the prophets" (Luke 24:27, 44). Luke directs the final verse to those in his community who, by neglecting the poor, do not heed the teaching or follow the example of Jesus who rose from the dead.

While the scenic parable of the rich man and Lazarus highlights one danger of riches—that they *cause blindness* to the presence of the suffering and needy neighbor, the rich fool, in its short compass, offers a second paradigm of the dangers of "the desire for more" and "superfluous possession." A desire to secure one's life through possessions is a *form of idolatry* and isolates one from community. The imagery of the parable is ominous: a rich man surrounded by material possessions, living and dying alone. Wealth also makes one deaf to God's presence—God has to interrupt the rich man's self-centered musings to deliver the death sentence: "this night your life will be demanded of you."

A third danger of wealth and power in Luke is harder to localize in one pericope but spans the whole Gospel: *wealth and power can be used to oppress others.* The journey of a pregnant Mary with Joseph to Bethlehem results from a census, a method of both control and economic exploitation by Roman occupiers. Luke juxtaposes the catalog of the "masters of the universe"—Tiberius Caesar, Pontius Pilate,

Herod, Philip, Lysanias, Annas, and Caiaphas who were to bring "salvation" with the coming of the "word of God" to John who proclaims a great reversal when "all flesh shall see the salvation of God." Jesus' death is orchestrated by a collusion of those very leaders mentioned at the beginning as Jesus begins his ministry.

When we come to the Acts of the Apostles, however, different perspectives emerge. Negative views of possessions remain. In Luke's version of the death of Judas (Acts 1:18–20), in contrast to Matthew (27:3–10), Judas does not return the money, but "buys a farm" with the "payment of his injustice." Ananias and Sapphira (Acts 5:1–11), by withholding the "proceeds of the land," are guilty of deceiving God, and Simon (8:9–24) tries to use money (v. 18) to buy power. The silversmiths of Ephesus riot because Paul's preaching threatens their market of little statuettes of Artemis (19:23–27). Positively, shared possessions rather than dispossession is the ideal of Christian communal life (2:41–47; 4:32–37). Almsgiving is praised (Acts 10:2, 4, 31; 24:17), which continues the shift in meaning in the later biblical tradition where "justice" is translated as "almsgiving," understood not as an optional activity but as a *mitzwah*, an obligation from the Torah. Lydia "the seller of purple" who was a worshipper of God, shows Paul hospitality; an example of good use of resources (16:11–15), and men and women of high standing further the spread of the gospel, and accept the gospel.

Luke–Acts embodies strains of reflection on rich and poor that are rooted in the Old Testament: the emphasis in the Torah on the treatment of the poor and marginalized as the touchstone of right relation to God, the prophetic invectives against those rich who abuse or forget the poor, and wisdom traditions on the right use of possessions. Paradoxically, these different perspectives from the Gospel and from Acts help to form Christian consciences today. In recent years, a consensus is emerging that Luke retains the calls for radical dispossession not as a lifestyle to be imitated, either by the community at large or by particular groups, but as symbolically powerful narratives. To say that Luke's statements on dispossession are symbolic or have a literary function is not to deny their power to address the real world, since in the Gospel and Acts, disposition of the heart is symbolized by the disposition of possessions (Johnson, *Gospel of Luke*, 201; *Acts of the Apostles*, 152). Through image and narrative, Luke creates a symbolic world that, by giving a different vision of reality, has power to shape the real world of his audience. There also seems to be a consensus that Luke directs his teaching on wealth and its dangers primarily to the rich in the community described as either the socially more respected or the economically more prosperous. Luke warns the well-off that their wealth and power can bring about greed, blindness, and ultimately loss of salvation, while he simultaneously summons them to conversion and offers them examples of the proper use of possessions, especially almsgiving, which should not be viewed as it often is today as simple charitable giving, but as an obligation in justice.

The Gospel narratives that Jesus was a poor man born among the poor of the land, and who lived an itinerant lifestyle and summoned his followers to a similar path, function as a story of origin and hallowed beginnings. As Paul will later remind the Corinthians, "consider your own calling, brothers. Not many of you were wise by human standards, not many were powerful, not many were of noble birth" (1 Cor 1:26). The hearers of Luke–Acts almost fifty years after the death of Jesus are summoned to remember their "godly ancestors" (cf. Sir 44:1) and to emulate their example. Today, when Catholics of the West are more prosperous than ever, they must be cured of an amnesia that blots out the history of their forebears who struggled and lived with far less, and be challenged to see in the new immigrants the reflection of their own roots and respond with effective compassion.

MALE AND FEMALE IN THE GOSPEL OF LUKE

Luke's inclusive vision of the ministry of Jesus and of the burgeoning Church is made manifest in both his vision of the role of women in the early community and in acceptance of the traditional "other," the Samaritan. An intriguing compositional technique is parallel narratives of man and woman: annunciation to Zechariah and to Mary (1:8–23); hymn of praise of Mary (1:46–55) and of Zechariah (1:67–79); miracle on behalf of the centurion of Capernaum and the widow at Nain (7:1–17); the Good Samaritan and Martha and Mary (10:25–42); God's kingdom is compared to the growth of a mustard seed planted by a man and leavened bread baked by a woman

(13:18–21); God seeks the lost in the image of a shepherd searching for a wandering sheep and a woman scouring the house for a lost coin (15:4–10); and true faith is found in a courageous woman and a prayerful tax collector (18:1–14); proclamation of the resurrection and appearance of the risen Jesus are to women (first) and to men. Jesus is accompanied by women listed with the Twelve during his ministry in Galilee (8:1–3), and only women lament Jesus' path to suffering and death (23:26–27), prepare the burial rites for the dead Jesus (23:55–56), and are the first to hear the resurrection proclamation and report it to the eleven (24:1–9).

Feminist scholars have reflected competently on gender issues in New Testament interpretation and on the Gospel of Luke. In surveying the field, as Amy-Jill Levine has pointed out so well, Luke has a Janus-like quality that "celebrates women's discipleship, self-determination and leadership even as it heralds a reversal of systemic inequities," but at the same time, "the Gospel of Luke threatens any attempt made by women, the poor or the disenfranchised to find a voice in either society or the church" (*Feminist Companion to Luke*, 1). Apart from the infancy narratives, women rarely speak or have a leading role; they do not teach (apart from Priscilla in Acts); nor are they sent out on mission, except perhaps among the mission of the seventy-two who are sent out in pairs—reflecting the missionary practice of married pairs in Acts and Paul (Acts 18:18–24; 1 Cor 9:5–6); they never cast out demons like the male disciples; and are never named "apostles."[10]

Women scholars call for and have employed a critical process of interpretation that moves beyond a description of women's activities in the text and uncovers the cultural biases of both text and reader. Hesitatingly, it could be argued that the most fundamental contribution Luke makes to the discussion is the constant emphasis on re-envisioning and reversing the structures of authority and power along with the Gospel's partiality toward those culturally marginalized. Mary proclaims a God who "has shown might with his arm, dispersed the arrogant of mind and heart. He has thrown down the rulers from their thrones but lifted up the lowly" (Luke 1:51–52); a widow, often an image of powerless-

---

10. See Barbara E. Reid, *Choosing the Better Part: Women in the Gospel of Luke* (Collegeville, MN: Liturgical Press, 1996).

ness, marches into the public arena and confronts a brutal judge to secure justice ("give me justice over my adversary" 18:6, *au. trans.*), while in the following periscope, a tax collector, often a cultural icon of power over others, is praised when he simply says, "be merciful to me a sinner" (18:13). Today, oppression on the basis of sex and gender discrimination is ultimately an issue of power that, despite massive changes in society over the past four decades, most often is claimed by men, especially in the Catholic Church—a continuing obstacle to the proclamation of the Gospel.

RESOURCE BIBLIOGRAPHY

REFERENCE COMMENTARIES

Barrett, C. K. *A Critical and Exegetical Commentary on the Acts of the Apostles*. 2 vols. ICC. Edinburgh: T & T Clark, 2002. See also Barrett, *The Acts of the Apostles: A Shorter Commentary*. London/New York: T & T Clark, 2002.

Bovon, François. *Luke 1: A Commentary on the Gospel of Luke 1:1—9:50*. Hermeneia. Minneapolis: Fortress Press, 2002; *Luke 2: A Commentary on the Gospel of Luke 9:51—23:17* (2013); *Luke 3: A Commentary on the Gospel of Luke, 19:28—24:53* (2012).

Fitzmyer, J. A. *The Acts of the Apostles*. AB 31. New York: Doubleday, 1998.

———. *The Gospel According to Luke, I—IX, and the Gospel According to Luke, X—XXIV*. AB 28, 28A. Garden City, N.Y.: Doubleday, 1981, 1985. One of the best commentaries in any language on Luke. The introductory essay, "A Sketch of Lukan Theology," in Luke I—IX, 143–270, is a fine synthesis of Luke's theology.

Green, Joel B. *The Gospel of Luke*. Grand Rapids, MI: Eerdmans 1997. A scholarly commentary with excellent pastoral insights.

Marshall, I. Howard. *Commentary on Luke*. International Greek New Testament Commentary. Grand Rapids, MI: Eerdmans, 1978.

Nolland, John. *Luke*. Word Biblical Commentary. 3 vols. 1. *Luke 1—9:20*; 2. *Luke 9:21—18:34*; 3. *Luke 18:35—24:53*. Dallas, TX: Word Books, 1989–93.

FURTHER STUDY OF LUKE

Bovon, François. *Luke the Theologian: Fifty-five Years of Research (1950–2005)*. Waco, TX: Baylor University Press, 2006.

Craddock, F. B. *Luke. Interpretation: A Bible Commentary for Teaching and Preaching*. Louisville, KY: Westminster John Knox Press, 1990.

Green, Joel B. *The Theology of the Gospel According to Luke*. New York: Cambridge University Press, 1995. An excellent overview of Luke's theology.

Hendrickx, Herman. *The Third Gospel for the Third World*. Collegeville, MN: The Liturgical Press, 1997–2002. A multivolume work. Hendrickx taught for four decades in Manila. His works draw on this experience while containing great insights.

Johnson, Luke T. *The Acts of the Apostles*. Sacra Pagina 5. A Michael Glazier Book. Collegeville, MN: Liturgical Press, 1992.

———. *The Gospel of Luke*. Sacra Pagina 3. A Michael Glazier Book. Collegeville, MN: The Liturgical Press, 1991. A very interesting commentary ideal for the "religious professional."

———. *Prophetic Jesus, Prophetic Church: The Challenge of Luke–Acts to Contemporary Christians*. Grand Rapids, MI: Eerdmans, 2011. A superb treatment of Jesus as prophet with insightful contemporary applications.

Kealy, Sean P. *The Interpretation of the Gospel of Luke*. 2 vols. Lewiston, NY: Mellen Press, 2005. An excellent resource covering the Patristic period to the present.

Navone, J. *Themes of St. Luke*. Rome: Gregorian University Press, 1970 (available from Loyola University Press, Chicago, IL). An excellent catalog of Lukan themes.

Powell, Mark A. *What Are They Saying About Luke?* New York/Mahwah, NJ: Paulist Press, 1989. An excellent synthesis and survey with an eleven-page annotated bibliography.

Rosner, Brian. *Greed and Idolatry: The Origin and Meaning of a Pauline Metaphor*. Grand Rapids, MI: Eerdmans, 2007. A careful history of the phrase, with examination of Jewish and Christian texts.

Talbert, Charles. *Reading Luke: A Literary and Theological Commentary on the Third Gospel*. Macon, GA: Smyth & Helwys, 2002. An insightful commentary by a scholar who has worked for decades on Luke.

Tannehill, Robert. *Luke.* Abingdon New Testament Commentary. Nashville, TN: Abingdon Press, 1996. Tannehill is one of the leading commentators on Luke, with a good pastoral sense.

THE GOSPEL OF POVERTY AND
THE GOSPEL OF PEACE

Comblin, José. *Called for Freedom: The Changing Context of Liberation Theology.* Maryknoll, NY: Orbis Books, 1998. While not a direct focus on Luke, this work discusses issues that are fundamental for the topic of wealth and poverty.

Donahue, John R. "Two Decades of Research on the Rich and the Poor in Luke–Acts." In *Justice and the Holy: Essays in Honor of Walter Harrelson,* edited by Douglas A. Knight and Peter Paris, 129–44. Atlanta, GA: Scholars Press, 1989.

Dunn, Geoffrey D., David Luckensmeyer, and Lawrence Cross, eds. *Prayer and Spirituality in the Early Church. Volume V, Poverty and Riches.* Strathfield, NSW: St Paul's Publication, 2009. More comprehensive than studies of Luke but with important essays, especially William Loader's, "Good News for the Poor" and "Spirituality in the New Testament: A Question of Survival."

Esler, Philip. F. *Community and Gospel in Luke–Acts: The Social and Political Motivations of Lucan Theology.* SNTSMS 57. Cambridge: Cambridge University Press, 1987. Very interesting and informative. Chapter 7, "The Poor and the Rich," presents excellent material on what it was to be "poor" in the Hellenistic world, and locates Luke in this context.

George, A., ed. *Gospel Poverty.* Chicago: Franciscan Herald Press, 1971. See especially "The Poor and Poverty in the Gospels," 25–52.

Gillman, John. *Possessions and the Life of Faith: A Reading of Luke–Acts.* Zacchaeus Studies. Collegeville, MN: Liturgical Press, 1991. A very good popular presentation that covers major texts and areas.

Grassi, Joseph A. *Jesus Is Shalom: A Vision of Peace from the Gospels.* New York/Mahwah, NJ: Paulist Press, 2006. Good for pastoral use and reading groups.

Green, Joel. "Good News to Whom? Jesus and the 'Poor' in the Gospel of Luke." In *Jesus of Nazareth: Lord and Christ*, edited by Joel Green and Max Turner, 59–74. Grand Rapids, MI: Eerdmans, 1994.

Hamel, Gildas. *Poverty and Charity in Roman Palestine, First Three Centuries C.E.* Berkeley: University of California Press, 1990. Though not on Luke, it is a magnificent study of poverty and attempts to alleviate it based on Jewish, Greco-Roman, and Christian sources.

Hays, Christopher M. *Luke's Wealth Ethics.* WUNT 275. Tübingen: Mohr Siebeck, 2010. A comprehensive study of all the "polyphonous" texts of Luke and Acts that deal with wealth and possessions, with the conclusion "that Luke calls his readers to a complete commitment of their goods to the service of the Kingdom of God" (261).

Johnson, Luke T. *Sharing Possessions: What Faith Demands.* Grand Rapids, MI: Eerdmans, 2011. Second edition of *Sharing Possessions: Mandate and Symbol of Faith.* Philadelphia: Fortress Press, 1981. While keeping the basic text of the first edition, the new introduction, epilogue, and study questions make this a major contribution to reflection on wider dimensions of the language of possessions.

Metzger, James A. *Consumption and Wealth in Luke's Travel Narrative.* Leiden/ Boston: Brill, 2007. An up-to-date survey of wealth and possessions in Luke; all major passages of travel narrative are discussed.

Pilgrim, Walter E. *Good News to the Poor: Wealth and Poverty in Luke–Acts.* Minneapolis: Augsburg, 1981. Good overview of the Lukan writings with fine sections on the Old Testament background.

Schmidt, T. E. *Hostility to Wealth in the Synoptic Gospels.* Sheffield: JSOT Press, 1987. This technical work covers more than Luke, but is comprehensive.

Schottroff, Luise, and Wolfgang Stegemann. *Jesus and the Hope of the Poor.* Maryknoll, NY: Orbis Books, 1986. See especially "The Following of Christ as Solidarity between Rich, Respected Christians and Poor, Despised Christians (Gospel of Luke)," 67–120. This book was updated in 2009 by Wipf & Stock Publishers

Stegemann, W. *The Gospel and the Poor.* Philadelphia: Fortress Press, 1984. An excellent short study that covers more than Luke. Ideal for pastoral ministry.

Swartley, Willard M. *Covenant of Peace: The Missing Piece in New Testament Theology and Ethics*. Grand Rapids, MI: Eerdmans, 2006. The chapters on Luke are part of a comprehensive study that is the fruit of decades of writing and research.

WOMEN AND THE GOSPEL OF LUKE

Brown, Raymond Edward, Karl P. Donfried, Joseph A. Fritzmeyer, John Reumann, eds. *Mary in the New Testament: A Collaborative Assessment by Protestant and Roman Catholic Scholars*. Philadelphia: Fortress Press; New York/Paramus, NJ: Paulist Press, 1978. A landmark ecumenical study that examines all Marian texts by careful historical-critical methods.

Dornish, Loretta. *A Woman Reads the Gospel of Luke*. Collegeville, MN: The Liturgical Press, 1996. A thorough and interesting study that argues for a positive view of women in Luke.

Fiorenza, Elisabeth Schüssler. *In Memory of Her: A Feminist Theological Reconstruction of Christian Origins*. Tenth anniversary edition. New York: Crossroad, 1994. A landmark historical reconstruction of women in the Jesus movement and in the early Christian missionary movement, preceded by important chapters on methods of research.

Gaventa, Beverly. *Glimpses of the Mother of Jesus*. Columbia, SC: University of South Carolina Press, 1995. This work offers original insights by a non-Catholic scholar.

Kitzberger, Ingrid Rosa, ed. *Transformative Encounters: Jesus and Women Re-visited*. Leiden: Brill, 2000. Essays on topics wider than Luke divided into three major sections: "Literary Approaches," "Historical Re-Construction," and "Actualizations." Most helpful in understanding different approaches and results of current scholarship.

Levine, Amy-Jill, ed. *A Feminist Companion to the Acts of the Apostles*. London/New York: T & T Clark, 2004.

———, ed. *A Feminist Companion to the Gospel of Luke*. London/New York: Sheffield Academic Press, 2002. An excellent collection of essays with a fine introduction by Levine and extensive bibliography.

Reid, Barbara E. *Choosing the Better Part: Women in the Gospel of Luke.* Collegeville, MN: Liturgical Press, 1996. This work combines theoretical perspectives on liberation with a fine study of particular texts.

Reimer, Ivoni R. *Women in the Acts of the Apostles: A Feminist Liberation Perspective.* Minneapolis: Fortress Press, 1995.

Schottroff, Luise. *Lydia's Impatient Sisters: A Feminist Social History of Early Christianity.* Louisville, KY: Westminster John Knox Press, 1995.

Seim, Turid K. *The Double Message: Patterns of Gender in Luke–Acts.* Nashville, TN: Abingdon, 1994.

CHAPTER 10

THE PAULINE WRITINGS

A paradox in contemporary discussions of issues of faith and justice is that while the Old Testament and the teachings of Jesus are called on to construct a theology of social justice, Paul, who cites the Old Testament, "The just man lives by faith" (Rom 1:17; Hab 2:4), and struggles with the relation of faith and justice in Romans and Galatians, is rarely treated in this context. A variety of reasons explain this neglect. Since the Reformation, Paul's teaching on the justice of God has been seen under the problematic lens of how the *individual* sinner can be accepted by a just God. This has led to an exegesis where Paul becomes, as Krister Stendahl has remarked, "the introspective conscience of the West."[1] While there is no doubt that Paul's language resonates with a modern quest for personal freedom and a struggle with guilt, much of the individualized and existential study of Paul was based on a misreading of his understanding of justice. Allied to this was a reading of Paul as one who rejected his Jewish heritage as slavery to law in contrast to the liberating work of Christ, so the Old Testament roots of Paul's thought were neglected. Recent exegesis has located Paul's thought not so much in the problem of how one who shares the legacy of Adam's sin can become a graced person, that is, a "just individual," but on his more foundational appropriation of the Christ-event and Jewish apocalyptic thought about the justice of God. Ernst Käsemann has captured the major influence of apocalyptic thought on Paul:

> Even when he became a Christian, Paul remained an apocalyptist. His doctrine of *dikaiosynē theou* (justice of God) demonstrates this: God's power reaches out for the world,

---

1. Krister Stendahl, "The Apostle Paul and the Introspective Conscience of the West," *Harvard Theological Review* 56 (1963): 199–215.

and the world's salvation lies in its being recaptured for the sovereignty of God.[2]

A third factor contributing to the neglect of social justice in Paul has been that Paul has been accused of teaching only an "interim ethic." Evidence for this would be in his exhortation to the people not to change their marital or social status, because "the time is short" (1 Cor 7:29). Paul's eschatological view that the shape of the world is passing away (1 Cor 7:31), and his own personal hope to be with the Lord (2 Cor 5:7), has made some interpreters doubt whether Paul's ethics offer any help for Christians settling in for the long haul of history.

In discussing Paul, we will first attempt to locate Paul's understanding of justice in the larger context of his theology and then address situations where he speaks to concrete issues that we view today as concerns for social justice: discrimination on the basis of status at the Lord's Supper (1 Cor 11:17–34) and the collection for the poor of Jerusalem (2 Cor 8—9).

PAULINE THEOLOGY AND CONCERNS
FOR FAITH AND JUSTICE

Central to Paul's thought is the proclamation of the Christ-event, which Joseph A. Fitzmyer has described as "the meaning that the person and lordship of Jesus of Nazareth had and still has for human history and existence" (*Paul*, 39, no. 32), and constitutes "a short way of referring to the complex of decisive moments of the earthly and risen life of Jesus Christ...his passion, death and resurrection," which "should also include his burial, exaltation and heavenly intercession" (*Paul*, 59, no. 6).[3] This Christ-event as proclaimed and lived by Paul has a number of implications for issues of social justice.

The Christ-event as the foundation of Christian faith demands responsibility for the world. Christian faith in the death and resurrec-

---

2. Ernst Käsemann, "Righteousness of God," in *New Testament Questions of Today* (Philadelphia: Fortress Press, 1959), 181–82.

3. Also in Joseph A. Fitzmyer, "Pauline Theology," *NJBC* 1389 (no. 32); 1397 (no. 67).

tion is not simply faith in the promise of eternal life, but faith in the *victory over death* achieved in Jesus. Through baptism, Christians participate *already* in this victory: "We have been buried with him by baptism into death, so that, just as Christ was raised from the dead by the glory of the Father, so we too might *walk in newness of life*" (Rom 6:4, emphasis mine). Here, Paul does *not* say, as does the author of Colossians (3:1), that the Christians "were raised with Christ." The resurrection has an ethical counterpart, "walking in the newness of life." Also in Paul, the Christian contrast is not between earth and heaven, or between material and spiritual reality, but between the "old age" and "the new" (cf. also Rom 8; 2 Cor 5:16–21). Fundamental to the new life in Christ is the experience of "power" (cf. Acts 4:33, "with great power the Apostles gave their testimony to the resurrection of the Lord Jesus"; 1 Cor 1:18–31; 2 Cor 12:9–13). The Christian is to be a witness in mission of the victory over death and the transforming power of the resurrection. To pursue the quest for justice in faith means that the Christian walks in confidence that evil is not Lord of life and that even death for the sake of others cannot separate a person from the love of God (Rom 8:28–39).

Justification of the sinner by God's grace through faith results in a personal and communal liberation that enables people to live for others rather than for themselves. Theologically, Paul states that the Christ-event frees the Christian from sin, law, and death. Equally important as this "freedom from," is the Pauline notion of "freedom for." Paul stated this succinctly, "For freedom Christ has set us free" (Gal 5:1a). Freedom for Paul is liberation from the self-serving and self-destructive aspects of "striving" and "boasting" in human achievements in order to direct one's attention to the needs of others. In Galatians, which, along with Romans, is his major theological statement on justification, after somewhat polemically rejecting those Christian opponents who want to reimpose Jewish practices on Gentile Christians, Paul says, "For you were called to freedom, brothers and sisters; only do not use your freedom as an opportunity for self-indulgence [flesh], but through love become servants of one another" (Gal 5:13). Paul then goes on to describe "walking according to the spirit," and "walking according to the flesh" (Gal 5:16–21). The virtues and vices listed here for the most part either foster or destroy life in community. Paul then concludes this whole section with the statement: "bear one another's burdens, and in this way you will fulfill the law of Christ" (Gal 6:2). Therefore, the justified and graced Christian is a person who seeks a community not of isolated individuals, but one in which concern for the weak and suffering is the touchstone of living according to the law of Christ.

Pauline eschatology does not warrant an "interim ethic," but summons Christians to responsibility for life in the world. Since Albert Schweitzer's challenge that Jesus and Paul provided only an "interim ethic," significant research has been done on the social context and meaning of Paul's eschatology.[4] For Paul, the Christian lives between the "already" and the "not yet." Through Christ, the evil powers have been subdued (Phil 2:10–11) and Christians live in the new age (1 Cor 10:11; 2 Cor 5:17). Yet Paul has an eschatological reservation. All creation is groaning (Rom 8:23) and Christians are to look forward to the final victory over death when the risen Christ hands over the kingdom to his Father (1 Cor 15:51–54). Between the "already" and the "not yet," Christians are to walk in the newness of life, and not let sin reign in their mortal bodies (Rom 6:12). They should yield themselves to God so that they might become instruments and servants of justice (Rom 6:13, 18). Eschatology thus provides a view from the end, a vision of a restored creation and of the kind of community that should exist in the world, and summons Christians to implement this vision, however incomplete, in their individual and social lives.

In his use of the terminology "this age," Paul shows himself to be an heir of apocalyptic Judaism. Paul asks, "Where is the debater of this age?" (1 Cor 1:20). He exhorts his community: "Do not be conformed to this age" (Rom 12:2). The rulers of this age are doomed to pass away, and it was the rulers of this age who crucified Jesus (1 Cor 2:6–8). The present age is transitory (1 Cor 7:31); it is an evil age (Gal 1:4) that is characterized by suffering and tribulation (Rom 8:18). Paul does not root the evil of this age only in an empirical description of sin, but sees this age as held captive by evil power. The gods of this world (2 Cor 4:4) and elemental spirits enslave humanity and hold it in bondage

---

4. For Schweitzer's concept of an "interim ethic," see Norman Perrin, *The Kingdom of God in the Teaching of Jesus* (Philadelphia: The Westminster Press, 1963), 32–34.

(Gal 4:3). Humanity is under the power of sin (Rom 3:9; Gal 3:22). Sin enters the world and takes it captive (Rom 5:21; 6:12, 14); enslaves humanity (Rom 6:16–17); and finally brings death (Rom 7:11; 8:10), which is both the consequence of and punishment for sin. Death is not simply an event but a power that "reigns" in this age (Rom 5:14, 17).

However, Paul parts company from apocalyptic Judaism in not contrasting this age with the age to come that will then bring victory over sin and death, but in locating the sending of Jesus at the turning of the age when this victory is inaugurated since Jesus "gave himself for our sins to deliver us from the present evil age" (Gal 1:4). The Christians are those who live in the period of the "eschatological now" and the end of the age has come upon them (1 Cor 10:11). For the Christian, the old has passed away and the new has come (2 Cor 5:17). Therefore, Paul has in one sense a "realized eschatology," yet, though the evil powers have been broken by Christ who is now Lord of all creation (Phil 2:10–11), the Christian lives between the times, a period when evil and injustice will continue to exercise their influence until the final victory. For Paul, all creation is groaning and "we ourselves, who have the first fruits of the Spirit, groan inwardly while we wait for adoption, the redemption of our bodies. For in hope we were saved" (Rom 8:23–24a). Although Jesus has risen and conquered death, death still reigns and will be the last enemy to be conquered (cf. 1 Cor 15:51–54). In the present time, Christians are the Body of Christ (Rom 12; 1 Cor 12), but "our citizenship is in heaven" (Phil 3:20).

When a discussion of justice in Paul is put in the context of his eschatology, certain conclusions are suggested. If the sending of Christ is salvation from the present evil age, and if this is a manifestation of the justice of God (Rom 4:25), then justice is not simply the quality of God as righteous judge over and against sinful man, but a relation of the saving power of God to a world captured by evil. God's justice is his fidelity, which inaugurates a saving victory over the powers that enslave and oppress humanity. Paul's eschatology suggests a Christian response to being in the world. On the one hand, if the world is still under the reign of sin and death, a prophetic stance of opposition to these powers is demanded. Such a stance demands an accurate diagnosis of what the powers are in contemporary experience. Along with the prophetic stance is an eschatological stance, which sees that the quest for realization of God's saving justice is always held in hope and anticipation. Paul sees the world in a process of transformation and Christians as coworkers in this process. On the other hand, precisely because the world is in process, is "groaning," no one crystallization of God's saving justice will be adequate, nor will any system ever be the final system. To hope to find a total incarnation of God's saving justice at any one time would, in Pauline terms, turn gift into law. The Christian who reflects on Paul's eschatology will be conscious that the quest for justice always operates between prophecy and vision, between realization and hope.

FAITH AND JUSTICE

There are two sets of texts in Paul that group faith and justice. In the first set, justice is joined with faith and Jesus Christ (for example, Rom 3:22, "the justice of God through faith in Jesus Christ"; cf. Phil 3:9; Rom 3:26; Gal 2:16). In the second set, there is the conjunction of simply faith and justice (Rom 3:28, 30; 4:5, 9, 11, 13; 9:30; 10:6; 10:10). Since faith in Paul is primarily faith in what God has done in Jesus, the difference between the two sets of texts is not significant. What is significant is what Paul means when he says that justice comes through faith.

In most current discussions the meaning of this statement is seen in terms of the "faith versus works" controversy. Justice or the acceptance of man by God is seen as the result of man's total surrender to the loving God, renouncing all claims on his love and not boasting in "works" as a way of attaining this love. While it is true that justification comes not from doing the works of the law, but from faith, limitation of these statements to this controversy misses the richness of the relation of faith and justice.

Like justice, faith in Paul is both central and protean. Joseph Fitzmyer has described faith in Paul as stated in Romans:

This experience begins with the hearing (*akoē* 10:17) of the "word" about Christ, and his salvific role...and ends with *hypakoē pisteōs* (1:5; 16:26)...personal commitment engaging the whole person to Christ in all his relations with God, other human beings and the world.[5]

Therefore faith is akin to the *metanoia* or conversion found in the Synoptic Gospels that demands a turning to the demands of the kingdom and engagement in the mission of the kingdom. Faith looks to the past: "I live by faith in the Son of God, who loved me and gave himself for me" (Gal 2:20); it also characterizes the present life of the individual: "I live by faith" (Gal 2:20); and of the community: "Your faith is proclaimed throughout the world" (Rom 1:8); and, as Paul's description of the faith of Abraham in Romans chapter 4 suggests, faith is living under a promise that must prove itself in the Christian life.

PHILIPPIANS 3:8–11:
THE CHRISTOLOGICAL BASIS OF FAITH

I regard everything as loss because of the surpassing value of knowing Christ Jesus my Lord. For his sake I have suffered the loss of all things, and I regard them as rubbish, in order that I may gain Christ and be found in him, not having a righteousness of my own that comes from the law, but one that comes through faith in Christ, the righteousness from God based on faith. I want to know Christ and the power of his resurrection and the sharing of his sufferings by becoming like him in his death, if somehow I may attain the resurrection from the dead.

The faith that justifies is the faith that leads to knowledge of Jesus Christ—a knowledge that involves personal sharing in the life and death of Jesus. The life and death of Jesus is his emptying (Phil 2:5–11), his renunciation of grasping, and the giving of his life for others. Therefore, the justice of God that comes from faith in Jesus is fidelity to the demands of a relationship—the relationship that the Christian is to have with Christ by being "in Christ" (a phrase used over 165 times in Paul's writings) and putting on Christ and the mind

---

5. Joseph Fitzmyer, "Pauline Theology," *NJBC* 1407.

of Christ. Käsemann describes well this Christological aspect of justifying faith:

> In justification it is simply the Kingdom of God proclaimed by Jesus which is at stake....The Christology inherent in the doctrine of justification corresponds to the existence led in the everyday life of the world. Justification is the stigmatization of our worldly existence through the crucified Christ. Through us and in us he simultaneously reaches out toward the world to which we belong.[6]

Therefore, to be justified by faith is to walk in the trust that God through Christ offers grace and redemption to a sinful world, that God is at work in history. A quest for justice that is from faith is sustained by the realization that the kind and quality of life Jesus lived and proclaimed still has transformative power.

ASPECTS OF PAUL'S CONTEXTUAL THEOLOGY

One of the more stimulating and informative movements in recent years has been the emphasis on "Paul and Empire." Earlier studies often portrayed Paul as either disengaged from concern for living under Roman rule, perhaps because of his anticipation of the near return of Jesus (1 Cor 16:22), or his desire not to alienate Roman authorities (Rom 13:1–7). Important works now stress that Paul is actually proposing a value system and lifestyle that is directly opposed to the cultural ethos of the Roman empire (see Elliott, *Arrogance,* and Horsley, *Paul and Empire*), while others have shown that the oppressed nations to whom Paul proclaims the gospel have their own subculture or "hidden transcripts" of survival that resist imperial values. Brigitte Kahl has opened up original ways of viewing Paul by combining detailed knowledge of the history, culture, and artistic works of the world Paul encountered, along with a sophisticated array of methods, for example, semiology and sociology of religion (*Galatians Re-*

---

6. Ernst Käsemann, "Justification and Salvation History in the Epistle to the Romans," *Perspectives on Paul* (Philadelphia: Fortress Press, 1971), 75.

Imagined: Reading with the Eyes of the Vanquished). She argues that "read before the Great Altar of Pergamon and in the scriptural code of Exodus and Deuteronomy, Galatians emerges as a passionate plea to resist the idolatrous lure of imperial religion and social ordering," and "the entire letter is the 'coded' theological manifesto of the nations under Roman rule, pledging allegiance to the one God who is other than Caesar" (*Galatians*, 287).

Certain themes emerge from these studies, such as rejection of the religious legitimation of empire; a stress on a counter-vision of egalitarian society in contrast to a world of stratified power and patronage; concern for the lives of poor and marginal people; a strong mission to the non-Jewish God fearers and to pagans; and affirmation of Jewish values and heritage, rather than opposition to Judaism.[7] In terms of a concern to plumb the richness of Paul on issues of social justice, these studies offer a promising future. We will now investigate two ways where Pauline theology and practice provide instances of a "contrast society" to the values of the imperial order.

ABUSES AT THE SUPPER OF THE LORD

Throughout 1 Corinthians, Paul addresses different pastoral and religious questions raised by the community in Corinth. In chapter 11, Paul turns to problems in the liturgical assembly. The first is an enigmatic section urging women to wear head coverings when prophesying (1 Cor 11:3–17). In the second, longer part of the chapter, he treats a serious problem surrounding the celebration of the Lord's Supper (11:17–24). At Corinth, this supper was celebrated in the context of an ordinary meal when Christians gathered in the evening at the end of an ordinary working day, most likely on a Sunday (the day of the resurrection). The only place with enough space for a community gathering would normally have been the home of one of the more prosperous members of the community.

Paul addresses the problem directly: "When you come together as a church, I hear that there are divisions among you; and to some extent

---

7. Behind the scenes in these studies is an awareness of the structures and values of empire that these authors feel are operative, often in hidden ways, in contemporary American policy and in civil religion.

I believe it" (1 Cor 11:18), and then gives his initial judgment on the situation, "When you come together, it is not really to eat the Lord's supper. For when the time comes to eat, each of you goes ahead with your own supper, and one goes hungry and another becomes drunk" (vv. 20–21).

This dispute has a social and ethical dimension. Apparently the more prosperous members of the community simply became hungry and tired waiting for the small artisans and day laborers to arrive after a working day that stretched from dawn to dusk. They began the celebration of the Lord's Supper and also ate special food and drink that they had prepared for themselves rather than sharing it with others. Paul reacts strongly to this practice, "Do you not have homes in which you can eat or drink?" (1 Cor 11:22), and highlights the evil effect of this practice: "Do you show contempt for the church of God, and humiliate those who have nothing" (the Greek here is literally, "the have-nots"). Paul is in effect saying that those social distinctions between upper-class and lower-class people, which are part of the fabric of the Greco-Roman world, have no place in the Christian assembly. One might recall here Paul's early statement to the Galatians that in Christ there is neither Jew nor Greek, slave nor free, male and female (Gal 3:26).

After this initial programmatic assault on the position of those who were shaming the have-nots, Paul cites the tradition of the institution of the Eucharist, which is parallel to accounts found in the Synoptic Gospels, and very similar to the words of institution used at the eucharistic celebration today (11:23–26). Having evoked this tradition, Paul then applies this to the situation in the community. He first says that anyone who eats the bread or drinks the cup of the Lord unworthily will have to answer for the body and blood of the Lord (11:27) and that anyone who eats and drinks without discerning the body eats and drinks judgment on himself (11:28).

For Paul, the words of institution make present again the self-offering of Christ, "my body for you." The "you" are all the Christians equally. As Paul has noted in other places, the death of Jesus is an example of one who did not choose his own benefit but that of others, and that Christ died for the weak or marginal Christian brother or sister as well as for the powerful (cf. Rom 14:7). The practices of the

Corinthians are a direct affront to the example of Christ. By preferring their own good, and shaming other members of the community of lower social and economic status, they are making a mockery of the Eucharist. They are importing into the celebration of the supper practices and values of their stratified society, which is in direct contrast to Paul's practice of a contrast community. The attitudes of the "early eaters" explain Paul's harsh judgment: "it is not the Lord's supper that you are eating" (1 Cor 11:20, *au. trans.*).

An added dimension of the abuse of the Lord's Supper, not stressed enough by commentators, is the stark statement that "for when the time comes to eat, each of you goes ahead with your own supper, and one goes hungry and another becomes drunk" (1 Cor 1:21). After the prosperous members of the community have eaten, there is virtually nothing left for the latecomers. In addition to humiliation, there is a more serious insult to the Lord's Supper. Commentators rarely advert to the issue of hunger, but famines were frequent in Paul's time and during his ministry. The hunger is real and perhaps the communal meal was one time in the week when the poor members of the community could have a decent meal. Paul returns to this issue after his critical remarks on the Corinthian practice (vv. 22–33) and tells "my brothers and sisters" to wait for one another and concludes rather ironically, "if anyone is hungry he should eat at home."

When Paul says that the one who eats without discerning the body, eats and drinks judgment on him or herself (11:28), the "body" is a reference not primarily to the body of Jesus (as the later concept of sacrilege affirmed) but the community as the Body of Christ (which Paul will discuss in great detail in the following chapter). Discerning the body for Paul means assessing the impact of one's actions on the good of the community, especially in regard to its weaker members, and asking how the actions of the community represent Christ in the world. Therefore, for Paul, ethical decisions are consequent on a prior theological vision and religious experience. The vision is the Christ-event; the reality is a society with opposing values and the hoped-for experience is the new life and new way of acting that the Christian assumes when he or she puts on Christ in baptism.

FRIENDSHIP IN PLACE OF DIVISION

Imperial rule was maintained by creating structures of division both in Rome and throughout the empire. Class divisions were fostered as aristocrats and wealthy people were favored over the poorer people called *humiliores*, literally, "the more lowly ones," and ethnic divisions were maintained. Paul's theology and pastoral practice were in direct opposition to these values, which is especially notable in his engagement in the dispute between the weak and strong at Rome, even before he visited the community at Rome. The area of contention was the eating of certain foods and religious observances, which Paul had addressed earlier in 1 Corinthians 6—8 and Galatians 4:10. Though seemingly arcane to modern readers, these issues threatened the nature and future of the Christian communities.

The final chapters of the Letter to the Romans (12:1—16:25) comprise a catechetical or hortatory section that applied the theology of justification by grace through faith to the demands of everyday life, followed by a letter of recommendation to the diverse Roman house-churches for Phoebe, deacon of the Church at Corinth. After a general description of the new life in Christ that is to characterize Christians (12:1—13:14), which concludes with the command "put on the Lord Jesus Christ" (13:14), Paul turns to the problem that threatens to divide the community (14:1—15:13). The specific issue and its ultimate solution are stated bluntly by Paul in Romans 14:1: "As for those whose are weak in faith; 'Welcome them!'" (*au. trans.*). This brief command reveals the situation that precipitated the problem. Paul is concerned that one group, called "threatened" or "weak in faith," are not welcomed to common assemblies by others except for "disputed opinions which lead to mutual judgments and feuding parties." It also highlights Paul's generic response to the problem, ("mutual acceptance," 14:1), to which he returns in 15:7 when he again urges: "Welcome one another as Christ has welcomed you to the glory of God." The imperative plural indicates that Paul is addressing another group, later identified as the "strong," with whom Paul himself identifies when he says "we who are strong ought to bear with the failings of the weak" (15:1). Paul is clearly involved in a serious dispute within the communities at Rome—one that tests the theology of the whole letter, and one that may threaten his future plans (15:14–33). Less clear is

235

the identity of the weak and the strong and the precise nature of the dispute. Since a lengthy discussion of this issue is beyond the scope of these present reflections, we will follow the majority opinion that the "weak" were most likely Jewish Christians or Gentiles who were Jewish "god fearers," prior to becoming Christians.

The initial and apparently major area of contention arises from the fact that: "Some believe in eating anything, while the weak eat only vegetables" (14:2). Other aspects of the dispute are that: one esteems one day as better than another, while another esteems all days alike (14:5), and at least some do not drink wine (14:21). Both the weak and the strong are criticized by Paul. The strong engage in contentious arguments with the weak (14:1) and "must not despise those who abstain" (14:3, Gk. *mē exoutheneito*, lit. "let him not reject them with contempt"; cf. also 14:10, *sy ti exoutheneis ton adelphon sou*, "why do you reject with contempt your brother?"). Their actions put a stumbling block in the way of others (14:13), which causes such harm that they are in danger of destroying the work of God (14:20). The weak are judgmental of others who do not share their practices; they interpret their observance of particular days as honor to the Lord (14:6).

Paul's response to the problem unfolds rhetorically in varied and expanding fashion. Initially, he counters the dispute over food with a brief rejoinder that mutual recriminations are to be rejected since everyone must stand in judgment before the Lord (14:3–4). He then counters in more detail the division over observances of certain days (14:5–6) by arguing that the true honor to the Lord is not living for oneself but for others, and introduces for the first time Jesus' death as an example for both sides (vv. 7–9). In 14:10, he takes up again the issue of mutual recriminations by invoking the universal judgment of all humanity (14:10–12), which should be a caution to the weak against judging others and to the strong against being a stumbling block to the weak.

The arsenal of theological perspectives Paul marshals in support of his argument testifies to the seriousness of the dispute. Considerations of the nature of God predominate, and throughout there is a stress on the authority and power of God: God accepts the strong whom the weak criticize (14:3); those with different observances and eating practices both give thanks to God (14:6); God will judge both the weak and strong (14:4, 10–12); God's reign does not consist in food and drink, but in justice, peace, and joy in the Holy Spirit (14:17); disputes over food destroy the work of God (14:20); a person's faith is known to God (14:22); and Paul prays that the God "of patience and consolation" will effect a resolution of the dispute (15:5–6). The Christ-event is also invoked constantly to challenge the behavior of both groups. People should live for others according to the example of Christ (14:7–9); each person should please his or her neighbor, for Christ did not please himself (15:2–3); the warring groups should welcome each other as Christ welcomed them (15:7); and Christ became a servant to the circumcised in order to confirm the promises to the patriarchs and so that the Gentiles might glorify God for his mercy (15:8–13). This combination of theocentric and Christocentric perspectives characterizes the theology of the letter as a whole. God is the impartial one who offers salvation to all people through the Christ-event.

In Romans 14:1—15:13, Paul addresses issues that threatened to undermine the fragile coalition of Roman communities. The positions of both groups rest on deeply held convictions. For the weak, who are most likely Jewish Christians or Gentiles who have come to Christianity through Judaism, the dietary laws and observance of the Sabbath and other feasts are identity markers that have sustained diaspora communities throughout the Greco-Roman world. Jews who converted to Christianity and non-Jews who had been "god fearers," that is, members of the synagogue communities, somewhat analogous to "catechumens" today, would have heard the stories of their ancestors who died horrible deaths rather than give up these practices that are rooted in God's revelation in the Torah (2 Macc 6:18—7:42).

Equally, former converts from Paganism and those from Judaism who accepted the vision of God's impartiality articulated by Paul, and who had heard of his "law-free" Gospel, may have seen continued observance of dietary laws, and so on, as an obstacle to bringing the Gentiles under God's promises articulated in Scripture. They could invoke Paul as their "patron" (Rom 15:1), and wanted to embody their convictions in religious practices, not so obviously identified as Jewish.

The issues had also social consequences. The first Christian communities in Rome, which existed before the arrival of Peter and Paul, were heavily Jewish in nature. The Roman historian, Suetonius, records that "all the Jews" were expelled from Rome, probably in AD 49 because of riots occurring *"impulsore Chresto"* ("at the instigation of Christ"), most likely a reference to disputes between Jews and Jewish Christians. This also suggests that Claudius and Roman officials had not yet begun to distinguish Jews and Christians. Claudius died in AD 54 and was followed as emperor by the nineteen-year-old Nero (AD 54–68). Despite the final horror of Nero's reign, when he murdered his mother and wife and persecuted Christians, the first five years of his tenure as emperor were marked by peace and progress. During this time, Nero took no actions against Jews and may have even been favorable to them. Jews and Jewish Christians expelled under Claudius would have been allowed to return to Rome. It is quite possible, however, despite having once been the largest group and leaders among the Christian communities, at the time of Paul's letter they may have been a minority.

Another factor that influences Paul is the organization of the early Christian communities at Rome. As Peter Lampe has carefully shown, "during the first centuries the Christians of the city of Rome met separately in privately owned locations scattered throughout the capital city." He also notes that these house-churches had "no central worship facility and a lack of central coordination that matched the profile of the separated synagogues in Rome."[8] He suggests at least five Christian groups in Romans: the one house-church of Prisca and Aquila (Rom 16:5, the only time in the letter Paul uses *ekklēsia* of a Roman Christian group); the two groups who gather around those named in 16:14, 15; those who belong to the household of Aristobulus (16:10); and those in the household of Nereus (16:15). A close reading of the names listed in Romans 16:1–16 reveals Greek and Roman names, Jewish and non-Jewish names, as well as names of upper-class figures and slaves or former slaves; and, of the twenty-six people mentioned, nine are women. The Roman Christian community was diverse and not unified under a single authority. (Paradoxically, given subsequent Church history, Christian Rome was not governed by a single bishop until the middle of the second century). The structure of the Roman communities

---

8. Peter Lampe, "The Roman Christians of Romans 16," in *The Romans Debate,* ed. Karl Donfried (Peabody, MA: Hendrickson, 1997), 229.

would allow for the emergence of diverse practices. Even among the "weak" one house-church could well manifest some ascetical practice that might not have been observed by every other "weak" Christian.

Paul is then faced with a major challenge of unifying different small Christian communities who lived in a hostile atmosphere but who also followed significantly different ways of living their Christian life. It is very important to understand Paul's specific goal. He does not urge either group to abandon their religious practices; the weak are not exhorted to abandon their special celebrations or to give up their observance of not eating certain foods; the strong are not told to observe the practices of the weak. What Paul desires and what he repeats three times is that all the different groups should "welcome each other" (14:1, 3; 15:7). The term that has been translated "welcome" (Gk. *proslambanesthe*) is taken from the moral glossary of friendship, and can be translated as "accept as a friend."

Friendship was not only discussed in writings of ancient philosophers and humanists, but was a large part of the popular culture, manifest in sayings such as "friends hold all things in common," or "friends are other selves," or "share a single soul." Such sayings are reflected in Luke's description of the early Christian community in Acts 2:44–47 and 4:32–37, where the community holds "all things in common" (2:44), or where all the believers were "of one heart and soul" (4:32). The highest form of friendship was only between equals and was directed to the benefit of the other person. Friendship was maintained by actual presence or through letters, by mutual gift-giving, and by hospitality. Friendship was thought to be a higher form of love than physical or erotic love, and the supreme instance of ancient friendship was to give one's life for a friend, again reflected in Romans 5:6–8, where Christ is an example of giving one's life for a good person, or John 15:12–16, where Jesus alludes to his own death as laying down his life for a friend and calls his disciples no longer servants but friends since he has shared the revelation of the Father with them.

Among the Classical writers, friendship existed almost exclusively between equals. It also existed very much in a culture of reciprocity, characterized by the giving and receiving of favors, and it quickly merged with a patronage system where favors were exchanged between patrons and clients. Since virtually every treatise on friendship comes from upper-class authors, it was somewhat class specific, that is, friendship rarely crossed social and gender barriers. This is vividly illustrated in a letter Cicero wrote to his beloved, Tiro, a slave who served Cicero most of his adult life, and to whom he wrote twenty-one letters. In 53 BC, Cicero granted Tiro, a slave and his long-term secretary, his freedom so that he would be "our friend instead of our slave."[9] A recent study of friendship by a noted scholar says that in antiquity friendship "involved an economic, political old-boys network, conferring favors."[10]

In the final section of the Letter to the Romans (12:1—15:33), where Paul exhorts the community to be transformed and adopt a lifestyle acceptable to God, Paul employs motifs from this moral teaching on friendship. The stress "on virtue as the basis of their mutuality" and the exhortation to "love one another with mutual affection; outdo one another in showing honor" (Rom 12:9–10), are motifs of the friendship tradition. The term "mutual affection," *philadelphia* (12:10), is one of the classic terms of the friendship tradition as is the stress on showing mutual honor. Shortly after this exhortation Paul tells the community to extend hospitality to strangers (12:13), and to "live in harmony with one another" (12:16; cf. also 15:5, lit. "to think alike among yourselves")—both friendship motifs. Terms for mutuality characterize this section. In his concluding exhortation, Paul notes expectation and support for his future travel (15:24), a friendship motif, and the whole section resonates with language of mutual affection. Most important, the command to welcome one another, which for Paul is the goal of his whole engagement in the dispute between the weak and strong, is part of the friendship vocabulary, and could be translated as "welcome as friends those who are weak in faith" (Rom 14:1, *au. trans.*).

The remarkable thing about Paul's use of friendship motifs here is that he stands the tradition on its head and releases it from its social and androcentric mooring among the upper classes. Far from exhorting people of like interests and like virtue to friendship, Paul wants the

9. D. R. Shakelton Bailey, trans, *Cicero. Letters to His Friends*, Loeb Classical Library 205 (Cambridge, MA: Harvard University Press, 2001), 16.16.1.

10. John Reumann, "Philippians as a 'Letter of Friendship,'" in *Friendship, Flattery and Frankness of Speech: Studies in Friendship in the Ancient World*, ed. John T. Fitzgerald (Leiden/New York: Brill, 1996), 104.

Roman congregations to form communities of friends that break down the walls erected between people of different ethnic backgrounds, "the weak," composed mainly of ethnic Jews or Gentiles who had been Jewish sympathizers, and "the strong," with their heavy predominance of Gentiles. As mentioned, there may also be a significant class and social distinction between the weak and the strong. Two of the neuralgic issues are eating meat and drinking wine, both of which were normally reserved to the more prosperous classes, while the poor of Rome existed mainly on the daily dole distributed to the people or on simple meals of grain and vegetables. Paul's statement that "some eat only vegetables," may reflect economic as well religious perspectives. When Paul summarizes his strategy for ending the dispute at Rome in the phrase, "Welcome one another, therefore, just as Christ has welcomed you, for the glory of God" (15:7), he is exhorting them to become communities of friends. This friendship does not involve even resolving the dispute. The weak can go on observing their food regulations and celebrating their special days, and the strong can go on eating whatever food they want. Deeply held convictions are not to be an obstacle to mutual acceptance since both groups have been accepted by God in Christ. Mutual acceptance in Paul does not result in some bland, lowest-common-denominator identity shared by all, but coexists with significant differences sustained by the radical new identity of being in Christ, and by a realization of the impartiality of a God who accepts radical difference.

The final verses of the letter, the letter of commendation for Phoebe (16:1–23), with its mixture of Jewish and non-Jewish names, its blending of upper-class names with those of slaves or people freed from slavery, and its prominence given to women Church leaders is a parade example of Paul's baptismal creed of Galatians 3:27–28: "As many of you as were baptized into Christ have clothed yourselves with Christ [like a garment or new identity]. There is no longer Jew or Greek, there is no longer slave or free, there is no longer male and female; for all of you are one in Christ Jesus." Thus Rome's marginal and often beleaguered communities can claim for themselves the most desired values that the aristocratic Romans would deny them, to be a community of friends and even to be friends of God, and to be a community that has broken down the walls of hostility. In our world today where religious divisions can be so destructive, Paul challenges our society to welcome people of different religious convictions and religious practice so that ultimately we can become those who share things in common (friends).

THE COLLECTION

While Paul is heralded as one who experienced and proclaimed the meaning of the Christ-event and provided a vision of life in contrast to the values of Roman imperial society, he also never forgot the sufferings of his Jewish brothers and sisters in Judaea. This collection has been the subject of important studies, most recently by David J. Downs (*Offering*). The earliest acceptance of Paul's Gospel by the Jerusalem leaders, James, John, and Cephas, was marked by an agreement that "only, we were to be mindful of the poor, which is the very thing I was eager to do" (Gal 2:10). The "poor" refers primarily to the Jerusalem Church that would have been most affected by the endemic food shortages and devastating famines that characterized the middle decades of the first century AD, not only in Palestine but throughout the empire.[11] The Acts of the Apostles describes the journey of Paul and Barnabas to Jerusalem for famine relief during the reign of Claudius in AD 41–59 (cf. Acts 11:27–29).

When writing to the Corinthians from Ephesus (c. AD 56), Paul returns to his concern for collecting funds for the Jerusalem community:

> Now concerning the collection for the saints: you should follow the directions I gave to the churches of Galatia. On the first day of every week, each of you is to put aside and save whatever extra you earn, so that collections need not be taken when I come. And when I arrive, I will send any whom you approve with letters to take your gift to Jerusalem. If it seems advisable that I should go also, they will accompany me. (1 Cor 16:1–4)

---

11. Peter Garnsey, *Food and Society in Classical Antiquity* (Cambridge University Press, 1999), 32–33.

Even amid contentious relationships with opponents manifest throughout 2 Corinthians, Paul seems to have written two distinct letters on the collection (2 Cor 8—9). In these chapters, Paul brings his great rhetorical skill to encourage the Corinthian Church to imitate the Church of the Philippians in Macedonia (cf. Phil 4:15):

> We want you to know, brothers and sisters, about the grace of God that has been granted to the churches of Macedonia; for during a severe ordeal of affliction, their abundant joy and their extreme poverty have overflowed in a wealth of generosity on their part. For, as I can testify, they voluntarily gave according to their means, and even beyond their means, begging us earnestly for the privilege of sharing in this ministry to the saints. (2 Cor 8:1–4a)

This letter is then followed by a second (or a fragment of one) in 2 Corinthians 9, where Paul again turns to the collection (called here in Greek a *diakonia*, which is "an act of service").

Throughout these letters, Paul weaves subtle theological arguments. In the first, which is also a letter of recommendation for Titus, Paul's agent for the collection, after praising the excellence of the virtues of the Corinthians: "faith," "speech," and "knowledge," Paul challenges them to a new kind of excellence, an excellence in generosity, and reminds them of "the generous act of our Lord Jesus Christ, that though he was rich, yet for your sakes he became poor, so that by his poverty you might become rich" (2 Cor. 8:7–9). While Paul is primarily referring to the poverty of Christ manifest in his emptying and taking on the cross (Phil 2:6–11), his readers would know that the Jesus who lived in Palestine was also materially poor and that their own roots are among the poor and vulnerable (1 Cor 1:26–31). He then goes on to suggest that their generosity will form a bond of community with the poorer churches, so that "as a matter of equality your surplus at the present time should supply their needs, so that their surplus may also supply your needs, that there may be equality" (2 Cor 8:14). Hans Dieter Betz, notes that "there is no alternative but to assume that the church of Jerusalem, though poor economically had spiritual wealth, while the church of Corinth while rich in every respect had its shortcomings," one of which was that it had not completed its contribution to the collection (2 *Corinthians 8 and 9*, 69).

In what may be a fragment of a second letter, Paul again urges the Corinthians to be generous in the collection, this time citing the example of churches in Achaia (most likely outside of Corinth) and again invokes the mutuality of gifts, since "you are glorifying God for your obedient confession of the gospel of Christ and the generosity of your contribution to them and to all others, while in prayer on your behalf they long for you, because of the surpassing grace of God upon you" (2 Cor 9:13–14).

Paul's final reflection on the collection comes at the end of the Letter to the Romans, written from Corinth before he sets out to Jerusalem with the collection where he recapitulates the major themes of meeting material needs and sharing in spiritual blessings:

> At present, however, I am going to Jerusalem in a ministry to the saints; for Macedonia and Achaia have been pleased to share their resources with the poor among the saints at Jerusalem. They were pleased to do this, and indeed they owe it to them; for if the Gentiles have come to share in their spiritual blessings, they ought also to be of service to them in material things. (Rom 15:25–27)

This journey to Jerusalem will ultimately bring about Paul's arrest and transfer to Rome, where he will die. In the New Testament, it is never revealed what happened to the money that was collected.

Paul's collection for the saints is a nest of literary and historical problems, and there is no consensus even on its theological significance. Four major understandings have been proposed. The collection was: (1) a prelude to the eschatological gathering of the Gentiles; (2) an obligation on Paul from the Jerusalem leaders; (3) an "ecumenical offering," to forge bonds of unity with the "mother church" at Jerusalem; and (4) to provide material sustenance. In his excellent survey of these views, David Downs argues for some combination of the last two (*Offering*, 161) and notes that, in the legacy of Paul (and I would add Luke–Acts), concern for the poor was a hallmark of Christian life. Paul's concern to alleviate hunger is at the fountainhead of an enduring tradition. The old Roman Church of Santa Maria in Cosmedin was constructed on the site of one of the food distribution centers, called *diakonia*, the same word that Paul used for his collection. Today, through the ministry (*diakonia*) of dedicated laypeople and religious, the Church sponsors major centers to feed the hungry in virtually every city of the United States.

REFLECTING ON THE COLLECTION

Today many beleaguered pastors and parishioners moan at the prospect of various collections, as most likely did Paul's hearers. Yet Paul's practice and theology can be a guideline for a just use of financial resources today. Fundamental to his practice was a concern for the sufferings of other Christians, even among those among whom he never worked or served. Concretely this involved alleviation of hunger. Second, he never lost sight of the dignity of those whom he was serving by the collection. He stressed mutuality of gifts in language that we could call today "solidarity."

AN OPTION FOR THE POOR

No less than the Lukan Jesus nor the practice of the early community in Acts, Paul is concerned about the social good of the communities he visited and founded. While the description may be contemporary, the reality is that Paul practiced "an option for the poor," that is, he provided a profound theological basis for justice where the Christ-event mandates a community where the poor and marginalized have claim on the resources of the whole group and where they share equal dignity. His theological vision was played out in diverse but similar ways when he wrote against the abuses of the Lord's Supper, took the cause of the weak in disputes over eating and other religious practices, and never lost sight of the need to provide material help to those who lived on the edge of starvation.

The legacy of the Gospels and Paul lived on as the Church grew in the Roman Empire. The eminent early Church historian, Peter Brown, has stated this powerfully:

The Christian community suddenly came to appeal to men who felt deserted. At a time of inflation the Christians invested large sums of liquid capital in people; at a time of universal brutality the courage of Christian martyrs was impressive; during public emergencies such as plague or rioting, the Christian clergy were shown to be the only united group in the town, able to look after the burial of the dead and to organize food supplies.[12]

When one looks at our contemporary world shattered by the greed of the super wealthy, the gap between rich and poor is the largest on record,[13] with 21 percent of children in the United States living in poverty.[14] More appalling is the prevalence of food shortage and famine in major parts of the world. Too often goes unheeded the ringing cry of Paul: "Bear one another's burdens, and in this way you will fulfill the law of Christ" (Gal 6:2).

RESOURCE BIBLIOGRAPHY

SELECT MAJOR ACADEMIC STUDIES

Beker, Johan Christiaan. *Paul's Apocalyptic Gospel: The Coming Triumph of God*. Philadelphia: Fortress Press, 1982.

———. *The Triumph of God in Life and Thought*. Philadelphia, PA: Fortress Press, 1982.

---

12. Peter Brown, *The World of Late Antiquity from Marcus Aurelius to Muhammed* (London: Thames and Hudson, 1971), 67.

13. Regarding income inequality, the "CBO [Congressional Budget Office] finds that over the past three decades, a growing fraction of income has gone to the top of the income distribution. The top fifth saw its share of pretax income rise from 43 percent in 1979 to more than 50 percent in 2010. Much of the gain went to the top 1 percent, whose share increased from 9 percent to 15 percent over that period. In contrast, households in the bottom two quintiles saw their income shares drop. The poorest 20 percent collected just 5.1 percent of pretax income in 2010, down from 6.2 percent in 1979. Households in the second quintile suffered a bigger decline—from 11.2 percent to 9.6 percent over the period." From an article in *Forbes Magazine*, Dec. 9, 2013, http://www.forbes.com/sites/beltway/2013/12/09/cbo-details-growing-u-s-income-inequality.

14. According to the United States Census Bureau, "The poverty rate in 2012 for children under age 18 was 21.8 percent. The poverty rate for people aged 18 to 64 was 13.7 percent, while the rate for people aged 65 and older was 9.1 percent." None of these poverty rates were statistically different from their 2011 estimates, http://www.census.gov/hhes/www/poverty/about/overview.

Dunn, James D. G. *The New Perspective on Paul: Collected Essays.* Tübingen: Mohr Siebeck, 2005. A collection of essays by Dunn, one of the most important interpreters of this shift in Pauline studies.

————. *The Theology of Paul the Apostle.* Grand Rapids, MI: Eerdmans; Edinburgh: T & T Clark, 1998. A comprehensive coverage by a leading Pauline scholar.

Sanders, E. P. *Paul and Palestinian Judaism: A Comparison of Patterns of Religion.* Philadelphia: Fortress Press, 1977. A landmark study that inaugurated the "new perspective on Paul." Sanders rejects a reading where Paul is opposed to a legalistic Judaism and stresses the conjunction of love and justice in both traditions.

Schnelle, Udo. *Apostle Paul: His Life and Theology.* Grand Rapids, MI: Baker Academic, 2005.

Wright, N. T. *The Climax of the Covenant: Christ and the Law in Pauline Theology.* Minneapolis: Fortress Press, 1992.

GENERAL STUDIES OF PAUL

Barrett, C. K. *Paul: An Introduction to His Thought.* Louisville, KY: Westminster John Knox Press, 1994.

Brown, Raymond E. *An Introduction to the New Testament.* New York: Doubleday, 1995. The section on Paul is one of the best presentations available.

Dunn, James D. G. *The Cambridge Companion to St Paul.* Cambridge: Cambridge University Press, 2003. A helpful collection of articles on Paul's life, letters, and theology.

Elliott, Neil. *Liberating Paul: The Justice of God and the Politics of the Apostle.* Maryknoll, NY: Orbis Books, 1994. Elliott stresses that Paul has been neglected in the struggle for justice and peace and suggests that by realizing that Paul spoke on behalf of the poor, we may better discover ourselves in his letters.

Fitzmyer, Joseph A. *Paul and His Theology: A Brief Sketch.* Englewood Cliffs, NJ: Prentice Hall, 1989. A short paperback that reproduces articles on the life of Paul and his theology from the *New Jerome Biblical Commentary*.

Gorman, Michael. *Apostle of the Crucified Lord: A Theological Introduction to Paul and His Letters.* Grand Rapids, MI: Eerdmans, 2004. A comprehensive introduction to the Pauline letters, though some-what marred by an overemphasis on Paul's theology of the cross.

Murphy-O'Connor, Jerome. *Paul: His Story.* Oxford/New York: Oxford University Press, 2004. Murphy-O'Connor has studied Paul for over forty years and brings a wealth of historical and archeological evidence to reconstruct the life of Paul.

Plevnik, Joseph. *What Are They Saying About Paul?* New York/Mahwah, NJ: Paulist, 1986. A fine survey of various studies of Paul.

Stendahl, Krister. *Paul among Jews and Gentiles.* Philadelphia: Fortress Press, 1976. A collection of important essays, especially "Call Not Conversion," and "The Apostle Paul and the Introspective Conscience of the West."

Witherup, Ronald D. *101 Questions and Answers on Paul.* New York/Mahwah, NJ: Paulist, 2003. An excellent overview of all aspects of Paul.

Wright, N. T. *Paul in Fresh Perspective.* Minneapolis: Fortress, 2006. This work covers essential aspects of Paul's theology.

PAUL IN THE CONTEXT OF THE ROMAN EMPIRE

Crossan, John Dominic, and Jonathan L. Reed. *In Search of Paul: How Jesus' Apostle Opposed Rome's with God's Kingdom.* San Francisco: HarperSanFrancisco, 2004.

Elliott, Neil. *The Arrogance of Nations: Reading Romans in the Shadow of Empire.* Minneapolis: Fortress Press, 2008.

Gill, David W. J., and Conrad Gempf, eds. *The Book of Acts in Its First-Century Setting.* Vol 2, *Greco-Roman Setting.* Grand Rapids, MI: Eerdmans, 1994. Important essays are: Bruce Winter, "Acts and Food Shortages," 58–78, and David W. J. Gill, "Achaia," 433–54.

Horsley, Richard A., ed. *Paul and Empire: Religion and Power in Imperial Society.* Harrisburg, PA: Trinity Press International, 1997. A collection by different authors; see especially Part III, "Paul's Counter Imperial Gospel."

———. *Paul and Politics: Ekklesia, Israel, Imperium, Interpretation. Essays in Honor of Krister Stendahl.* Harrisburg, PA: Trinity Press International, 2000. See especially Neil Elliot, "Paul and the Politics of Empire"; N. T. Wright, "Paul's Gospel and Caesar's Empire."

Kahl, Brigitte. *Galatians Re-Imagined: Reading with the Eyes of the Vanquished.* Minneapolis: Fortress Press, 2010. Part of the important new series "Paul in Critical Contexts."

Lopez, Davina. *Apostle to the Conquered: Reimagining Paul's Mission.* Minneapolis: Fortress Press, 2008. Lopez worked with Brigitte Kahl and pursues similar goals.

Trebilco, Paul. *The Early Christians in Ephesus from Paul to Ignatius.* Grand Rapids, MI: Eerdmans, 2004. An encyclopedic study of available evidence on the location and life of Christians in Ephesus, also important for Johannine writings.

PAUL AND THE POOR

Betz, Hans Dieter. *2 Corinthians 8 and 9: A Commentary on Two Administrative Letters of the Apostle Paul.* Hermeneia. Minneapolis: Fortress Press, 1985. A detailed study of these chapters with a focus on the rhetoric used by Paul to support the collection.

Downs, David J. *The Offering of the Gentiles: Paul's Collection for Jerusalem in its Chronological, Cultural and Cultic Contexts.* Tübingen: Mohr Siebeck, 2008. A clear summary of this aspect of Paul's life.

Georgi, Dieter. *Remembering the Poor: The History of Paul's Collection for Jerusalem.* Nashville: Abingdon, 1992. Covers not only the history of the collection, but also offers powerful reflections on its significance in relation to Paul's theology of the cross.

Joubert, Stephan. *Paul as Benefactor: Reciprocity, Strategy and Theological Reflection in Paul's Collection.* Tübingen: Mohr Siebeck, 2000. This work investigates the collection from the perspective of the social convention of benefit exchange and expresses the reciprocal relationship between the Jerusalem leadership and Paul, and also with the rapidly growing early Christian movement under Paul's supervision.

Longenecker, Bruce W. *Remember the Poor: Paul, Poverty and the Greco-Roman World.* Grand Rapids, MI: Eerdmans, 2011. A comprehensive scholarly study of the social and historical context of Paul's statements on the poor, followed by careful study of individual texts, with a powerful conclusion: "The devotion to the cause of the poor that Paul says had marked his early ministry (Gal 2:1) seems to have continued throughout the 50's as shown by his willingness to put his life on the line in his delivery of the collection…" (315–16).

Meggitt, Justin. *Paul, Poverty and Survival.* Edinburgh: T & T Clark, 1998. Not specifically on the collection, but it describes the economic location of Paul and the Pauline churches, and their various survival strategies as a group located among the "poor" of the first century.

Nickle, Keith F. *The Collection: A Study in Paul's Theology.* London: SCM Press, 1966. Seminal work that studies history of collection, analogies to Paul's collection in contemporary Judaism, and its theological significance.

THE LORD'S SUPPER

The literature is vast and mainly treats the relation of 1 Corinthians 11:17–33 to the Gospel institution narratives. The listed works focus on its implication for social justice.

Coutsoumpos, Panayotis. *Paul and the Lord's Supper: A Socio-Historical Investigation.* New York: Peter Lang, 2005.

Lampe, Peter. "The Corinthian Eucharistic Dinner Party: Exegesis of a Cultural Context (1 Cor 11:17–34)." *Affirmatio* 4 (1991): 1–15. An interesting article that describes supper as an *eranos* ("potluck") meal provided by food brought by different groups.

Murphy-O'Connor, Jerome. "Eucharist and Community in First Corinthians," *Worship* 50 (September 1976): 370–85; cf. also 51 (January 1977): 56–69. Excellent articles that relate Paul's theology to the social situation.

Schottroff, Luise. "Holiness And Justice: Exegetical Comments on 1 Corinthians 11:17–34" *Journal for the Study of the New Testament* 19 (2000): 51–60. Lord's Supper was the locus "where just relationships were tried out" (55).

Theissen, Gerd. *The Social Setting of Pauline Christianity.* Philadelphia: Fortress Press, 1982. A seminal study of social stratification at Corinth.

Winter, Bruce. *After Paul Left Corinth: The Influence of Secular Ethics and Social Change.* Grand Rapids, MI: Eerdmans, 2001. See especially 142–63.

CHAPTER 11

THE JOHANNINE WRITINGS

The title of this chapter oversimplifies the challenge of its content. In the early Church, three works were attributed to a "John," often identified with the "beloved disciple," who was considered the author of the Gospel, the Book of Revelation (the Apocalypse), and the three Letters of John. Virtually no scholar today would agree with this, mainly because the literary genre, the style, and theological content of the Book of Revelation and the Gospel/Letters are so utterly different. The grouping of this chapter is partly for convenience, but I will also propose that, though the authorship is different, the three works reflect a similar setting and fundamental theological perspectives. All appear near the end of the first century in a Greco-Roman environment when the nascent communities are setting sail into a Hellenized world that is dominated by the religious and political ideology of the Roman Empire. Each Johannine writing, in its own way, offers an alternate vision to its domineering ethos.

THE GOSPEL WITH A NOD TO THE LETTERS

Two of the very best recent studies on John repeat the description of John as "a stream where a child can wade and an elephant can swim" (Anderson, *Riddles*, 1, citing Augustine and Pope Gregory) since "the Gospel has a mysterious quality to it: easily graspable, in one sense, but profoundly elusive in another" (Lee, *Hallowed*, 22). Jesus is clearly "from above," described as "a stranger from heaven," and characterized by Ernst Käsemann as "god walking on the face of the earth."[1] He talks in apparent riddles that humans "from below," cannot understand, and no single perspective or description exhausts its richness. On first

---

1. Ernst Käsemann, *The Testament of Jesus* (Philadelphia: Fortress Press, 1968), 73.

reading, the Gospel lacks the concern for issues of social justice found not only in the other Gospels, but elsewhere in the New Testament. Jesus does not associate with marginal groups, but chooses a band of disciples that are his constant companions. There are no direct commands to disciples to abandon possessions. There are no exhortations to care for the poor, nor any warnings against the dangers of wealth. Though Jesus reaches out and heals various maladies, the narratives of the actual healings are brief and serve mainly to introduce long discourses about his identity and relation to the Father. Though "otherworldly," Jesus was sent by the Father to save the world (1:29; 3:17; 4:42; 12:47) and yet "world" most often symbolizes alien forces opposed to the revelation of Jesus (see especially 1:10; 3:19; 7:12; 12:46; 14:17, 27; 15:18–19; 16:33; 18:36), and the future work of the disciples (15:18–19; 16:33; 17:15–18). The ambivalence of "the world" as the place where "salvation" will unfold as well as the center of opposition to the Gospel message foreshadows the contemporary efforts to proclaim and enact social justice, in situations of deep structural evil.

Important studies have examined both direct and indirect elements in the Gospel that foster reflection on its relevance to social justice. Over two decades ago, Robert Karris underscored important elements of Jesus' concern for the marginalized in John (*Jesus and the Marginalized*). Jesus heals the physically afflicted: the son of the Galilean official (4:43–54), the lame man at the pool of Bethesda (5:1–15), and the blind beggar (9:1–41), and welcomes people on the fringes of his society: the Samaritan woman, who leads other Samaritans to Jesus (4:1–42). He feeds the hungry (6:1–14), and he and his disciples are to follow the Passover custom of giving money to the poor (12:5–8; 13:29). Women, often marginalized in first-century society, follow him on the way to the cross; Mary Magdalene is first to meet the risen Jesus who commissions her to bring the news of the resurrection to "my brothers" (20:11–18).

Despite the relative absence of concerns for the poor and the marginalized found in the Synoptic Gospels, the theology of John provides resources for a community today dedicated to issues of social justice. Since the purpose of this book is to offer reflections and resources, let us also reflect on the context of these writings, with an emphasis on "John and Empire" that helps better to understand the challenges facing readers of John then and today. A community that is united around the teaching of Jesus and lives as friends can embody resistance to an empire founded on oppressive power.

THE JOHANNINE JESUS: REIMAGINING DIVINITY

The Prologue (John 1:1–18) is widely acknowledged as an overture to the Gospel and contains John's fundamental understanding of Jesus. Its opening words, "in the beginning," Creation through the Word, and the arrival of life and light, echo the beginning of Genesis when God's Word brought forth light and culminates in the Creation of life. In rhythmic cadence it moves from the preexistence of the Word to his role in Creation (as light and life) to becoming enfleshed among us, so that "we have seen his glory, the glory as of a father's only son, full of grace and truth." Yet darkness remained but could not overcome the light, yet "the world did not know him" and "he came to what was his own, and his own people did not accept him." Especially striking here is the alternation between transcendence and presence, power and weakness (flesh), light and darkness, revelation and ignorance, gifts (grace, truth, adoption into the very family of God) and rejection. Interspersed in the original hymn are comments on the proper relation of John, the man sent from God, to the incarnate Word, not as the light but as a witness to the light, and an anticipation of other followers of Jesus as witnesses. As the Gospel unfolds, Jesus is above all the revealer who discloses God. To know God is not to begin with some preconceived idea of God based on attributes, for example, all-powerful, all-knowing, but to realize that Jesus embodies and reveals the *persona* of a God who invites his followers into deepest communion.

Just as in Genesis the creative Word of God culminates with the first humans, Adam and Eve, the first major section of the Prologue heralds the new creation with the startling statement "the Word became flesh and dwelt among us" (1:14). The hymn changes here from narration to a first-person confession: "we have seen his glory" (1:14b), and "from his fullness we have all received" (1:16). Most shocking is the term *flesh*, which suggests finitude and the solidarity of Christ with all of humanity as well as sharing human mortality, and indicates how "the divide between the divine and human is traversed" (Lee, *Hallowed*, 42).

Here the Divine does not simply create a human, but becomes human. "Flesh" has the overtones of the weakness and vulnerability of being human, yet now humanity becomes the very bearer and presence of the Divine. At a later stage in the life of the Johannine communities, failure to accept this results in a schism: "Many deceivers have gone out into the world, those who do not confess that Jesus Christ has come in the flesh; any such person is the deceiver and the antichrist!" (2 John 1:7).

In discussing Genesis above (see chapter 2, 29–30), we argued that creation in the image and likeness of God is the foundation of all respect for people regardless of things such as race, gender, or social status. That the Word become flesh at this new creation is the basis of solidarity with every human; all humanity has been objectively changed, and everyone alive bears the stamp of the eternal and incarnate Word, who is "the true light, which enlightens *everyone*" (John 1:9, emphasis mine). The universal scope of the incarnation of the Word is a fundamental disposition for all those who seek justice in a broken world.

Such a reimaging of divinity reflects the context and concerns of those who will hear and live the Gospel. By the end of the first century, Christian authors are offering a vision of God as more powerful than heavenly and earthly rulers and summoning people not to abject obedience but to a share of divine life (Colossians and Ephesians). At the same time, especially in the eastern provinces (Asia and Syria), Roman emperors were pursuing active campaigns of divinization of themselves and their predecessors. Early Christianity began to flourish in the cities of these provinces, especially Antioch and Ephesus.

The Gospel of John clearly reflects the life and teaching of Jesus in first-century Judaea and Galilee, but embodies many different stages and community interests in its development (cf. Brown, *Community*.) However, Ephesus remains the most agreed upon setting for the final edition of the Gospel, mainly because of the almost universal testimony of the early Church. Acts and the Pauline corpus show that early communities began to flourish in Ephesus, where multiple house-churches existed, and among which was a group that claimed "John" as their patron (Trebilco, *Early Christians*, 263). While different settings and communities are claimed for the final edition of each Gospel, the genre itself suggests that the Evangelist envisioned a "wide-ranging Christian audience" (Trebilco, *Early Christians*, 236).

In the context and culture of Ephesus, John's portrait of Jesus receives a distinct coloring (Carter, *John and Empire*). With the arrival of the Roman Empire under Augustus (63 BC to AD 14) came the gradual divinization of the emperor. An inscription from Priene in Asia Minor (9 BC) celebrates the birth of Augustus "the birthday of the god [emperor] was for the world the beginning of joyful tidings which have been proclaimed on his account." Throughout the first century AD, emperors were designated as a "son of God," well summarized by Warren Carter:

> A number of the inscriptions from Ephesus attest the use of the title "Son of God" for Roman emperors through the first century (Greek: *theou huios*; Latin: *divi filius*). Augustus is "son of God." Nero is "son of God Claudius and descendant of God Caesar Augustus." Titus is "son of God Vespasian." Domitian is also "son of God Vespasian." Trajan is "son of God" and "son of God Nerva." The title denotes origin as well as divine legitimation or sanction for the exercise of ruling power. (*John and Empire*, 194–95)

The massive temple of the Sebastoi in Ephesus dedicated to the emperors Trajan and Domitian is but one indication that emperor worship flourished especially in the Roman province of Asia. Throughout this area, the titles, the shrines, and the architecture directed people to feel the power of the emperor, and to obey his mandates.

For the community, hearing John's Gospel, "Son of God," could have diverse meanings. In the Old Testament, "Son of God" is applied to Israel as God's people (Hos 11:1), the king at his coronation (Ps 2:7), angels (Job 38:7), and the suffering righteous person (Wis 2:18). In John, it appears at crucial places, as John points to Jesus early in the Gospel: "I myself have seen and have testified that this is the Son of God" (1:34), which provides an *inclusio* to the testimony of the Evangelist, "these are written so that you may come to believe that Jesus is the Messiah, the Son of God" (20:31). Life and death, belief and unbelief hinge on the power of the Son of God and "according to the law," Jewish leaders say Jesus deserves death "because he has claimed to be the Son of God" (19:7).

No single meaning can be ascribed to the title in John since it evokes multiple associations from the Jewish Scriptures and its use in other Christian writings prior to John and from the surrounding culture. Amid this diversity, the fundamental notion is a special relationship to divinity and the exercise of power.

John presents a "high Christology" of preexistence and incarnation of Jesus, where many feel that the divine so dominates that he only "seemed" to be human, which leads to Docetism, which was opposed explicitly by the Johannine letters. But the exaltation of Jesus and the stress on his heavenly origin and destiny could provide a counter vision to the ideology of empire that surrounds the readers' lives. The divinization of the reigning monarchs and their predecessors developed strongly in the province of Asia, and these rulers were heralded as benefactors and shepherds of their people—activities that characterize Jesus in the Gospel of John. Here the small communities of Asia Minor can find an ideology of nonviolent resistance to the injustice that arises from a dominating power. Such resistance is always a component of the quest for social justice, and will be epitomized in the trial of Jesus before Pilate that we will consider below.

A COMMUNITY OF DISCIPLES

John's understanding of discipleship, while in agreement with the Synoptics, is the most original of the Gospels. The disciples are initially disciples of John the Baptist who is a witness to Jesus and points to him as "the Lamb of God"; they then turn to follow Jesus who asks, "What do you seek," (*au. trans.*), and they respond, "Rabbi, where are you staying" (that is, "abide," *meneis*, John 1:29–42). A disciple is called by Jesus to be with him, to witness his mighty works, and to continue his work in the world. Especially characteristic of John, however, is that the relation between the disciple and Jesus is one of personal love and attachment, which springs from radical faith in Jesus (Lee, *Hallowed*, 134–35). No book in the New Testament stresses as strongly as John the power of faith. John's somewhat peculiar expression of believing "into" Jesus (*pisteuein eis*) underscores that belief is not simply intellectual assent, but a profound personal attachment. The believer in John is one who will have eternal life (John 3:15; 6:40–47), which is not simply life forever with God after death, but the fullness of life that begins before death. Those who believe will not only do the works that Jesus does, but even greater works (14:12).

While in the Book of Signs (John 1—12), the disciples are mainly witnesses to the work of Jesus, hovering in the background rather than central figures in the narrative, the farewell discourses (13—17), when Jesus and the disciples gathered alone, present the principal values that should characterize a community. Jesus is described as one who loved his own until the end (13:1), and he washes their feet to give them an example of love (13:1–12). Unlike the Synoptics, where the final testament of Jesus comprises warnings about the coming apocalyptic trials, in John 13—17, Jesus reveals to his disciples the depth of his relationship to the Father and of theirs to the Father through him, consoles them about his imminent death, and promises a Paraclete or advocate who will bear witness to him and dwell within them. Throughout the final discourse, Jesus prays that the lives of his disciples may be characterized by mutual love (13:34–35; 17:26), faithful prayer (14:12–14), peace (14:27), and joy (17:13), and that by abiding in him they will bear fruit (15:1–11). Jesus also prays for those who "will believe in me" through the words of the disciples (17:20), and the whole Johannine theology of discipleship is summed up in the final words of the farewell discourses, "I made your name known to them, and I will make it known, so that the love with which you have loved me may be in them, and I in them" (17:26).

Among the four Gospels, John has a distinctive egalitarian quality. Personal attachment to Jesus is paramount (vine and branches); there is no explicit choice of an inner group of twelve; no primacy given to Peter, but to "the disciple whom Jesus loved." After Jesus departs to prepare a place for the disciples, the guiding force of the community is the Paraclete, the advocate and spirit of Jesus who will continue the work of Jesus in the Church (Brown, *Gospel According to John [XIII—XXI]*, 1145).

In chapter 10, we noted that friendship was the subject of considerable reflection in Greco-Roman society, and is reflected in the language and practice of the Pauline communities. The highest form of friendship was only between equals and was directed to the benefit of the other person. Friendship was maintained by actual presence or through letters, by mutual gift-giving, and by hospitality. Friendship was thought to be a higher form of love than physical or erotic love, and the supreme instance of ancient friendship was to give one's life for a friend. But as noted, friendship rarely, if ever, bridged social or economic divisions.

Friendship is also important in appreciating the depth of relations between Jesus and the disciples in the Gospel of John. Distinctive to John is not only that Jesus washes the feet of the disciples and gives them an example of loving service, but that he calls them "friends." John the Baptist is a "friend" of the bridegroom (3:29) and Lazarus is described as "our friend" (11:11). As Jesus prepares to leave the disciples, he tells them that "no one has greater love than this, to lay down one's life for one's friends," and calls them friends rather than servants (15:13). When Jesus, whom Thomas will address with the imperial title, "my Lord and my God" (John 20:28), calls his disciples friends, he is countering one of the most fundamental divisions of class and status in the ancient world. The Gospel then confers on the Christian community a respect and dignity that counters the destructive values of the surrounding culture, which were maintained by social and economic factors. Breaking through similar divisions today remains as a mission for all concerned about social justice, so that Christian communities can truly become societies of friends.

THE TRIAL BEFORE PILATE:
THE CLASH BETWEEN GOSPEL AND EMPIRE

While the conflict between Gospel values and the Roman Empire is often latent or subtle throughout John, the dramatic trial of Jesus before the Roman prefect, Pontius Pilate, presents an overt "inversion of empire" (Thatcher, *Greater*, 122–39). The narrative is carefully structured with an introduction (18:28), "seven brief scenes that take place either inside or outside the praetorium (18:29–32, 33–38a, 38b–40; 19:1–3, 4–7, 8–11, 12–15), and a conclusion (19:16a)" (Moloney, *John*, 493). Multiple themes characterize the narrative: Jesus as king (18:33, 37, 39; 19:3, 12, 14, 15), culminating in the inscription on the cross (19:19, 21); the outcome of the conflict between "the Jews" and Jesus; and the contrast between Pilate representing "the power of empire," and Jesus as "the truth of God's power."

The narrative, which contains the longest dialogue between Jesus and another person in the Gospel, moves quickly with a contrast between incidents that take place inside the praetorium ("courtyard" of the official residence), where Pilate questions Jesus, and those outside, where Pilate confronts the Jewish leaders. The atmosphere differs; Jesus speaks only inside and the mood is somber but quiet; outside Jesus is silent and Pilate engages in a shouting match with Jewish leaders. "Inside" also suggests that the readers are given privileged revelation by Jesus that Pilate rejects; "outside" is the place where Jesus finally appears after being scourged, crowned, and wearing a purple (royal) robe, and where Pilate calls him simply "the human one" (*anthropos*). Thatcher makes the interesting observation that "'outside' presents a stage that parades the public values of the Roman power, while 'inside,' for Pilate represents a 'safe zone,' that Jews cannot enter and where he can exercise his power in an unfettered way, but the dialogue with Jesus shows that Jesus is ultimately more powerful than empire" (Thatcher, *Greater*, 70–71).

Certain elements of this trial call for further reflection. Of particular importance is that it has fostered anti-Semitism. Older commentaries portrayed Pilate as weak, vacillating, and manipulated by the "Jews," in an apologetic attempt to excuse and gain favor of the Romans (Brown, *Gospel According to John [XIII—XXI]*, 860). Since the question of the negative picture of "the Jews" over the centuries has contributed to hatred and persecution of Jewish people, attempts to clarify the meaning of the term are a paramount social justice issue.

First, Jesus and his followers are all Jewish, and observe Jewish festivals (2:13; 5:1; 10:22), and John gives more information about Jewish religious life than any other Gospel. Jesus is proud of his Jewish heritage and says, "we worship what we know, for salvation is from the Jews" (4:22). Various Jews believe in him (8:31); Jews come to console Martha and Mary and believe in Jesus (11:19, 33–36, 41). Yet hostility by the Jews permeates the narrative (cf. 5:15–18; 7:1); they believe his claims are false (7:10–13; 45–52); and call him a blasphemer (5:16–18; 19:7). Jesus' attacks on the Jews are bitter and virulent; they do not

keep the law that Moses gave them (7:19); they have a false understanding of Abraham and the devil is their father (8:39–43). Finally,
before Pilate they loudly call for Jesus' death and deny their own heritage by choosing Caesar as their king (19:15).

Second, a plethora of responses has emerged: One claim is that
"the Jews" (hoi Ioudaioi) should be translated as "the Judeans" and
means not all Jews but mainly Jewish leaders closely allied to the temple authorities who were concerned about their own positions of
power. Those "Jews" who appear at the trial before Pilate are primarily
Jerusalem temple officials who, historically, were seen as an oppressive
group by ordinary Jewish people of the time, and cooperation with the
Roman prefect was essential to maintaining power.

But the most dominant explanation of the conflict with "the Jews"
is that the opposition reflects a situation at the end of the first century
when Jews and Christians were embarking on "the parting of the
ways." Allied to this the comments on the text that followers of Jesus
would be put out of the synagogue (9:22; 12:42; 16:2) that some
authors argued reflected a widespread Jewish synagogue prayer against
Christians (birkat ha minim) that forced Christians to leave. The widespread existence of such a prayer and practice is now denied and the
expulsion may represent sporadic events in the lives of Johannine
Christians at the end of the first century, for example, in Ephesus. With
some variation, "the Jews" are constructed actors in a narrative and
represent values of "the world" that could not accept Jesus. Similarly,
the opinion of Frank Moloney has gained currency: "'The Jews' are
those characters in the narrative who have made up their minds about
Jesus." They are one side of a christological debate, that does not reflect
the situation of the historical Jesus, but later bitter Jewish-Christian
debates (see esp. Brown, Introduction, 160–72).

Third, while no definitive solution to the problem has emerged
and all have some grain of truth, neither the Jewish people at the time
of Jesus, nor those throughout history can be blamed for the rejection
of Jesus. Those engaged in preaching or teaching the Gospels have a
serious obligation to explain these texts and to counter the constant
misuse of them for covert or overt anti-Semitism.

The appearance before Pilate is a fundamental clash between the
standards of empire and gospel values where, though the main char-

acters reflect the social situation of Jews and Christians at the end of the first century, they become paradigmatic for subsequent centuries. Recent studies have underscored this in different ways. Richey stresses that the trial before Pilate should not be viewed as an anti-Semitic diatribe, but as anti-imperial narrative (*Roman Imperial*). Carter sees it more as part of the Gospel's rhetoric of distance "to create greater cultural distance from the empire, a distance secured by devotion to Jesus alone" (*John and Empire*, 197).

One aspect of the dialogue embodies the clash between two understandings of power. When Pilate asks Jesus if he is king of the Jews, he responds: "My kingdom is not from this world. If my kingdom were from this world, my followers would be fighting to keep me from being handed over to the Jews. But as it is, my kingdom is not from here" (18:36). The double statement that the kingdom is not of this world (or from here) provides an *inclusio* that frames the kind of kingship Pilate would understand, one of violent resistance to unjust power. That the kingdom proclaimed by Jesus is "not of this world," does not mean that Jesus' kingdom is purely spiritual or otherworldly, which would certainly contradict the Synoptic presentation of the kingdom. In contrast to the way of power and violence that Pilate understands, the kingdom of Jesus is one that does not adopt the ways of the world, and Jesus has come into the world to testify to the truth and his followers are "of the truth."

"Truth" is a major theme of the Gospel of John. The Prologue concludes with the glory of the Word made flesh, full of glory and truth (1:14); Jesus tells Jewish believers, "you will know the truth, and the truth will make you free" (8:32) and Jesus is "the way, and the truth, and the life" (14:6); the Advocate (Paraclete), the Spirit of truth will testify on behalf of Jesus (15:26) and "will guide you [the disciples] into all the truth" (16:13). Truth (*alētheia*, lit. "not hiding") is fundamentally the revelation or disclosure of God's saving plan in Jesus, and its opposite is often blindness: "I came into this world for judgment so that those who do not see may see, and those who do see may become blind" (9:39).

Warren Carter sums up well what is at stake in the confrontation with Pilate over "truth":

By declaring that his mission is to witness to "the truth," Jesus tells Pilate that he witnesses to God's faithfulness in saving the people. He witnesses to God acting faithfully to God's own commitments to save (3:33). When Jesus declares that he is "the truth" (14:6), he claims to reveal God's faithful saving action. When he declares that the truth shall set you free, he claims that God's saving actions, manifested in him, will free people from everything that resists and rejects God's purposes (8:32). Jesus comes from above (8:23), from heaven (3:13), where he has heard (8:26) and seen (5:19) the Father, so that he can reveal God's "truth" about God acting powerfully and faithfully to save the world (3:16–17; 8:14–18). This is not good news for Rome or its representative Pilate. (*John and Empire*, 303)

A motif running through the Gospel of John is that Jesus is on trial and "witnesses" appear in his defense: John the Baptist, the word of Jesus, the Spirit of truth will testify, and so will the disciples. The Greek verb, *martyreō* and all its cognates are the basis of the terms "witness" and "testify," and have given us the legacy of the "martyr." The trial before Pilate where Jesus stands as a witness to the truth and discloses the kind of power wielded by empire: vested in a single leader, sustained by force, arbitrary, brutal, and self-serving; truth unmasks the culture of empire. The quest for social justice today often involves a confrontation with such power, and as with Jesus, the result is the murder of those who are witnesses for justice. Karl Rahner has argued that the classical concept of martyrdom, which is fundamentally conditioned by an *odium fidei* ("hatred of the faith"), needs to be widened to include those who have been killed by an *odium iustitiae* ("hatred of justice"), and the past century contains a cloud of such witnesses who unmask and confront those whose resistance to truth and embrace of lethal power engender massive injustice.[2]

---

2. Karl Rahner, "Dimensions of Martyrdom: A Plea for the Broadening of a Classical Concept," *Concilium* 163 (1983): 9.

A MANDATE FOR SOCIAL JUSTICE

An initial impression may be that John, in comparison with the Synoptic Gospels, offers little for those who want to draw on Scripture as they reflect on social justice. But pathways open that invite more exploration. The incarnation of the Word and presence of Jesus as the revelation of God can be the basis of a deeper understanding of human dignity and of God's care for the world. The call to discipleship and the quality of community portrayed in the Gospel is a mandate that those who pursue justice must themselves mirror the kind of world they seek. Burgeoning studies on "empire" as the context of the Gospel situate the Gospel where many "divine" powers are competing for loyalty, but the Gospel provides the community an assurance that the incarnate Jesus was truly "Lord and God." This context also portrays the dynamics of oppressive power and control, that not only characterized first-century imperial rule but infect major areas of modern society. Above all, the Gospel summons people to a deep faith that, out of love, God sent his Son to bring life and peace to the world, and even when a distorted world rejected and murdered Jesus, death could not contain him, and he has sent the Paraclete or Spirit of truth, who continues his mission and presence.

THE LETTERS OF JOHN

Not surprisingly, multiple critical problems surround these short letters, concerning genre, authorship, dating, social context, and their relation to the Gospel of John. Thankfully, excellent commentaries and studies help one to navigate through these questions, with some agreed-upon perspectives, especially on 1 John, the longer and more theological of the three and the focus of these comments. Its author, who frequently uses the first-person plural "we," is not identified, and the work, which reads more like a treatise, lacks the normal greetings proper to a letter.

This first letter of John is clearly influenced by the theology of the Gospel with its emphasis on the incarnation of Jesus, the frequent use of the love command, and the ethical dualism between light and darkness. Yet there are significant differences. In 1 John, the "Jews" are never mentioned and the conflict with the synagogue is past, while now arises the conflict with other Christians, who "went out from us, but they did not belong to us; for if they had belonged to us, they would have remained with us. But by going out they made it plain that none of them belongs to us" (2:19), and the community must "test the spirits to see whether they are from God; for many false prophets have gone out into the world" (4:1).

The fundamental issue is that those who remain faithful confess "that Jesus Christ has come in the flesh is from God, and every spirit that does not confess Jesus is not from God" (4:2–3). The principal aims of the letter are to counter the claims of the secessionists also dubbed "antichrists" (1 John 2:18, 22; 4:3; 2 John 1:7), and to affirm again the radical truth of the incarnation of Jesus, and to instruct and encourage the community by intensifying the love command of Jesus.

In thinking of social justice and 1 John, two passages stand out. At the conclusion of a reflection on the implications of the love command the author writes: "Whoever loves a brother or sister lives in the light, and in such a person there is no cause for stumbling. But whoever hates another believer is in the darkness, walks in the darkness, and does not know the way to go, because the darkness has brought on blindness" (2:10–11). The author warns the community against loving "the world or the things in the world" (2:15), which then unfold in rhythmic sequence: "human nature full of desire" (*epithumia tes sarkos*); "eyes hungry for all that they see" (*epithumia ton omphalmōn*); and "material life that inflates self-assurance" (*alazoneia tou biou*, 2:16, trans., Brown, *Epistles*, 294). Each of these terms reflects social realities faced by the community.

The first two, "full of desire" and "eyes hungry," (NRSV, "desire of the flesh" and "desire of the eyes") reflect a language (*epithumia*) most often directed toward evil objects. Philo, for example, traces all wars to "the desire for money, glory or pleasure," (*On the Decalogue*, 28.153; Brown, *Epistles*, 306), and in the New Testament is frequently coupled with "flesh," in relation to sexual urges (1 Cor 7:27; Gal 5:16–17, 24; Eph 2:3). More important, in the Old Testament, "desire" appears in two of the Ten Commandments against "coveting" (*epithumein*) a neighbor's house, or wife (Exod 20:17; Deut 5:21), which is the background also of the failure of the sowing in Mark 4:19: "But the cares of the world, and the lure of wealth, and the desire [*epithumia*] for other things come in and choke the word, and it yields nothing."

In 1 John, "eyes hungry for all they see" refers to the same kind of "covetousness" for possession excoriated in the Decalogue and in the New Testament. This becomes even more clear in the third element of the worldly triad, "material life that inflates self-assurance" (NRSV, "pride in riches"). Desire then escalates into *alazoneia*, which evokes a wide range of meanings: pride, arrogance, boastfulness, ostentation (Brown, *Epistles*, 311). The community in 1 John is fractured, not only by different understandings of the incarnation of Jesus, but by socio-economic practices that characterize those who "went out from us," because they were never really "part of us" (2:19).

In 1 John, the heritage of the love command of Jesus (John 13:34–35; 15:9–10) becomes a virtual touchstone of Christian life (1 John 2:10; 4:7–9; 20–21) and becomes concrete in the treatment of a poor neighbor, again captured in the vivid translation of 1 John 3:16–18 by Raymond Brown:

> This is how we have come to know what love means: for us Christ laid down his life; ought we in turn to lay down our lives for the brothers. Indeed, when someone has enough of this world's livelihood and perceives his brother to have need, yet shuts out any compassion towards him how can the love of God abide in such a person? Little children, let us not give lip service to our love but show its truth in deeds. (*Epistles*, 439)

Even though the Gospel of John, unlike other parts of the New Testament, does not reflect the constant biblical call to be concerned for the poor and powerless, 1 John evokes this heritage in vivid language. Concretely, possessions—having enough of the world's livelihood—and perception of another's need without compassion, shown not simply in word but in actions, destroys any possibility of sharing in the benefits of Christ's self-gift of love or "abiding" in love. Love must be concrete, and Brown notes that the author of 1 John 3:16–17, "in being specific about the need to show love by helping the poor is

265

not holding up a new moral demand, rather, he is reaching into the heart of Christianity's Jewish heritage," and grounds this in Deuteronomy 15:7: "If there is among you anyone in need, a member of your community in any of your towns within the land that the Lord your God is giving you, do not be hard-hearted or tight-fisted towards your needy neighbor" (*Epistles*, 474). Shutting out compassion is the equivalent of being hard-hearted, for in Luke 10:25–37, it is rather the compassion of the Samaritan that leads him from merely "seeing" a wounded neighbor to stopping and saving him from death. In the Letter of James, fulfilling "the royal law" of loving your neighbor as yourself (2:8) consists in helping in word and deed a brother or sister who is naked and lacks daily food (2:15, see Brown, *Epistles*, 474–75).

Therefore, in two brief but powerful exhortations to the community, the author of 1 John stands in the biblical tradition of a right relation to God (justice) expressed in compassion and acts of loving kindness to a suffering neighbor. The love command of Jesus and his laying down his life for his friends is realized and embodied in concrete actions of care for a suffering neighbor. This letter joins the canon of those works that engender a theology of social justice.

THE BOOK OF REVELATION (THE APOCALYPSE)

In the words of Winston Churchill (speaking of Russia), the Book of Revelation "is a riddle, wrapped in a mystery, inside an enigma," and recently Elaine Pagels has captured its awesome power:

> The Book of Revelation reads as if John had wrapped up all our worst fears—fears of violence, plague, wild animals, unimaginable horrors emerging from the abyss below the earth, lightning, thunder, hail, earthquakes, erupting volcanoes, and the atrocities of torture and war—into one gigantic nightmare. Yet instead of ending in total destruction, his visions finally open to the new Jerusalem—a glorious city filled with light. John's visions of dragons, monsters, mothers, and whores speak less to our head than to our heart:

like nightmares and dreams, they speak to what we fear, and what we hope. (Pagels, *Revelations*, 171)

With its startling visions of the grand finale of human history, it is also the final work of the New Testament canon. Though accepted in the Western Church as early as the third century, it was rejected in the East and not completely accepted until the ninth century. It offers a panoply of images and symbols that make it the delight of artists, and a fascination for interpreters.

The solemn opening verse describes its origin and purpose: "The revelation of Jesus Christ, which God gave him to show his servants what must soon take place; he made it known by sending his angel to his servant John" (1:1). The work is a disclosure both from and about Jesus, Messiah, and future events for his servants, and which was made known to a certain John, most likely in exile at Patmos because of his witness to the Word of God. The designation, "revelation," (*apokalypsis*) links it with a large genre of literature best described by John J. Collins as a "genre of revelatory literature with a narrative framework, in which a revelation is mediated by an otherworldly being to a human recipient, disclosing a transcendent reality which is both temporal, insofar as it envisages eschatological salvation, and spatial, insofar as it involves another supernatural world."[3]

This genre has traditionally been viewed as "persecution literature," giving hope to suffering people that God's justice would ultimately prevail as their oppressors would be destroyed and that they would share in the benefits of a new creation. Paradoxically, its often brutal images of mass destruction do not sanction violent reaction by those suffering since salvation will originate from God at a set time, and in God's manner. Its main ethical thrust is to counsel faithful witness to God's Word amid suffering.

The book unfolds in two major sections, where John's visionary commission (1:9–20) is followed by Christ's proclamations to the seven churches of Asia Minor 2:1—3:21, which are a prelude to the main part of the work in 4:1—22:5. The use of symbolic numbers characterizes all apocalyptic literature, and the Book of Revelation may

---

3. John J. Collins, "Introduction: Towards the Morphology of a Genre," *Semeia* 14 (1979): 9.

set the gold standard, with seven, the traditional symbol for completeness, mentioned fifty-four times in conjunction with a host of other symbols, for example, seven stars (the angels of the seven churches) and the seven golden lampstands (the seven churches, 1:20). There are three important groups of seven seals, trumpets, and bowls (4:1—5:14; 8:1–5; 15:1–8). Though not numbered, there are seven beatitudes that frame and permeate the work: "Blessed is the one who reads aloud the words of the prophecy" (1:3, cf. also 14:13; 16:15; 19:9; 20:6; 22:7, 14: "Blessed are those who wash their robes, so that they will have the right to the tree of life and may enter the city by the gates"). Since the number seven signifies completeness or totality, such proliferation broadcasts the totality of revelation and the abundance of salvation proclaimed throughout the book.

Apocalyptic literature in general and the Book of Revelation in particular, with its emphasis on otherworldly hope, on first reading, seems to have little *direct* relevance for reflection on social justice. Yet, over the past quarter century, significant works have shown how its major themes contribute to a concern for liberation (Fiorenza, *Revelation*), nonviolent resistance to oppression (Kraybill, *Imperial Cult*), a community of faithful witness against "idolatry," and the delusions of dominating power. The book also conveys a sense of hope with the realization that its hearers will be "a kingdom and priests serving our God" that "will reign on earth" (5:10). Our aim, influenced by these writings, is to highlight certain aspects of the work that bear more directly on issues of social justice.

Among the seven churches mentioned, Ephesus was the most important, both in the Roman province of Asia Minor and as an early Christian center. It was visited by Paul and was most likely the setting for Johannine writings. The other churches were within a hundred-mile radius and possibly formed a circuit for itinerant Christian prophets and teachers. The social location and lifestyle of the seven churches is a concern of the prophet, John. An overriding concern seems to be that the communities are beginning to assimilate their values to those of the surrounding culture, for example, by eating food offered to idols (2:14 in Pergamum; 2:20 in Thyatira). This was a problem faced by Paul when writing to the Corinthians, and one that had socioeconomic ramifications since the more prosperous in the community would attend banquets where "idol meat" was served—perhaps also in two of the seven churches.

The most explicit warning about the danger of wealth occurs in the letter to the Laodiceans with the scathing comment: "because you are lukewarm, and neither cold nor hot, I am about to spit you out of my mouth" (3:16), because, "you say, 'I am rich, I have prospered, and I need nothing.' You do not realize that you are wretched, pitiable, poor, blind, and naked" (3:17). The city was a wealthy, self-sufficient town, and the Laodiceans are a wealthy, self-sufficient community of faith (Blount, *Revelation*, 82). The criticism of wealth as engendering self-sufficiency and its corresponding neglect of the poor echoes the familiar prophetic invective against wealth and is also reminiscent of the Lukan parables of the rich fool and the rich man and Lazarus (cf. chapter 9, 207–10, 212–14).

The second and major section of the Book of Revelation offers a fundamental rejection of the worship of dominating power and economic exploitation that characterized the Roman Empire—and that remains valid today as characteristics of social injustice (see Bauckham, *Theology*, 37–39). The tone shifts from prophetic critique to a panorama of apocalyptic visions (4—22), comprising two major collections, first of seven seals and seven trumpets (4:1—11:19) followed by three chapters of inaugural visions, which introduce the major symbols of the second half of the book: the dragon, the beasts, and the Lamb (12:1—14:20), followed by another grouping of seven plagues and bowls (15:1—16:21), and concluding with a contrasting parallel of final judgment on the great harlot and Babylon (Rome and the Empire, 17:1—19:10), the victory of Christ and the end of history (19:11—22:5). The visions throughout the book do not unfold chronologically or even thematically, but portray a fundamental theme: wars in both heaven and earth between dominating powers and the power of God, along with visions of hope for those on earth who remain victims of the conflict. Often they intensify and recapitulate a particular theme or image and anticipate a subsequent treatment. Though the rejection of Rome's practices and values is a subtext of the total narrative, two sections are most significant.

In Revelation 12—14, three figures, the dragon and the two beasts, are introduced and are prominent throughout the rest of the book. The section begins with the struggle between the "woman clothed with the sun, with the moon under her feet, and on her head a crown of twelve stars" who "gave birth to a son, a male child, who is to rule all the nations with a rod of iron" (12:1, 5), who is then attacked by the ancient symbol of evil, the dragon, who attacks the woman and her offspring. Though the references for the woman and the dragon are disputed, when the woman is saved, "the dragon was angry with the woman, and went off to make war on the rest of her children, those who keep the commandments of God and hold the testimony of Jesus" (12:17).

The war now unfolds in a vision of the power of the Roman Empire in the multiple images of the two beasts of Revelation 13. The first beast arises from the sea and is most likely Rome and its emperors, especially Nero, who in the eastern empire was thought to have come to life again (*Nero redivivus*, 13:1–11), while the second beast, "that rose out of the earth…exercises all the authority of the first beast on its behalf, and it makes the earth and its inhabitants worship the first beast." This chapter is a coded polemic against the dominating power of the emperor, and the spread of emperor worship in the territories of the seven churches.

In a pattern that again characterizes the book, the following chapter counters with images of hope and the ultimate victory of those who are murdered by the beast and are called blessed, since "they will rest from their labors, for their deeds follow them" (14:13). The following two chapters contain visions of seven bowls and seven plagues that portent the final judgment.

Since the visions in the Book of Revelation unfold often as recapitulation or intensification of a particular theme, the final judgment of Rome and all dominating power culminates in Revelation 17 and 18 applying to Rome, the traditional Old Testament image of "the harlot" for cities characterized by idolatry or godlessness, luxuriating in wealth from commerce and those who accept their authority as fornicators (Isa 23:47; Nah 3; Jer 50–51; Ezek 16:23, 26–27), "the great whore" (17:5), or Babylon (18:2). The author is not only attacking Rome, "the great harlot," but also its client rulers, "the kings of the earth [who] are the inhabitants of the earth [who] became drunk on the wine of her harlotry" (17:2). The images again allude to the woman as Rome, which has also become drunk with the blood of the saints and of the witnesses to Jesus (17:6).

The final judgment then unfolds when an angel proclaims, "Fallen, fallen is Babylon the great" (18:2). Faithful people are to come out from her, "for her sins are heaped high as heaven" (18:5). The destruction is the consequence of her (Rome's) slaughter of the innocent in general (18:24, cf. 18:6), her idolatrous arrogance (18:8), and her self-intelligent luxury at the expense of her empire (18:7). The economic element of the judgment has received too little attention but features prominently in the cause of Rome's destruction (Bauckham, *Prophecy*, 350). The cargoes carried by the trading ships provide insights, found nowhere else in the New Testament, into Rome's mercantile empire. They represent exploitation of the geographical scope of the empire, and most are luxury items and an index of "the newly conspicuous wealth and extravagance of the rich families of Rome in the period of the early empire" (Bauckham, *Prophecy*, 352). The list of cargo ends with the transport of "slaves—and human lives" (18:11–13), which is the starkest condemnation of slavery in the New Testament—and John's wording is significant. The Greek of "slaves and human beings" (*sōmatōn kai psychas anthrōpōn*) can also be read as "slaves who are human beings," and Bauckham has captured its significance:

> He (John) is pointing out that slaves are not mere animal carcasses to be bought and sold as property, but are human beings. But in this emphatic position at the end of the list, there is more than just a comment on the slave trade. It is a comment on the whole list of cargoes. It suggests the inhuman brutality, the contempt for human life, on which the whole of Rome's prosperity and luxury rest. (*Prophecy*, 370–71)

This evil commercial network is a prelude not only to the destruction of Babylon, but destroyed also will be "all the nations [that] have drunk of the wine of the wrath of her fornication, and the kings of the earth [who] have committed fornication with her, and the merchants of the earth [who] have grown rich from the power of her luxury" (18:3). Those who supported and benefited from the power of the empire will

271

be involved as "all shipmasters and seafarers, sailors and all whose trade is on the sea...wept and mourned, crying out, 'Alas, alas, the great city, where all who had ships at sea grew rich by her wealth! For in one hour she has been laid waste'" (18:18–19). This lament is followed by the counter visions of the victory of Christ, the end of history, and the arrival of the new Jerusalem as a counter image to Rome, inaugurated in chapter 19, when a great multitude proclaims, "Hallelujah! Salvation and glory and power to our God, for his judgments are true and just" (19:1–2).

Let us now make some suggestions of the relevance of the work to issues of social justice. First, for the Book of Revelation, the medium (imaginative language) is the message, as Bauckham eloquently notes:

> One of the functions of Revelation was to purge and to refurbish the Christian imagination. It tackles people's imaginative response to the world, which is at least as deep and influential as their intellectual convictions. It recognizes the way a dominant culture, with its images and ideals, constructs the world for us, so that we perceive and respond to the world in its terms. Moreover, it unmasks this dominant construction of the world as an ideology of the powerful which serves to maintain their power. In its place, Revelation offers a different way of perceiving the world which leads people to resist and to challenge the effects of the dominant ideology. (*Theology*, 159)

Second, as the seven letters indicate, a major concern of the author is that the values and ethos of their environments are compromising their following of Christ. The visions of the power and ultimate destruction of Rome and its empire do not simply offer hope to a people threatened with persecution, but are warnings against the seductive power of the empire. The far-flung empire brought peace and prosperity to the major cities of Asia Minor. Temples, festivals, statuary, and even coins supported the quasi-divine status of Roman rule. This power threatened even Christians, which may explain the use of the harlot image (rightly offensive to women), and that of devouring beasts. The destruction of the beast and of the merchants is a warning to Christians perhaps overly engaged in reaping the rewards of commercial engagement.

Third, as J. Nelson Kraybill notes, "While some imagery in Revelation is violent and vindictive, *the counsel for actual Christian behavior is non-violence*" and "the *controlling metaphor* or governing symbol is the slain lamb" (*Apocalypse*, 135, emphasis in original). In the face of violence, the vocation of the Christian, then and now, is faithful witness and resistance to the divinization of power and prosperity.

Fourth, behind all injustice that permeates the whole Bible is the craving and exercise of dominating power, from the desire of Adam and Eve to "be like God, knowing good and evil," and snatch immortality from God (Gen 3:8, 22), through idolatry and abandonment of God's covenant, to the blindness and neglect of the poor, excoriated by prophets and chanted in psalms, to the rejection of the teaching and life of the Word of God made flesh. Yet Revelation depicts the apex of idolatrous power, and offers the counter vision where the "might of God is the might of suffering and death freely chosen...where God chooses to intervene in the world...to bring an end to its suffering and its sin" (Lee, *Hallowed*, 238).

Finally, this last book of the Bible completes an arch with the first book, Genesis, the book of beginnings. God, who created the world out of chaos, rhythmically pronounced it good, and blessed man and woman created in his image, will create a new heaven and a new earth (Rev 21:1) and a new dwelling place nurtured by "the tree of life with its twelve kinds of fruit, producing its fruit each month; and the leaves of the tree are for the healing of the nations" (22:2).

JOHANNINE SPIRITUALITY

Paradoxically, these writings, which on first reading seem to offer little material for reflection on the Bible and social justice, contain fundamental beliefs and attitudes that undergird a theology necessary for those committed to the quest for justice. Dorothy Lee has presented the most powerful summary of the theology and spirituality of the three writings, which merits quoting in full:

To sum up: Johannine spirituality in all three texts is grounded in the life of God, the dynamic presence of the Spirit, the gracious love of the Father, and the incarnate presence of Jesus, crucified and risen. The story of God's dealings with the people of God is the framework which makes sense of believers' lives. In the incarnation, Jesus identifies with the human story and with the story of creation. In turn, believers are invited to encase their small stories within that larger tale. Such an outlook is both community oriented and personal. It is spirited and embodied, celestial and terrestrial, with the capacity to ascend from earth to heaven and heaven to earth. Nor need such spirituality be restricted to the human domain: the extent of redemption is the extent of creation itself. Divine judgment is the obverse side of salvation, not alien to its spirituality but framed by it. It looks expectantly, beyond judgment and negation, to divine affirmation. God's future as the source of life and hope, a future that already permeates the present, as the dawn begins to lighten the night sky. Such spirituality awaits the future: the divine promise to wipe away all tears in the final overthrow of sin and death; yet it lives now within that anticipated reality, transforming the present. The spirituality of the Fourth Gospel, the Johannine epistles, and the Book of Revelation, is rich and variegated. It is pervaded by the conviction that is found on the spiritual path for believers and for the community of faith: the hallowing of their lives before God in truth and love. (*Hallowed*, 248)

RESOURCE BIBLIOGRAPHY

THE GOSPEL AND LETTERS OF JOHN

Since the available bibliography is so vast, this bibliography will list some standard commentaries, studies of Johannine theology, and works that provide a resource for issues of social justice. A major resource for literature on the Johannine writings is provided by Felix Just, SJ at http://catholic

-resources.org/John/index.html, see especially John Traxler, "Johannine Themes and Social Justice," http://catholic-resources.org/John/Justice.html.

Anderson, Paul N. *The Riddles of the Fourth Gospel: An Introduction to the Gospel of John*. Minneapolis: Fortress Press, 2011. An excellent and comprehensive work that captures the character and content of John.

Brown, Raymond E. *The Community of the Beloved Disciple*. New York: Paulist Press, 1979.

————. *The Epistles of John*, AB 30; Garden City, NY: Doubleday, 1982.

————. *The Gospel According to John*. 2 vols. AB 29, 29a. Garden City, NY: Doubleday, 1966–70.

————. *An Introduction to the Gospel of John*. Edited, updated, introduced and concluded by Francis J. Moloney. The Anchor Bible Reference Library. New York: Doubleday, 2003. When Raymond Brown died suddenly on Aug. 8, 1998, he was working on a revision of the *Anchor Bible Commentary*. The revision was mostly complete and Francis Moloney has done a wonderful job of editing and updating it. This *Introduction* is an outstanding survey of Johannine scholarship over the last forty years.

Carter, Warren. *John and Empire: Initial Explorations*. New York/London: T & T Clark, 2008.

Cassidy, Richard. *John's Gospel in New Perspective: Christology and the Realities of Roman Power*. Maryknoll, NY: Orbis Books, 1992. An early and important study with the thesis "that John's Gospel generally responds to the phenomenon of Roman claims and Roman power" (5).

Friesen, Steven. *Imperial Cults and the Apocalypse of John: Reading Revelation in the Ruins*. New York/Oxford: Oxford University Press, 2001.

Harvey, A. E. *Jesus on Trial: A Study in the Fourth Gospel*. London: SPCK, 1976.

Herzog, Frederick. *Liberation Theology: Liberation in the Light of the Fourth Gospel*. New York: Seabury Press, 1972.

Howard-Brook, Wes. *Becoming Children of God: John's Gospel and Radical Discipleship*. The Bible and Liberation. Maryknoll, NY: Orbis Books, 1994. The book argues that John's Gospel does not so much focus on "economic exclusion as on the social barriers of ethnicity, ritual impurity and lack of 'proper' belief" (5).

Karris, Robert J., OFM. *Jesus and the Marginalized in St. John's Gospel.* Collegeville, MN: Liturgical Press, 1990.

Keener, Craig. *The Gospel of John: A Commentary.* 2 Vols. Peabody, MA: Hendrickson Publishers, 2003.

Lee, Dorothy. *Hallowed in Truth and Love: Spirituality in the Johannine Literature.* Eugene, OR: Wipf & Stock, 2012.

Lincoln, Andrew T. *Truth on Trial: The Lawsuit Motif in the Fourth Gospel.* Peabody, MA: Hendrickson Publishers, 2000. Author proposes a more wide-ranging exploration of the trial motif than previous studies (for example, Harvey) using various methods and approaches.

Moloney, Francis J. *The Gospel of John.* Sacra Pagina 4. Collegeville, MN: Liturgical Press, 1998.

Philo, *On the Decalogue,* 28.151–53 in *The Works of Philo: Complete and Unabridged,* trans. C. Yonge, 530–31. Peabody, MA: Hendricksen, 1993.

Rensberger, David K. *Johannine Faith and Liberating Community.* Philadelphia: Westminster Press, 1988.

Richey, Lance B. *Roman Imperial Ideology and the Gospel of John.* Washington, DC: Catholic Biblical Association, 2007. Richey argues that the "Gospel is a conscious effort on the part of John to address issues which would unavoidably have been raised for his community by the Roman Imperial Ideology, or, as it is more commonly called, Augustan Ideology" (xii).

Ringe, Sharon. *Wisdom's Friends: Community and Christology in the Fourth Gospel.* Louisville, KY: Westminster John Knox Press, 1999.

Schneiders, Sandra. *Written That You Might Believe: Encountering Jesus in the Fourth Gospel.* Rev. ed. New York: Crossroad, 2003.

Smith, D. Moody. *The Theology of the Gospel of John.* Cambridge/New York: Cambridge University Press, 1995.

Thatcher, Tom. *Greater Than Caesar: Christology and Empire in the Fourth Gospel.* Minneapolis: Fortress Press, 2009. The author of important works on John, Thatcher shows that John's Christology is a form of resistance to imperial power.

Trebilco, Paul. *The Early Christians in Ephesus from Paul to Ignatius.* Grand Rapids, MI: Wm. B. Eerdmans Publishing, 2007.

Van Tilborg, Sjef. *Reading John in Ephesus*. Supplements to *Novum Testamentum*, LXXXIII. Leiden: Brill, 1996. Using archeological, literary, and epigraphical data, this work presents how John might have been read in first-century Ephesus.

THE BOOK OF REVELATION

Bauckham, Richard. *The Climax of Prophecy: Studies on the Book of Revelation*. Edinburgh: T & T Clark, 1993. A collection of essays spanning two decades of research, especially chapter 10, "The Economic Critique of Rome in Chapter 18."

————. *The Theology of the Book of Revelation*. Cambridge/ New York: Cambridge University Press, 1993. An excellent synthesis and introduction, now in its eighteenth printing.

Blount, Brian K. *Can I Get a Witness: Reading Revelation through African American Culture*. Louisville, KY: Westminster John Knox Press, 2005. A creative exposition and appropriation of the work from an African American perspective.

————. *Revelation: A Commentary*. New Testament Library. Louisville, KY: Westminster John Knox Press, 2009. An excellent commentary, original and well-written with sensitivity to the contemporary importance of Revelation.

Collins, Adela Yarbro. *The Apocalypse*. Wilmington, DE: Michael Glazier, 1979. A very helpful introduction.

Fiorenza, Elisabeth Schüssler. *The Book of Revelation: Justice and Judgment*. Philadelphia: Fortress Press, 1985. An excellent introduction with fine survey of ways of approaching Revelation with exposition of individual chapters.

————. *Revelation: Vision of a Just World*. Minneapolis: Fortress Press, 1991. An excellent introductory work.

Friesen, Steven. *Imperial Cults and the Apocalypse of John: Reading Revelation in the Ruins*. New York/Oxford: Oxford University Press 2001.

Gonzalez, Justo. *For the Healing of the Nations: The Book of Revelation in an Era of Cultural Conflict*. Maryknoll, NY: Orbis Books, 1999.

Howard-Brock, Wes, and Anthony Gwyther. *Unveiling Empire: Reading Revelation Then and Now*. Maryknoll, NY: Orbis Books, 1999. In the Bible and Liberation series, this work presents expositions of text with deliberate relevance to contemporary issues.

Kirsch, Jonathan. *A History of the End of the World: How the Most Controversial Book in the Bible Changed the Course of Western Civilization*. San Francisco: HarperSanFrancisco, 2006. A lively and readable depiction of mostly bizarre and baleful interpretations in literature and art.

Kovacs, Judith, and Christopher Rowland. *Revelation*. Blackwell Bible Commentaries. Oxford: Blackwell Publishing, 2004. In a series devoted to the reception history of the Bible, this work integrates excellent commentary on the text with presentation on its impact on theology, literature, and art through the centuries.

Kraybill, J. Nelson. *Apocalypse and Allegiance: Worship, Politics and Devotion in the Book of Revelation*. Grand Rapids, MI: Brazos Press, 2010.

————. *Imperial Cult and Commerce in John's Apocalypse*. Sheffield: Sheffield Academic Press Ltd., 1996.

LeMoignan, Christine. *Following the Lamb: A Reading of Revelation for the New Millennium*. London: SCM, 2000.

Pagels, Elaine. *Revelations: Visions, Prophecy and Politics in the Book of Revelation*. New York: Viking, 2012.

Portier-Young, Anathea E. *Apocalypse Against Empire: Theologies of Resistance in Early Judaism*. Grand Rapids, MI: Eerdmans, 2011. A major scholarly study of Second Temple Jewish apocalyptic works, indicating that this literature does not function only to give oppressed people a hope of future vindication, but is itself a form of resistance.

Royalty, Robert M. *The Streets of Heaven: The Ideology of Wealth in the Apocalypse of John*. Macon, GA: Mercer, 1998.

CHAPTER 12

FROM TEXT TO LIFE

Amid the vivid images of the call of Ezekiel (1:1—3:27), the prophet hears this command, "O mortal, eat what is offered to you; eat this scroll, and go, speak to the house of Israel" (3:1). This remains a call today to gather up the scrolls of the Bible, open them, be nurtured by them, and share them as the bread of life for contemporary believers. Interpreting the Bible (hermeneutics) is a major and challenging component of biblical study, involving philosophical foundations, theological reflection, and pastoral sensitivity. In the bibliography for this chapter, and also for chapter 1, are listed select works on this task, but here we will present approaches that may help those who teach and read the Bible with concerns for social justice.

ENGAGING BIBLICAL TEXTS

The reflections and resources in this work have been offered to those engaged in different ways in the quest for social justice. A major and continuing task is engagement with the biblical texts, which involves not only a conversation with biblical texts and themes but also reading "the signs of the times." This phrase is derived ultimately from the warning of Jesus to those seeking a miracle: "You know how to interpret the appearance of the sky, but you cannot interpret the signs of the times" (Matt 16:3). The Second Vatican Council stated that "Christ entered this world to give witness to the truth, to rescue and not to sit in judgment, to serve and not to be served. To carry out such a task, the church has always had the duty of scrutinizing the signs of the times and of interpreting them in the light of the gospel" (*Gaudium et Spes*, Pastoral Constitution on the Church in the Modern World, nos.

3–4). Such an approach is similar to the task of theology described by Paul Tillich as one of correlation of the symbols of the faith, where symbol includes sacred text and sacred tradition, with the existential question of a given age.[1] In our present national and global context, the vast reaches of poverty, the ever-expanding gap between rich and poor, and the idolatry of dominating power are clearly signs of the times and provide existential questions that call for dialogue with the biblical heritage.

As an entrée to this dialogue, and in debt to the writings of Paul Ricoeur, as mediated primarily through Sandra Schneiders and Dorothy Lee, I will propose an admittedly oversimplified approach to the biblical material. Ricoeur argues that, "as readers, we begin to read a text naïvely, opening ourselves to its dynamic in the same way that children listen to stories; this first movement is a 'naïve grasping of the meaning of the text as a whole'" (*Interpretation Theory*, 74). When reflecting on the biblical meaning of justice, this means that often, especially for those Catholics not nurtured on the biblical tradition, simple exposure to biblical texts is a prerequisite to any significant use of these texts. Subsequent explanation and exegesis may simultaneously challenge and enrich this initial engagement, but always as a preparation for an appropriation that leads to individual and social transformation.

Following initial engagement, the next movement involves explanation of the text: "the reader steps back from the text and engages in the kind of research necessary for a deeper comprehension at a number of levels. Here, the historical-critical method and related tools of biblical study play their part" (Lee, *Flesh*, 6). This movement also involves "distanciation" as the reader moves beyond initial and naïve interpretations that arise from an initial engagement, culminating in a "second naïveté" (Schneiders, *Revelatory Text*, 143–44; 169–74), which enables an informed explanation of the text.

This is the stage when traditional methods of exegesis and explanation of texts are employed, which involve (among others) the following procedures:

---

1. Paul Tillich, *Systematic Theology: Three Volumes in One* (Chicago: University of Chicago Press, 1967), I, 59–66.

1. Close reading of the text itself, which is not specific to biblical studies, but part of engagement with any literature, especially imaginative or poetic literature, and which attends to the meaning of particular terms or phrases, especially when the text is a translation from another language. The English term *text* is from the Latin, *tegere*, "to weave." A text is an interwoven network of meanings that gives rise to the "hermeneutical circle." The meaning of a particular text must be determined from the meaning of the whole, but study of the individual parts is necessary to arrive at the meaning of the whole. Reading texts involves an expanding contextual analysis, where one studies the immediate context of a passage, what follows or precedes, its proximate context, for example, the location of the parable of the Good Samaritan following the lawyer's question (Luke 10:25–37) and the larger context of the completed document near the beginning of Jesus' journey to Jerusalem; or the "call of Moses" (Exod 3:1–12) at the beginning of the confrontation with Pharaoh and the leading out of the people from slavery.

2. Awareness of the historical and social context of texts. Joseph A. Fitzmyer, a longtime advocate and practitioner of historical criticism has well described this task:

   > It recognizes that the Bible, though it is the inspired written Word of God is an ancient record, composed by many human authors over a long period of time. As such, it has to be read, studied, and analyzed as other ancient records of human history. Since the Bible narrates events that affected the lives of ancient Jews in early Christians, its various accounts have to be read, compared, and analyzed in their original languages against their proper and historical backgrounds, and within their contemporary context. (*Scripture*, 19)

3. Knowledge of the genre or kind of literature treated. The Dogmatic Constitution on Divine Revelation of Vatican II (*Dei Verbum*) stated interpretation should be based on the meaning of a biblical text as intended by the authors and

that "for the correct understanding of what the sacred author wanted to assert, due attention must be paid to the customary and characteristic styles of feeling, speaking and narrating which prevailed at the time of the sacred writer, and to the patterns men [and women] normally employed at the period in their everyday dealings with one another" (no. 12).

4. Attention to the canonical context. The term, *canonical criticism*, though rooted in past approaches, was coined by James A. Sanders to describe two main interests: the canonical *process*, by which texts in the Bible itself were used and reinterpreted, which then gives *guidelines for subsequent reinterpretation* and appropriation of biblical texts.[2] In the work of Brevard Childs and others, the focus is on the canonical context in its final form, as a source itself for interpretation.[3] The canonical shaping and form then become a resource for theological interpretations of texts in context.

5. Realization of the possibility of multiple interpretations: While scholars recognize multiple interpretations of a given text, not every interpretation is valid. There are criteria in the texts that historical and literary criticism will always provide. Sandra Schneiders offers a helpful list: respect for the text as it stands; an interpretation consistent with itself that elucidates the whole text; an interpretation that explains anomalies; one that its compatible with what is known from other sources (for example, comments of the Jewish historian Josephus on the ministry of John the Baptist); and one that uses appropriate methods (*Revelatory Text*, 165–66). Biblical literalism and fundamentalism are not methods of interpretation but world views.

---

2. James A. Sanders, *Canon and Community: A Guide to Canonical Criticism* (Philadelphia: Fortress Press, 1984). Cf. also R. W. Wall and E. Lemcio, *The New Testament as Canon: A Reader in Canonical Criticism* (Sheffield: JSOT Press, 1992).

3. Brevard Childs, *The New Testament as Canon: An Introduction* (Philadelphia: Fortress Press, 1985).

APPROPRIATING BIBLICAL TEXTS

Beyond the study of the texts in their historical and literary context, Ricoeur addresses the semantic autonomy of a text, whereby its meaning is not limited to the "intention" or original setting of an original author. This autonomy does not imply that "authorial meaning has lost all significance," but that there will always be a dialectical relationship between authorial intention and subsequent meaning (*Interpretation Theory*, 30). The "semantic autonomy" of texts opens them to interpretations beyond their original context, which occurs within the Bible itself. Texts engender traditions of interpretation, which often involve genres and settings quite different from the originating discourse. For example, the exodus is celebrated, perhaps originally by the hymns at the sea (Exod 15:20–21; 1–18) and in Psalms 78 and 105, and the sagas of the "taking of the land" in Joshua and Judges reflect exodus motifs (Josh 3:14–17). The return from exile in Isaiah is seen as a second exodus from oppression to liberation, and the exodus motif shapes much of New Testament theology. The "effective history" (*Wirkungsgeschicthe*) of texts and traditions continues beyond the canonical Scriptures and can continue to influence the interpretation and appropriation of the originating narratives.

Ricoeur, among others, offers guidelines for the *ongoing appropriation* of biblical texts. In a seminal essay, he states that "interpretation concerns essentially the power of the work to disclose a world," and that "interpretation" overcomes distanciation and "actualizes the meaning of the text for the present reader."[4] He then notes that "appropriation is the concept which is suitable for the actualization of meaning as addressed to someone," and "as appropriation, interpretation becomes an event." Ricoeur understands "appropriation" in the sense of the German *aneigen*, which conveys the sense of making one's own what was initially "alien." An English paraphrase would be also "ownership." Appropriation involves both dispossession and a new possession. It involves moving beyond both sedimented meanings of texts, as well as

---

4. Paul Ricoeur, *Hermeneutics and the Human Sciences: Essays on Language, Action and Interpretation*, ed. and trans. John S. Thompson (Cambridge: Cambridge University Press; Paris: Editions de la Mason des Sciences de l'Homme, 1981), 182. Quotes in this paragraph are taken from this essay.

the myth of subjectivity where the person "subjects" meaning to intention. Appropriation follows the "arrow of meaning" in a text and engenders a new self-understanding. The cryptic phrase "arrow of meaning" is important, since, throughout his works on biblical interpretation, Ricoeur speaks of the "surplus of meaning" of biblical texts and following the direction of the text itself, rather than literal reproduction. In matters of social justice the direction to which the text points opens ways to new applications and new appropriations.

Sandra Schneiders, who has herself appropriated carefully the methods of Paul Ricoeur and Hans Gadamer, describes the process of appropriation as primarily the "fusion of horizons," whereby "the world horizon of the reader fuses with the horizon of the world projected by the text." She then states:

> Appropriation of the meaning of a text, the transformative achievement of interpretation, is neither mastery of the text by the reader (an extraction of its meaning by the application of method) nor mastery of a reader by the text (a blind submission to what the text says) but an ongoing dialogue with the text about its subject matter. (*The Revelatory Text*, 172)

COMMUNITIES OF INTERPRETATION

The dialogue between text and interpreter is not simply an individual act, but in the quest to join biblical reflection to social justice concerns, summons the Church—understood as believers within and across denominational lines—to become communities of interpretation. Such communities fall into four general categories.

The first, but not necessarily the most important, comprises communities of informed reflection, involving biblical scholars among themselves and with different disciplines (see especially Richard Hays, *Moral Vision*). In a programmatic essay, James Gustafson argues that "comprehensive and coherent theological ethics must be adequate with reference to the four following sources": (1) the Bible and Christian tradition; (2) philosophical methods, insights, and principles; (3) scientific information and methods that are relevant; and (4) human experience, broadly conceived.[5] Since each of these reference points has its own methods and challenges, dialogue between them must involve communities of interpretation that engage in multiple conversations—between the disciplines themselves, as well as between sacred texts, traditions, and possible applications. Without critical interchange among disciplines, today's application of the Bible could easily become tomorrow's horror—as history sadly confirms.

A second community of interpreters would arise from official statements by Church leaders. The collection of mainly papal documents under the heading of "Catholic Social Doctrine" are a prime example as are statements by local bishops' conferences, along with documents issued by other Christian communities. They can set the agenda for debate and can provide documentation and justification for those working in particular areas of social justice. Yet while often prophetic and powerful, apart from theologians and Church leaders, they are too infrequently known or used.

Individuals and groups sensitive to suffering and injustice, with a growing consciousness that these violate the biblical revelation also comprise communities of interpretation "from below." Like the mustard seed in the Gospel, where small beginnings are contrasted to an abundant harvest, justice arose from groups concerned with issues such as the rejection of slavery and struggle against racism,[6] the quest for the rights and dignity of women,[7] opposition to war and the quest for peace,[8] concern for social and economic oppression,[9] along with the early liberation theologians. To these movements must be added early

---

5. James Gustafson, *Protestant and Roman Catholic Ethics: Prospects for Rapprochement* (Chicago: University of Chicago Press, 1978), 142. Lisa Sowle Cahill has developed these in *Foundations for A Christian Ethics of Sexuality* (Philadelphia: Fortress Press; New York/Ramsey: Paulist Press, 1985), especially 1–13. Various authors have noted that these reference points have their origin in the Methodist "quadrilateral" of Scripture, tradition, reason, and experience.

6. James Stewart, "Abolitionists, the Bible and the Challenge of Slavery," in Sandeen, *Bible and Social Reform*, 30–57, and Peter J. Paris, "The Bible and the Black Churches," in Sandeen, *Bible and Social Reform*, 133–54.

7. Barbara Brown Zikmund, "Biblical Arguments and Women's Place in the Church," in Sandeen, *Bible and Social Reform*, 85–104.

8. Charles Chatfield, on "The Bible and American Peace Movements," in Sandeen, *Bible and Social Reform*, 105–31, and William Miller, on "Dorothy Day and the Bible," in Sandeen, *Bible and Social Reform*, 155–77.

9. William McGuire King, "The Biblical Basis of the Social Gospel," in Sandeen, *Bible and Social Reform*, 59–84.

opponents of anti-Semitism (Connelly, *From Enemy to Brother*, ch. 4, "Catholics against Racism and Anti-Semitism). In Catholicism, for example, many of those who initially spoke out against racism were rejected by Church leaders.

While the above movements arose for the most part from educated religious professionals within churches, concerns for social justice can flourish among individuals and parish groups attempting to bring the Bible to bear on their everyday lives. Especially pertinent are the conclusions of Jerome Baggett, a theologian and sociologist, in his important survey of Catholic attitudes in *Sense of the Faithful*. On the basis of over 150 extensive interviews at seven parishes in the San Francisco Bay area, with people varied in ethnicity, socioeconomic background, and religious attitudes, from conservative to progressive, Baggett offers a panorama of faith lived on the ground. His research shows that virtually all those interviewed have assimilated often negative values of the surrounding culture in areas of social justice. The teaching of bishops and of the Vatican have little direct bearing on their practice of the faith, though most of those interviewed hold core beliefs such as the resurrection, the importance of the Eucharist, and consider helping the poor to be a strong value. But, of special interest in this work is that, when people are asked to discuss particular biblical texts (for example, Matt 19:16–26, the parable of the rich young man or Matt 25:31–46, the parable of the sheep and the goats), they grapple seriously with questions of wealth and alleviating the suffering of others. Even amid diverse interpretations, the Bible often becomes a far better entrée into social justice concerns than official Church teaching, however powerful the latter might be.

The fourth "community of interpretation" for Catholics could and should be the weekly celebration of the Eucharist. The command, "Do this in memory of me," is not simply a mandate to recall the words of Jesus, but a call to the mission of imitating the deepest meaning of the Lord's Supper, that the body of Jesus was to be broken and his lifeblood poured out because he died for others at the hands of oppressive and unjust power.

From the earliest centuries, this took concrete form. We noted that for Paul, concern for the "have-nots" informed his description of the Lord's Supper. Less than a century later, Justin Martyr, in his *First*

Apology (AD 155–57) addressed to the Roman emperor, Antonius Pius, describes the weekly Christian worship:

> "[Where] the memoirs of the apostles or the writings of the prophets are read, for as long as there is time; then, when the reader has stopped, the president in an address makes admonition and imitation of their good things" and at the conclusion of the meeting, "they who are well-off and willing give—each what he wishes according to his own choice—and what is gathered together is deposited with the president. And he assists the orphans and widows and those who are in need because of illness or through some other cause, and those who are in chains, and the foreigners (sojourners) who are staying among us. And he is the protector of all in general who are in need." (ch. 67)[10]

Listening to the Scriptures, reflection and application to the lives of the community, and concern for those same groups that inform the faith of ancient Israel—the poor, the widow, the orphan, the stranger or sojourner (cf. Exod 22:21–27)—are at the very essence of Christian worship. To divorce celebration of the Eucharist and preaching from concerns for social justice is to betray the very essence of Catholic faith, while to join them is an enduring mandate and challenge.

FINAL REFLECTION OR NEW BEGINNING

A frequent pattern in biblical literature is the *inclusio* or "A-B-A" structure where similar statements bracket longer comments. So we end where we began by emphasizing that the purpose of this work has been to stimulate reflections on biblical texts, which should be part of any conversation on social justice, and to present resources that will enable people to move well beyond the reflections, and to garner more resources. The legacies of a wide survey of biblical thought are first, that the Bible resonates with concern and compassion for the down-

---

10. Text and translation from *Justin, Philosopher and Martyr: Apologies*, edited with commentary by Denis Minns and Paul Parvis (Oxford/New York: Oxford University Press, 2009).

trodden and powerless people who live at the margins of any society. This concern takes three forms that thrive today among those who seek justice: direct care and advocacy; empowering those most affected by injustice in their struggle for justice and peace; and prophetic and critical confrontation with individuals and institutions that contribute to and benefit from the social deprivation of others. Though motivated by love and informed by wisdom, the ultimate aim of all groups working for social justice is the transformation of culture and society, which begins with laws that protect the vulnerable and enable them to achieve human dignity.

A second legacy of the Bible is the rejection of grasping for power: from the desire "to be like God" (Gen 3:5), through the polemic against the worship of false gods by a prophet from Jerusalem, "When you cry out, let your collection of idols deliver you! The wind will carry them off, a breath will take them away" (Isa 57:13), and the joyful paean by a young woman of Nazareth to the Lord who shatters the trappings of power:

> His mercy is for those who fear him
>> from generation to generation.
> He has shown strength with his arm;
>> he has scattered the proud in the thoughts of their hearts.
> He has brought down the powerful from their thrones,
>> and lifted up the lowly;
> he has filled the hungry with good things,
>> and sent the rich away empty.
>
> (Luke 1:50–53)

Today's idols are not wood and stone that stare down on us from temple porches, but the quest for wealth almost beyond imagining and its symbols of power and influence that populate the caverns of Wall Street. The cancer of dominating power invades both the body politic and all too often the Body of the Church.

The words and Word of God in the Bible are its most enduring legacy that echo through the centuries. They have given birth to the Jewish people who, despite centuries of mordant hatred and appalling persecution, remain "a light to the nations" by speaking out for *tsedaqah* and *mishpat*. For Christians the Word became flesh, a poor man who shared his meals and his life with marginal people, a prophet who gave a voice to the poor, and "came into conflict with those clerical and civil authorities who collaborated in his death." But by dying, he conquered death and "the reason for his speaking and acting remained in the memory of the people" and his living presence sustains their lives.[11] As we move from text to life, the voices of a prophet from Jerusalem and a prophet who was to die in Jerusalem call out to us:

> Learn to do good;
> seek justice,
>   rescue the oppressed,
> defend the orphan,
>   plead for the widow.
>
> (Isa 1:17)

You know that among the Gentiles those whom they recognize as their rulers lord it over them, and their great ones are tyrants over them. But it is not so among you; but whoever wishes to become great among you must be your servant, and whoever wishes to be first among you must be slave of all. For the Son of Man came not to be served but to serve, and to give his life a ransom for many. (Mark 10:42–45)

RESOURCE BIBLIOGRAPHY

Baggett, Jerome P. *The Sense of the Faithful: How American Catholics Live Their Faith*. New York: Oxford University Press, 2009. See especially chapter 6, "Civil Society: Private and Public Good," which treats of parish-level attitudes toward issues of social justice.

Barton, John. *Ethics and the Old Testament*. Harrisburg, PA: Trinity Press International, 1998. Barton, a long-term commentator on Old

---

11. Dorothea Sölle, "The Role of Political Theology in the Liberation of Man." In *Religion and the Humanizing of Man*, ed. James M. Robinson (Los Angeles: Council on the Study of Religion, 1972), 131–32.

Testament ethics, has argued for a "natural law" type of ethics within the biblical texts.

————. *Understanding Old Testament Ethics: Approaches and Explorations*. Louisville, KY: Westminster John Knox Press, 2003. An important collection of essays.

Bergman, Roger. *Catholic Social Learning: Educating the Faith that Does Justice*. New York: Fordham University Press, 2011. Drawing on both theoretical models and long-term experience as an educator, Bergman shows how one moves from knowledge of Catholic Social Teaching to appropriation and practice.

Birch, Bruce C. *Let Justice Roll: The Old Testament, Ethics and the Christian Life*. Louisville, KY: Westminster John Knox Press, 1991. This work surveys the literature in a canonical and historical order from Genesis through the Wisdom literature.

————. *What Does the Lord Require? The Old Testament Call to Social Witness*. Philadelphia: Westminster Press, 1985. More popular presentations of material that Birch later develops in *Let Justice Roll*.

Birch, Bruce C., and Larry L. Rasmussen. *The Predicament of the Prosperous*. Philadelphia: Westminster Press, 1978. This work arose from discussions in both academic and pastoral settings.

Connelly, John. *From Enemy to Brother: The Revolution of Catholic Teaching on the Jews, 1933–45*. Cambridge, MA: Harvard University Press, 2012. Although anti-Semitism is not strictly speaking a social justice issue, many of those biblical texts that address issues of social justice are especially pertinent when countering this evil.

Fitzmyer, Joseph A. *Scripture: The Soul of Theology*. New York/Mahwah, NJ: Paulist Press, 1994.

Green, Joel B., ed. *Hearing the New Testament: Strategies for Interpretation*. Grand Rapids, MI: Eerdmans, 1995. An excellent collection of essays on traditional and contemporary methods of interpretation.

Haynes, Stephen R., and Steven L. McKenzie. *To Each Its Own Meaning: An Introduction to Biblical Criticisms and Their Application*. Louisville, KY: Westminster John Knox Press, 1993.

Hays, Richard B. *The Moral Vision of the New Testament: Community,*

Cross, New Creation, A Contemporary Introduction to New Testament Ethics. San Francisco: HarperSanFrancisco, 1996.

Lee, Dorothy. *Flesh and Glory: Symbolism, Gender and Theology in the Fourth Gospel*. New York: Crossroad, 2002. An original and interesting study with an important introductory chapter on biblical interpretation.

Ogletree, Thomas W. *The Use of the Bible in Christian Ethics: A Constructive Essay*. Philadelphia: Fortress Press, 1983. A sophisticated attempt by an ethicist to bridge the gap between biblical studies and ethics. The chapter on "Covenant and Commandment" (47–85) is one of the best treatments of the implications of covenant for a theology of social justice.

Petersen, Eugene. *Eat This Book: A Conversation in the Art of Spiritual Reading*. Grand Rapids, MI: Eerdmans, 2006.

Ricoeur, Paul. *Interpretation Theory: Discourse and the Surplus of Meaning*. Fort Worth, TX: Texas Christian University Press, 1976.

Sandeen, Ernest, ed. *The Bible and Social Reform*. Chico, CA: Scholars Press, 1982. A fine overview by various scholars of the impact of the Bible on social reform movements of nineteenth and twentieth centuries.

Schneiders, Sandra. *The Revelatory Text: Interpreting the New Testament as Sacred Scripture*. 2nd ed. Collegeville, MN: Liturgical Press, 1999. The best resource available for combining historical-critical and literary methods with religious appropriation, with fine use of the works of Paul Ricoeur and Hans-Georg Gadamer.

Spohn, William C. *What Are They Saying About Scripture and Ethics?* 2nd. rev. ed. New York/Mahwah, NJ: Paulist, 1995. An excellent survey of various ways Scripture is used in addressing ethical issues.

LITURGY, PREACHING, AND SOCIAL JUSTICE

Baldovin, John F. "The Liturgical Year: Calendar for a Just Community." In *Liturgy and Spirituality in Context*, edited by E. Bernstein, 98–114. Collegeville, MN: Liturgical Press, 1990.

Burghardt, Walter J. *Preaching the Just Word*. New Haven, CT: Yale University Press, 1996. An excellent work bringing together reflection on justice with great wisdom on how to preach about justice.

————. *When Christ Meets Christ: Homilies on the Just Word*. New York/Mahwah, NJ: Paulist Press, 1993. Powerful examples of how to preach the just word.

Empereur, James L., and Christopher Kiesling. *The Liturgy That Does Justice*. A Michael Glazier Book. Collegeville, MN: The Liturgical Press, 1990. An excellent study that covers all aspects of liturgy with fine insights. The annotated bibliography is worth the price of the book and should be consulted as a supplement to this present brief bibliography.

Gonzalez, J. L., and C. G Gonzalez. *Liberation Preaching: The Bible and the Oppressed*. Nashville, TN: Abingdon, 1980. This work offers some good suggestions on preaching about social justice.

Grosz, Edward M. ed. *Liturgy and Social Justice: Celebrating Rites—Proclaiming Rights*. Collegeville, MN: Liturgical Press, 1988. Papers presented at the 1988 meeting of the Federation of Diocesan Liturgical Commissions. See especially Dianne Bergant, "Liturgy and Scripture: Creating a New World," 12–25; and J. Bryan Hehir, "Liturgy and Social Justice: Past Relationships and Future Possibilities," 40–61.

Guroian, V. "Bible and Ethics: An Ecclesial and Liturgical Interpretation," *Journal of Religious Ethics* 18 (1990): 129–57. Written from an Orthodox perspective, this essay offers interesting suggestions on the Bible, liturgy, and social justice, using examples from John Chrysostom.

Hamm, Dennis. "Preaching Biblical Justice: To Nurture the Faith That Does It." *Studies in the Spirituality of the Jesuits* 29, no. 1 (St. Louis: Seminar on Jesuit Spirituality, 1997). A good and brief discussion of justice, along with suggestions on preaching with some sample homilies.

Hessel, Dieter, ed. *Social Themes of the Christian Year: A Commentary on the Lectionary*. Philadelphia: Geneva Press, 1983. A collection of essays on the lectionary cycle. Most helpful as a way to think differently about biblical texts, though the specific applications are uneven. (Available through Westminster John Knox Press).

Hughes, Kathleen, and Mark R. Francis, eds. *Living No Longer for Ourselves: Liturgy and Justice in the Nineties*. Collegeville, MN: The

Liturgical Press, 1991. A good collection of essays. See especially Hughes, "Liturgy and Justice: An intrinsic Relationship," 36–51 and R. A. Kiefer, "Liturgy and Ethics: Some Unresolved Dilemmas," 68–83.

Searle, Mark, ed. *Liturgy and Social Justice*. Collegeville, MN: The Liturgical Press, 1980. Important essays by Walter Burghardt, Mark Searle, Edward Kilmartin, and Regis Duffy.

Silberman, Louis H. "Boldness in the Service of Justice." In *Preaching Biblical Texts: Expositions by Jewish and Christian Scholars*, edited by Frederick C. Holmgren and Hermann E. Schaalmann, 29–35. Grand Rapids, MI: Eerdmans, 1995.

Weakland, Rembert G. "Liturgy and Social Justice." In *Shaping the English Liturgy*, edited by P. Finn and J. Schellman, 343–57. Washington, DC: Pastoral Press, 1990.

INDEX